I0210710

The characters and events portrayed in this book are real.

ISBN-13: 978-0-6453854-3-4

Cover design by: Eszter Pungur

Auschwitz 5.0 - The Empire of Hell
Birkenau, Auschwitz, Gross-Rosen, Dachau, Mühldorf

Story of the survivor No: A-17854 Sandor SCHWARCZ
from 7 forced labour camps and 5 concentration camps.
An International football player of Auschwitz

A	n
U	ntold
S	tory of
C	onstant
H	ope
W	here
I	nmates
T	ogether
Z	ombifying

Book cover designed and drawn by Eszter Pungur
This book and all context of it is protected by copyright law. All
right reserved by the writer.

From the 1st of December, 2021

Contents

Foreword from the Author

I was born in Hungary in 1972 and in 2004 emigrated to Australia with my wife.

My parents moved from the Western Hungarian city of Veszprém to one of the largest Eastern Hungarian cities, Debrecen, in 1977. I was aged 4 and my brother was 7.

From 1979, my mother started collecting special edition stamps which were released from time to time. If you wanted to "put your hand" on one of these, you had to line up early morning before the Post Office Central had opened. She became a friend of Sándor Schwarz, a Jew who often kept the waiting crowd "entertained" with his miraculous survival stories from the Concentration Camps of the Second World War. My mother introduced us to Sándor and took us to see him in his apartment. I remember the first time very clearly as our mother made us dress up nicely as if we were going to a great celebrity party. When we entered his small studio apartment, I noticed that on the right side of the living area there were books from the floor almost to the ceiling. On top of the bookshelves there also were black and red covered bound books.

During our visit I could not settle my curiosity until I found out what those books were, so I had to have the strength to stop Sándor immediately telling another story.

"Excuse me Sándor, what are those black and red books on top of the bookshelves? I asked.

"They are summarizing my life" he replied.

"All of them? You must have had a lot of stories to tell!" I said with childish curiosity.

"No," he said with a smile, "they are all the same. I have made 30 copies of the book."

"And why are they black and red?" I asked.

"Because they are the colour of the Nazi flag" he replied.

After that we visited him very often. Every time he surprised us with new memories. It is my memory that he never repeated himself. I am not sure how he managed to keep track of which story he had told to which visitor. He was always calm, very energetic and spoke with a very soft and calm voice.

Later, some time after our parents had divorced and my mother had moved back to the city of Veszprém, my brother and I continued to visit our dad in Debrecen a few times each year. On these visits we always made sure we dropped by to see Sandor, with a 2 litre bottle of his favourite grape flavoured soft drink, "Traubi-Szoda".

He greeted us with no surprise at all, as if we saw him every other week. He was always happy to see us and mentioned our surprise visits as a great gesture in his letters to our mum.

His small studio apartment had not much in it, but enough for him: a comfortable bed, a flushable toilet, clean running hot and cold tap water, a kitchen and a window overlooking the main train station from which he was taken away in the summer of 1944.

His entrance door not only had his name on it, but also his number that was tattooed on his forearm: "**Auschwitz: A-17854**".

When we knocked on the door, it was flung open energetically. In fact, he preferred us to enter unannounced as the door was never locked. He had no one to fear any longer. He had survived the "living hell" which had become the final "resting place" of millions of unfortunate humans as part of the Holocaust.

During one of our visits many years later, I noticed there were only a few of his red and black bound books left.

"Sorry Sándor, but whatever happened with the red-black books you had on the top of the bookshelves?"

"I have given them away" he replied.

"To whom?" I asked.

"You see, I have visitors almost every day and I have been educating the young generation about this black history of the 20th Century. I have been asked to visit many schools, I have been speaking on the radio about it and I have appeared on the TV as well. My story has touched many people all over the country. Since my story got out a bit I have been visited by many journalists as well. They have been very fascinated with my story and they have promised me they will publish my book. However, so far nothing has been published."

"Well, that is not nice, is it?" my brother said. "If they promised to do it, then they should have kept their word".

"Look, I have lived through so much inhumanity in my life, I just cannot be bothered about it. I cannot allow myself to be upset about it either," he said it calmly. "These kinds of disappointments have been happening to me time after time. The recent one is this," he said as he stood up from the small dining table which was in the middle of the living area and walked over to the bookshelves. He returned with a thin book in his hand and set it on the table and continued. "This book has recently been published. This is a book about a small part of my story in the Birkenau concentration camp. However, the author has forgotten to mention my name on the front page. He has claimed this book as his own story. I did not even receive a complimentary copy from him," he said with some disappointment in his voice. "I have purchased this copy and a few more with my own money".

All Sándor was looking for was respect, not financial wealth by sharing his story. All he wanted was to educate the ones in need, by telling the younger generation, and to warn the world not to let this happen ever again. So, when all channels were closed for him to continue his teaching, he decided to publish his own book and not to wait any longer for anyone else to do it for him. He had had enough of the number of disappointments with the journalists, the movie writers, the reporters. I have never forgotten this, nor his disappointment.

Sandor's story has given me a lot of strength to live through the difficult days and years of my own life. I believe sharing this unbelievable story will help others to face the challenges life throws at them. Because of my long-standing relationship with Sándor, the collection of resources relevant to his life that I have acquired during that period, and my understanding of the cultural environment during which they occurred, I am in a unique position to have the opportunity of bringing his experiences to the attention of a wider community. I never thought I would ever have the honour of putting his life story together and translating it to another language.

During the time I have taken writing it, I have talked to many of my friends and people with whom I have come into contact. When I have mentioned my project, I have found that many people knew or were related to someone who had been in one of the concentration camps, but they had never found out what actually happened to them behind the electric barbed wire fences. I believe these grandparents and relatives where too embarrassed to tell how inhumanly they had been treated. I would like to help people to understand why a grandfather never told his grandchildren how he has been treated, how he lost his name along with all his family, his friends and his home, why many of them have never returned to their hometown, and why they never trusted the government of their country any longer.

I hope this book will give strength and help to many through the tough days ahead and will bring peace for the others in need.

This is his story.

Statement by Sándor Schwartz

In 2005, after sixty years, I am the living witness to the following events. This is not a fiction, nor a liturgical reading, but a real story in every sentence. I, as the living witness, on the 30th of August 1964, on my 53rd birthday celebration, have written down the most tragic event of the world's history, taking care of the punctual accuracy of the reality.

After 60 years surviving five concentration camps - Birkenau, Auschwitz, Gross-Rosen, Dachau, Mühldorf - I wish to publish my memories of these ordeals.

I recommend this reading to everyone, but especially high school and university students, so they can get a real picture about these inhuman, terrible years. I see it as necessary, so the young people of the 21st century can learn and understand how a concentration camp resident could survive when more than 700,000 Hungarian compatriots did not.

I hope these words will not only be interesting reading, but will help in the fight against the difficulties of everyday life. During our weakest moments we should never give up, and we need to believe and hope in a better future. To be able to do this, we must lay down the correct bases and pathways in the young years of our life, as I did when I was 16 and 17 years of age.

Sandor Schwarcz
A-17854 numbered and tattooed survivor from Auschwitz
26th April 2005

Being selected

My special destiny was handed to me by the eternal good God. "You will go through a period of hell where you have to pay attention to everything and then tell all, write down what you saw as a witness, because you will have a long life and use that to improve people." In the 5th camp, the Bavarian Mühldorf, beside the skeleton-like dying and dead, I knew that my survival did not happen by accident. I am not a religious person. However, I have never denied my Judaism for which I have had to suffer.

So far, I have been able to do enough through the favour of the Upper Power which keeps me alive. In the past 50 years I have lived a double life. I use every opportunity to speak, to write about the tragic scenes, and explain what Hitler and his allies have done with more than 700,000 Hungarian Jews, and with the 6 million European Jews.

I speak about this to the thousands of young students at the primary schools, high schools, vocational institutes, and universities. I have spoken many times on the radio and in more detail on the television screens. I usually tell how I served the

Hungarian Homeland as a yellow arm-banded citizen for four years - as a second-class citizen - as a labour servant humiliated by the gendarme hitman. I usually tell how I felt when I left the gate of our house on the early morning of April 5th 1944 with a yellow star blooming on my jacket. I also tell of our sadness in the ghetto when we had to traverse the wooden barriers having been robbed of our homes. I tell about the inhuman, difficult circumstances of the brick factory where we just had to wait for our transport which would take us to Germany, for the promised work - which was a lie. I tell how I was compressed with 80 people into a cattle car with the help of gendarme and SS-soldiers, without water, food, and utensils to meet our human needs. This is how our homeland was removed and replaced with homelessness, with the help of the Hungarian authorities.

Antecedents

On January 30, 1933, when German President Paul von Hindenburg appointed Adolf Hitler (who subsequently formed a government with Franz von Papen) as Reich Chancellor of Germany, no one did anything! The world just ignored his appointment. Germany immediately started to build a very strong army, which was against the Peace Treaty of Versailles[1]. Nations around the world did not believe that Germany would take this action which resulted in the Second World War.

"The instability created in Europe by the First World War (1914-18) set the stage for another international conflict, World War II, which broke out two decades later and would prove even more devastating. Rising to power in an economically and politically unstable Germany, Adolf Hitler and his National Socialist (Nazi Party) rearmed the nation and signed strategic treaties with Italy and Japan to further his ambitions of world domination. Hitler's invasion of Poland in

[1] Signed on June 28, 1919, Part V reduced Germany's armed forces to very low levels and prohibited Germany from possessing certain classes of weapons, while committing the Allies to eventual disarmament as well.

September 1939 drove Great Britain and France to declare war on Germany, and World War II had begun. Over the next six years, the conflict would take more lives and destroy more land and property around the globe than any previous war.
Among the estimated 45-60 million people killed were 6 million Jews murdered in Nazi concentration camps as part of Hitler's diabolical "Final Solution," now known as the Holocaust." (From www.History.com)

Amsterdam, Paris, Warsaw, Prague, Debrecen – it did not matter when the German Empire appeared, even if the citizens protested. The Third Reich sent the citizens into abolition camps. Some countries fought against this evil plan and some, like Hungary, has assisted the faster deportation of the Jews.

The crocked nose

I was born on 30 August 1911 in the Eastern Hungarian city of Debrecen as the third boy of the family. My older brother Zoltán was born in 1905 and József in 1907. Béla, my youngest brother, was born in 1913 and my younger sister Erzsébet in 1919. My father, who was a corporal gunner in World War I, left the army in 1918 and became a shoemaker. My mother was a housewife looking after the family of five children.
We lived at the address of 60 Hatvan Street, which was an old-fashioned courtyard with many small houses. Many travellers' horses were stationed there for rest after long overnight trips. I was about four and a half years old when I decided to play between the horses with my toy made of an old corn cob[2].

---

[2] **Corn dollies** or **corn mothers** are a form of straw work made as part of harvest customs of Europe before mechanization.
Before Christianisation, in traditional pagan European culture it was believed that the spirit of the corn (in American English, "corn" was the "grain" that lived amongst the crop, and that the harvest made it effectively homeless.

Photo from: harvest-party.jpg (1296×1944) (bloominthyme.com) – Children toys made of corn leaf

I started to tickle the leg of a horse which kicked back and one edge of the horseshoe ended up breaking the base of my nose and the other ripped one of my eyebrows open. There was blood everywhere and my Mum carried me back to the house in her arms making a terrible scream. Many of the housewives from the neighbourhood came to her assistance and managed to stop the bleeding. When my father came home after work, he was very sad to see my face which had swollen up. The swelling took a long time to come down, and my parents realized only then, that my nose had shifted towards my right eye and was not in the middle of my face anymore. We had no money to see the doctors, so I wore this twisted face from then on.

I managed to finish the first four years of the primary school as an "OK" but not brilliant student, but at age 12 my father told me I would have to go to work as we had no money and I could not continue with study any longer.

I had to push a heavy wheelbarrow and deliver pieces of leather to the shoe and boot makers. I was very sad to see other kids of my age playing and going to school.

Later on I became an apprentice at a store, but my job there was the same as before, moving heavy bags and items. I was hoping for some tips from the shop owners to whom I made deliveries so I could go and see a movie or to watch my favourite sport game, football. Usually, I climbed up on the tall trees around the football field and from there I watched the games. I loved the ball so much that I decided to make my own as we had no money to buy a real leather ball.

On one occasion, I was punished severely by my Mum because I used one of her tights and stuffed it with old clothes and pieces of rugs to make my own ball. Occasionally, it was a privilege to be invited by the richer kids to play with them and kick their leather ball - a real ball.

We had very little money but my father made sure there was a duck or a chicken on the table on Fridays. When I was hungry I picked wild berries and wild pears or lingered around the fruit stores hoping there would be a few apples rolling from the barrows on which they were delivered. My Mum sometimes bought small - actually, I must say, tiny -fishes at the market and made fish soup. Fresh bread was always an extra joy for us as well. We lived very poorly.

After three years of work and study I moved to the local textile factory. I was doing very heavy physical loading work, but twice a week we gathered for football training with my younger brother and colleagues from the factory and played games on Sunday. There was no trainer - just us, training each other. We had to look after our own football uniform. There was no extra money after the games, not even a free dinner if we won. If we were not able to play a game every Sunday, it was a punishment and a disappointment for us. We played the game for the pure joy - the joy of the football.

At my own instigation I went three or four times a week for an 8 to10 kilometre run. On the "Hatvan Street" the government had planted 91 trees. During my run I jumped up at all 91 trees and aimed to "header" the lower branches to practice my ball heading.

I was playing at right forward most of the time as I was very fast. I ran the 100 metres in 11.5 seconds. I was in my early twenties when our team was facing the university team (DEAC), and there was already an anti-Semitism comment from one of the university players, "Now you little Jew, you will get it now!" he said. But I stood up for myself and threw back a strong comment at him, to stop the argument then and there, as I wanted to focus on the game.

During one of the games on the newly-built grass field stadium (which had been built by the many jobless citizens as a government operated construction) I had a powerful shot which has bounced back from the goalkeeper. As I tried to place the ball in the net with my left leg, the goalkeeper accidently grabbed my lower leg instead of the ball. I flipped over his shoulder while he was still holding my leg and my knee hyper-extended, rapturing my ligaments and also causing a meniscus tear. In the '30s, medical science wasn't advanced enough to repair such an injury, nor we would have had the money to pay for it, so from then on I had to train and live with this injury.

When I turned 18 I had to attend to the government-operated weekly trainings – "Leventeszervezet" (Levente association)[3]. The teacher, Gyula Gésuta had seen my talent in football and also in running and he always asked me to display my ball handling skills. He entered me into short distance athletic sprint competitions. I have won many medals in these competitions. He also introduced me to the drama group, which was held every Sunday afternoon. Here I made friends and no one made me feel like a Jew, despite the anti-Semite machine of Germany being well under way. It was also here, for the first time in my life, I started to date beautiful girls. Unfortunately, as we were very poor, I was ashamed of the quality of my clothing, so I had to be smart. One night I was walking home in the dark after a

---

[3] It was established in 1921 with the declared purpose of physical and health training. Since mid-1930s they had become a de facto attempt to circumvent the ban for conscription imposed by the Treaty of Trianon and over the time it had openly become a pre-military organization under the leadership of veterans. Since 1939, by the Act of Defens, all boys of ages 12–21 who had no regular physical activities (ex. high school or university) were required to take part in *levente* 2 hours a week, after 1938 3-4 hours a week. It is usually compared to Hitler Jugend of Nazi Germany and Opera Nazionale Balilla of Italy

drama group rehearsal and the girl I liked was heading home the same direction. I slowed down so she could catch up with me. This way, in the dark, I could hide the terrible state of my "outfit" from her.

Finally, my luck had turned on in the "clothing department".

The winner - A new roll of textile

As I was part of the drama group we used to rehearse and perform at the local youth theatre. One day my eyes noticed a sign on the wall in the theatre's hallway. It was an invitation to the young dressmakers' dress-up ball, which featured a competition where the best dressed could win (amongst other prizes) a roll of brand new textile. I was interested only in obtaining the textile. For days leading up to the dress-up competition, I could not sleep. I was dreaming about winning the prize that aroused my interest, although many different other prizes could be won.

From the drama school, I could borrow a costume and dress up as a hunter. I made a dog for myself. It was a very simple dog. I attached a cardboard box on to a string and wrote the name of "my first dog", Hector, on the side.

I felt very proud of myself and was happy to display my costume and my dog, which followed my lead like one of the best hunting dogs in the world. It was midnight when the winners have been announced. And …… I won. I won a bolt of new textile which was enough to make some new pants. I ran home like the wind and ran into the dark house and started to yell, "I won, I won, I won!"

All my family were in a deep sleep. They did not know what had happened. It took a while for my father to light up the petroleum light in the pitch dark, to see what on earth was happening. When I explained what had occurred, I got a big hug from my parents and my father reassured me he would get the money to pay the dressmaker. They then all went back to sleep, but I was so excited I was the only one who could not. I kept picturing myself in the new pants and how I wouldn't have to be shy anymore for the quality of my clothing.

I now had much more self-esteem and would be able to ask the girl I liked out for a date. I felt like a different man!

I remained part of the Levente association from 18 to 21 years of age. Even until today I am very grateful for the physical exercises and for the organized youth activities, they provided for us all. I believe today's youth communities would benefit from something similar too.

The labourer - The new job

From the 1930's I was employed in the local textile factory. I was doing mainly physical work. This involved boxing up products, loading them onto trucks up at the end of the day for a transport company called Müller, shifting many items of equipment, and other various tasks.

In 1938 a new regulation was promulgated which stated: '*Anyone who is a Jew cannot fulfil intellectual jobs and positions any longer.*'

The factory leader was German-born Steiner Selényi (Antal Selényi) who knew me very well as I had been working there for more than eight years. Because of the new regulation, many Jews who were lawyers, doctors, and many other different professions, asked for my help to try to assist them to get a physical job at the factory. I went to Mr Selényi: "Would you be able to help one of my friends to get a physical job here?

"Is he a Jew?" he asked me.

"Yes," I said with no hesitation.

"No problem," he responded.

In the same way as this first "employment", later he ended up employing a further 39 Jews in different positions. Although he was a Hitler sympathiser, on no occasion did he treat people inhumanely or assault anyone who belonged to the discriminated race.

However, the local Ispan [4] found out about how he was helping out the community and he ordered him to attend a meeting at which Mr Selényi got into trouble for lending a hand to the Jews.

The insulted one - My first antisemitic experience

In early 1939, WWII was close to its beginning.

I was walking home and a female friend of mine was coming out of the Apollo cinema. As it was dark, I offered to accompany her home, for which she was very grateful. It was a cold night and as we passed the Vadászkürt (hunting horn) ristorante on the Wesselényi Street I suggested to her we grab a shot of spirits to warm us up. Not long after we placed the order, four men walked into the pub and closed the doors. I knew right away that something was wrong. They were two policeman and two detectives. They started to check everyone's papers. When they came to our table, the girl handed over her ID. They did not find anything wrong as she was a good Christian girl. My ID was a grey coloured, small army booklet with a big red ZS, which meant Zs=Zsidó[5] on the front.

"Are you a Jew?" they asked me.

"Yes, I am."

"What are you doing here and having a drink with this Christian girl?" they asked.

"Why? I didn't do any harm to anyone. We are just having a drink together," I stated.

"Both of you have to come with us to the station!" they ordered. They took us to the police station at 20 Kossuth Street. I was ordered to follow them to the second level. They beat me up there and then, very badly. In addition, they wanted the girl to sleep with them, and in return they would not notify the authorities about her "wrongdoing", which was going out with a Jewish boy.

---

[4] The **ispán** or **count** was the leader of a castle district (a fortress and the royal lands attached to it) in the Kingdom of Hungary from the early 11th century.

[5] Zsidó= Jew in Hungarian

Luckily for her, one of her uncles was a police officer and they let her go early the following morning.

The Football player – My last football team

After the textile factory had no money to keep the football team running, it was closed down in 1939 and I joined the local team called "The Labour's Exercise Team of Debrecen"[6] (DMTE). This was openly a communist sport team, and we also had red football jerseys. Each time we went on the field, the fans of the opposition team yelled anti-communist words and slanders. I played for this team from 1939-1940 until my first forced labour camp.

---

[6] Debreceni Munkás Testedzö Egyesület

Hitler - The enemy

The news about Hitler, the Nazi ideology, Dachau, and a place in Poland was something we had heard about on the radio. A few relatives and friends who lived on the same Hatvan Street listened to the secret radio. We knew that at Dachau, Nazi Germany was collecting the political prisoners and the Jews. We heard about a place in Poland which had concentration camps, gas chambers and crematoriums. We were very self-confident, almost cocky in a way, and we did not believe anything could happen to us here in Hungary. We trusted the Hungarian Government very much and we strongly believed they would not permit anything terrible to happen to us.

I heard from other friends that sometimes there were trains crossing by our main train station and they were filled with people. One Saturday in 1939, my walk took me towards the station. I saw a long train which was filled with people. I am not sure what nationality they were, but I heard the voices and they were yelling for help. This much I could understand even if I did not speak their language.

I was very sorry for them and just acknowledged the fact but could not do anything about it. I went home, had lunch and forgot about this experience. I was in church with my father in 1941 when the Hungarian authorities entered in the building. They asked about anyone who had moved here to Hungary from Galilee[7] and had fathered children here. There were a few people who stood up. Two of our friends (Vári and Wulbrant) who were part of our Hatvan Street physical activity group, which was mainly a football team competing against other street's football teams, were taken away with many more men and their children and were executed. Even then we did not think it would happen to many of us who had been living in Hungary a long time as good citizens.

---

[7] Galilee is a region located in northern Israel and southern Lebanon.

My younger brother Béla

My two older brothers Zoltán and József had both moved to Budapest, got married and had children. Our big family in Debrecen had become smaller - just me as the oldest now at home, my younger brother Béla, younger sister Erzsébet, Mum and Dad.

The call to join the forced labour camp arrived in the mail, just like a military call. The difference was that we had to go in our civilian clothes and we had a yellow armband to show we were from a different outcast race. We didn't think of it much as it was war, and we understood that we had to help to defend our country in any way we could.

Béla was a successful army officer as a border protector for more than two years in the city of Berettyóújfalu[8]. He was a good soldier. His Major was Mr Pál who liked him so much he even presented my brother with a watch as a gift. Unfortunately, after 1942, Jews were no longer allowed to hold a position in the army.

The First Forced Labour Work Service

From 1940 to 1944 I was called up seven times for forced labour camps. According to the politicians and military officers we could also serve the homeland with shovels and pickaxes.

At the end of the summer in 1940, I received my first "work-service" call for unknown length of duty. Because it was war time it was normal to help the government and the army. Every citizen had to understand, "Help needed!" This was my first experience, where all 140 of us, young Jew men from Debrecen, turned up in civilian clothes. However, we had to wear a yellow

---

[8] A town in eastern Hungary

armband, which identified that we belonged to a different level of citizenship. We were considered a different race. I was in great physical condition, so the work was not difficult for me.

During three months at Hajdúnánás[9] we had to dig water wells and some of us helped out in the straw[10] factory. We had good quality food and living conditions. We stayed in a straw factory. Things were normal and humane. The situation concerning the treatment of Jews had not yet emerged as an issue. My relatives came to visit me three times and I could keep all the food and anything else they brought with them. Every Saturday we could go to the local church and every Sunday was also a day off. After our discharge from the labour camp I went home and returned to work at the textile factory for a few months before I received my second call.

The gardener - Püspökladány[11] – The notorious labour camp

My second call for duty was in 1941. Here, things got ugly. We were placed in a gunners' barracks outside of the city. From here we were transported to nearby cities like Szolnok[12] and Szajol[13] for work like digging ground, cleaning the train tracks or packing different items.

These barracks were notorious. The guards and officers where very selective in their methods of making our lives miserable. In June 1941 the grass on the barracks yard grew only a few centimetres "tall". The instructions were to bend over and tear the grass shoots off one by one. Our muscles were overstretched,

---

[9] Hajdúnánás is a town in Hajdú-Bihar county, in the Northern Great Plain region of eastern Hungary

[10] Straw is an agricultural by-product

[11] Püspökladány is the sixth largest town of Hajdú-Bihar county in North Eastern Hungary with a population of approximately 16,000 people.

[12] Szolnok is the county seat of Jász-Nagykun-Szolnok county in central Hungary. Its location on the banks of the Tisza river, at the heart of the Great Hungarian Plain, has made it an important cultural and economic crossroads for centuries.

[13] Szajol is a village in Jász-Nagykun-Szolnok county, in the Northern Great Plain region of central Hungary.

and the heat was uncomfortable. By using their beating sticks, the guards made sure we were not picking more than one grass shoot at a time. Instead of providing the water we needed in the heat, they sought to encourage greater effort by beating anyone who fell over from dizziness or lost consciousness. Our lips cracked from the dehydration and our bodies were dripping with sweat but we were not given even a single mouthful of water.

I picked the grass blades anxiously and cursed the existence of every one of them. I wished that the yard had consisted of sand and clay.

Luckily, I managed to get through the day without fainting or getting a heat-stroke.

After this "work" we were sent back to our barracks which had no windows - and they closed the door on us in the early afternoon. Of course, instead of cooling off, many more of us ended up getting heatstroke because we had not received any water either while "at work" or at the end of the day. Some men's condition was so severe it had to be medically treated. They were taken to the local doctor called Dr. Székely. He had "developed" his own special treatment for heatstroke. He would hammer the forehead with a small hammer to let the heat out. Consequently, many men came back with a cracked skull. He did not use any medicine other than a hammer.

In these unventilated barracks without any water, we had to get through the night. We had no access to toilets, so we had to satisfy our bodily needs into an internal community pot. Many of us suffered from the heat and dehydration all night.

The horseman

Next morning before the guards announced the next tedious work, the officer had a question to all of us, "Is there anyone, who can look after horses?" he asked.

As I was always very adventurous, which helped me for the rest of my years, I raised my hand a bit fearfully. Since I had that accident with a horse when I was four years old, resulting in me having a broken and shifted nose, I was sceptical if this venture would be a disaster or a glory.

The officer signalled at me to step forward, then looked at me from head a toe a few times. I must have made a positive impression on him as he just signalled again to follow him. As we left the barracks he finally started to talk to me. "We have a mare which has lost her foal, and you need to milk her to ease its pain". This task had a significant message as well. The horse and its pain was more important and had a higher status in the biological chain then us Jews.

As this conclusion ran through my mind, we arrived to see this magnificent huge dark horse which was tied to a tree. As beautiful this horse was, my knees started to shake and I felt all the blood exiting my face. I had to be careful of myself as the guard was watching me closely. I already regretted my decision of putting my hand up for this job, but I had to proceed if I did not want to be beaten up. I approached the horse from the front and gently reached under its belly to grasp the teats.

I watched horse's back leg closely. I was half on my knees and I started to milk the horse as I had seen cows getting milked. The horse was very unsettled at the start but then became relaxed.

I was very thirsty since we had not been given any water since the day before and I was swallowing my dry throat big time as the fresh milk got soaked up by the soil and disappeared in front of my eyes. I must have done a great job as the horse became very settled until I finished my job. Most importantly, I also pleased the guard and he noted my expertise as I climbed out from under the horse. Then, I received a new mission. He ordered me to look after the horse, give her water and food and start milking her again if she became unsettled. I was delighted to accept the order.

I walked around to savour my triumph, for she had saved me from being inside the barracks, away from the guards, the officers, and their wooden beating sticks. I was given some fodder and a bucket. I was afraid to drink at the well in front of the guards, so I had to wait until I returned to the horse. I knew horses will drink only fresh water, so I managed to spoon out some from the bucket with my hands as she was loudly sipping away. We made friends and she let me to drink with her from the same bucket. My golden time lasted only for two days. My drinking mate was taken away somewhere, but I was surprised that they did not send me back to the barracks. I had gained so much respect that I had been promoted to become a coachman. At that time, not only the men were affected by the calls for duty, it went on to the animals, the vehicles and the horse-drawn carriages from the nearby villages and towns.

There were about 40 carriages in the yard of the gunner barracks, most of them drawn by two horses. All the horses were fed next to the carriages, and with an assigned partner of mine, we walked around the animals and the carriages, checking out everything and chatting, but wittingly avoiding the subject of horsemanship. Both of us put our faith in the trust of the other. We had to get the horses harnessed to the wagon and get more straw from the train station. We were instructed to get ready. All we were waiting for was the command. My companion was looking very timidly towards me, and I towards him. I started to have a feeling that both of us were very uninformed in this profession.

"Harness the horses!" the sergeant commanded us.

Everybody started to move fast around the horses and with quick hands started to put all the gear on the horses in a systematic order. We were trying to watch and learn from the others, but it was impossible to pick up their professional skills quickly. The horses started to rear up and neigh. The commander understood what was going on, and came towards us yelling. He was calling us names, like "amateur" and "duffer" and suggesting we did not even deserve air and water. He sent us back inside the hot barracks where I remembered with disappointment my short golden days as a "horse-carer".

Most of the days were slow as we had to stay inside the barracks in the heat lying on the straw. Sometimes we were given some so-called "job" like picking grass blades one by one.

The other job we were given was to clean the local sewage pit. It was quite a deep hole. We had to lower each other with a rope to collect the human excrement in a bucket and bring it up to the surface. The smell was unbearable, our skin was soaked in it and it stayed with us for days.

Usually when the mail arrived, the guards took it and shared the packages amongst themselves. There was a very beautiful young Jewish woman called Eva Kolb. One day she delivered the mail to the barracks and somehow managed to talk the guards into distributing the mail to their rightful owners.

The Partisan

One day I organized a small partisan movement in the barracks. We found out that the wife of one of our colleagues had come to see her husband, but because we did not have permission to leave the site, he was very sad. Subsequently, I came up with an idea. I told a few guys to get the horses in the carriage and the rest was my job. They did so, then Dr János Madár, Dr György Gál, Dr Sándor Dán (whose wife we wished to meet outside) and myself, jumped up on the carriage and drove it to the gate. "Where are you guys going? "asked the guard at the gate. "We have to get to the train station to get more straw for the animals!" I said without blinking an eye, and off we went. They were very happy to see each other even if it was for a short period of time. This made me feel great. I had again helped out another friend in need.

One day a new order was announced from the Hungarian ministry stating that "The Jews must be entitled to a church visit once a week during forced labour." As a result, the guards had to take us to the local church. When the wives and women from the church saw us entering with all the soldiers, they all ran home to collect food (bread, milk, cheese, salami, home baked goodies, etc.) for us. When we arrived back to the barracks, it all had been taken away and the guards had split it all up amongst themselves.

From these barracks, human transports were sent, not only inside Hungary to other labour camps, but also into the Soviet Union. There they would pick up landmines, dig infantry entrenchments, build roads or off-load goods carried on the wagons. Whoever was chosen for these transports did not have much chance of returning alive.

On top of the usual inhumane work, the guards used hundreds of "smart" tortures including making men work without warm covering, like upper body clothing, in the minus 40 degrees Celsius temperatures. Not surprisingly we were afraid of these "selection days".

Such a selection was very hectic and draining as we watched anxiously to see who would be chosen to step forward from the line-up. The fate of anyone chosen was sealed when they were asked to step forward.

The brave one

This kind of marching battalion to the Soviet Union war front was about to be selected in the spring of 1942. In the barracks of Püspökladány about 300 of us were ordered to line up in the yard. A corporal walked between the lines and pulled our scared companions from it. The chosen ones had to walk away in front of officer Hegede, who was approving the selections. During the selection process I didn't even dare to look up, like an ostrich which will dig its head into the sand. I was trying to avoid the look of the corporal, even though this was a mistake. As much I was avoiding his look, the corporal saw all of us, even me. I winced when he grabbed my arm and pulled me out of the line. He jostled me towards all the other selected men. I had nothing to lose anymore and I tried the impossible as I stepped front of officer Hegede. I officially saluted and addressed him. "I have a bad knee," I said. "I have a meniscus tear. I suffered this injury during a football game. After forced marching I usually suffer from symptoms of swollen knee."

"You will fully recover in Ukraine!" said officer Hegede, yelling his refusal into my face as a response to my plea. I could do nothing, I had to accept the decision. In my exasperation I stepped into line with the others, who were also sorrowful. The weaker ones had tears rolling down on their cheeks as we waited for further orders. Less than five minutes later officer Hegede turned towards us. "Where is that man with the crook knee?" he yelled. "Step forward," he ordered. Completely forgetting my bad knee, I jumped out of the line like a gazelle. Hegede looked at me very closely and with a very loud voice he said, "I'm having a great day today. I'm selecting you into the transport to Szolnok city. Move over into the other line." The other group greeted me with happy and joyful looks but no one would dare to speak. Here all men were weak, old, or ill. They were not fit enough for the forced march to Ukraine. Officer Hegede's inexplicable decision helped me to remain inside the country. I have never found out why this grumpy and ruthless officer made this decision – one which spared my life, at least for now. On the same night that we left the barracks of Püspökladány we were ordered to move to Szolnok. Very quickly the news about the selection process escaped from the barracks and relatives and friends tried to receive some information at the gate as we marched out. We had one eye smiling and one was crying. We had to say goodbye to many relatives and friends who had gone with the other transport. Many never returned from the battles at Voronezh[14] where they lie in an unmarked grave.

In Szolnok we had to fix the railways. The guards required very hard work, and all of us did as required as we were happy to still be in Hungary. We found out later what had happened to the ones who had been sent to the Soviet front to perform forced labour work. Many froze to death or ended up being beaten to death by the guards.

---

[14] In late June 1942, the German military launched Case Blau, the operation designed to capture the oil-rich Caucasus region. Voronezh is a city and the administrative centre of Voronezh Oblast, Russia, straddling the Voronezh River and located 12 kilometres from where it flows into the Don. The city sits on the South-eastern Railway, which connects European Russia with the Urals and Siberia, the Caucasus and Ukraine, and the M4 highway. - https://thegreatpatrioticwar.wordpress.com/battle-of-voronezh-june-july-1942/

A few months later I was discharged and after returning home I once again went back to work in the textile factory. The German owner was aware of what had happened to the Jews, so he was happy to see me back at work.

The injured one

I was home for only a few weeks when I have received a new call for forced labour, this time to Gyoma[15]. After all 600 of us had arrived from Debrecen, we were allocated to one of three commands, the 7th, 8th and 9th, where we lived under very strict conditions. I was allocated to the 9th command with my brother, Béla. Because from 1942 no Jews were any longer allowed to be part of the army, he had been discharged from the Hungarian armed forces and been called up for forced labour work like me. There was no "selecting" being conducted there and they immediately told us we would be departing to the Soviet-Union. We were treated by the guards as having been given the death sentence.

The guards did not allow us the smallest amount of "luxury". We were not allowed to receive any kind of mail (letters and packages) and we could not even see our closest relatives as visitors. One of the commanders even ordered that the visitors be beaten up as well. We felt like we were prisoners for life. We did not have to work there - we were just waiting for our departure. On one occasion I checked in to the medical staff with my knee but I was sent back to the barracks. The doctor from Debrecen knew me from the football fields and said to me, "The army needs strong young men like you to do the labour work".

One Saturday morning, the three companies had to line up after marching to the football field of Gyoma where we waited in columns of five for something to happen.

---

[15] Gyomaendrőd is located in the Great Hungarian Plain upon the river Körös, 177 km southeast from Budapest. The smaller towns of *Gyoma* and *Endrőd* were united in 1982

Our commander was a very young man called Radnóti, whom we best knew as being very inhumane towards us. He walked around the columns and always managed to find something wrong, such as the yellow armband not being put up exactly the way it should have been on the sleeve of the jacket. As he was walking around his path led him towards me. Perhaps driven by some sort of instinct, I stepped out from the line right in front of him. To step out of the line without permission already showed bravery as it was forbidden. I had nothing to lose. I was sentenced to death one way or another.

I was prepared to be penalized even with a physical punishment. Radnóti's look showed surprise. I repeated the same line I had previously said to Hegede. "I have a bad knee. I have a meniscus tear. I suffered this injury during a football game." He studied me for a long time and I could not read anything good from his look.

My companions around me admired my bravery, even my younger brother, Béla, who was close to me. I had not told him about my intention as I had acted only in that moment, spontaneously. If the commander had not walked towards me I may not have been able to write down my story of survival. I do not know if it was my bravery that impressed him, or whether he had some human feelings inside him deep, deep down.
He didn't start to yell at me nor send me back into the line. My companions and myself were impressed to see that he did not become violent against me. After studying me he ordered, "Step out of the line, walk to the football goalkeeper box and lay down on the grass." The irony of the situation didn't pass me by. I am lying down on the football field next to the goalbox and waiting for my sentence - which could be to live or die. A few years ago, I had been racing with a football ball towards the goal to score with a passion and now I was waiting for amnesty or my death sentence. My thinking and dreaming were distracted by the trumpeting of the horns. Army vehicles had arrived and high ranked army leaders stepped out of them. Commands were called out and the battalions were frozen in their formation during an inspection. A Lieutenant-Colonel from Debrecen delivered his speech. He brought to the attention of the 600 men

that they would be transported to the Soviet Union where they all must serve our country to their absolute best.

After his speech he walked through the lines and his eyes noticed me as he was very close to the goal. I heard as he enquired why was I lying down over there. Radnóti told him,"He has a meniscus tear in his knee." The Lieutenant-Colonel right away said to him, "He needs to be discharged immediately. We have no use for a man with sore legs." A corporal came to me and started to write down my details. Looking down with my eyes almost shut I dictated my name, date of birth and where I had been born, hoping he would not see the endless happiness in my eyes. After the inspection they also arranged my transport. A two horse-drawn carriage came and picked me up and took me back to the barracks. I received my discharge documents, but they did not allow me to say goodbye to my brother. He did manage to yell through the small gap of the office door, "I'm leaving on my long journey with peace in my heart as I know someone will be able to look after our old and ill parents after all."

It was getting dark when I walked by myself to the train station of Gyoma to catch the train to Debrecen. I was heading home, and the rest of the 600 men were leaving to a one-way journey. None of the men ever returned and this was the last time I saw my young brother Béla.

Unfortunately, I was home only for a few weeks and in the beginning of 1942[14] I was called for duty once again - to Püspökladány and Gyoma.

They had been waiting for the new arrivals of our forced labour group with a job in mind. However, it was one which clearly did not serve the country which was at war. The cesspool was full of human waste and it had to be emptied and cleaned out.

It was a very cold winter. As our family had been living very poorly, it had also showed in the lightness of my clothing. Many who had better financial status had proper warm winter clothing and winter shoes on. I had only a very light jacket and just normal shoes. Maybe my poor clothes brought me luck.

We had been sent over to Szolnok again. In an early cold morning we had to clean the snow and ice from the railways with a pickaxe. It was a very difficult job in the freezing weather. My clothing was not exactly the best against the cold.

One morning a man in his railway uniform approached me along with one of our guards. I was ordered to follow the railwayman. I was happy to follow him leaving my "army shadow" behind and hoping to get some job easier than hacking. The man in the railwayman uniform did not say a word, he did not ask a question, and I just followed. We arrived at his little railroad house and he waved at me to enter. It was nice and warm inside. He ordered me to sit and suddenly he became friendly. "My name is Veres and I'm the group leader of the Szolnok railway locksmith brigade. I was sorry for you wearing this light clothing in this cold. I asked the guard to let you come with me as I have a very important job for you - to clean the railway switches."

So, I went outside and did a bit of that for a few minutes when he asked me again to come into the house.

"Here", he said, "eat some bread and pork specks." I was very grateful for that. He kept me with him for the rest of the afternoon and did not let me go back to my battalion. Somehow he managed to make an arrangement and I'm sure he also had to take responsibility for me.

Next morning, I got a further surprise. I was called by name, "Schwarcz, step forward!" the guard ordered. "You must go to the railway's locksmith building to see Mr Veres," he ordered. I ended up working there for the next few days.

In the beginning no one would look at me (the one with the yellow armband) with kindness, especially when they all found out I could not even operate a simple blower machine. However, as the days went by, they all started to help me, not just with the jobs but also by testifying to the guards what a great workman I was and how much help I was in the repair centre.

I had a lot to thank Veres for. He looked after me and he liked me. I saw lots of solidarity between the railway workers, even up in the higher ranks.

I believe he was responsible for my next placement when I had to work in the wagon factory in Szolnok. The locksmith workshop was far too much within in the view of the guards and he wanted me to be further away from them.

The work was not easy. We had to carry very heavy items from one pit into the next but the workers were very friendly and that made the very heavy physical job easier and bearable. This was the first time I had met a workman who was a communist thinker since I had begun my forced labour work.

There was an older man with lots of deep wrinkles on his face working with a grindstone. He made sure I did not feel the indignity of the forced labour. He spoke bravely about the future fall of Nazism and he deeply disagreed with the idea of us, the Jews, being treated as non-citizens. All the other workmen looked up to this man and treated him with high respect. It was clearly visible he was the spokesman of the service station. His guidance was effective as they all talked about Horthy[16] with hate and the bad decision of fighting against the Soviet Union in the war. They always had great news for me because they knew a lot about the updates of the war and reported the retreat of the German army with great happiness and provided me even more support. They brought me so much I was able to share with my inmates at night at the sugar factory where we all stayed overnight.

Their brave and courageous words brought me happiness, especially when they started to share their sandwiches with me. A few days later they started to bring me some more food from home - sausages, salamis, specks, bread. I thanked them for their work and care at the Szolnok wagon factory and the locksmith station for a few weeks. I met many great people who were bravely supportive of the weak ones. They proved with their humanitarian behaviour that not everyone had joined the inhumane Fascist ideology. I always remember these workers and the group leader, Veres, with great respect.

---

[16] **Miklós Horthy**, (born June 18, 1868, Kenderes, Hung., Austria-Hungary—died Feb. 9, 1957, Estoril, Port.), Hungarian naval officer and conservative leader who defeated revolutionary forces in Hungary after World War I and remained the country's head of state until 1944.

Mikló
s Horthy

Miklós Horthy and Adolf Hitler
Picture from: https://www.pinterest.com.au/pin/327707310361741650
https://upload.wikimedia.org/wikipedia/commons/thumb/3/30/Miklós_H
orthy_and_Adolf_Hitler_1938.jpg/1200px-
Miklós_Horthy_and_Adolf_Hitler_1938.jpg
More info about : **Miklós Horthy**
https://www.britannica.com/biography/Miklos-Nagybanyai-Horthy

One early morning the guards asked if anyone felt sick or
incapacitated. If so, it should be reported, as there would be a
visit of a doctor during the day. An army doctor arrived and
listened patiently to the problems of all those who lined up next

to the main building of the train station. I used this opportunity to pay a visit to him regarding my knee which was very swollen. We had to walk a very long distance every morning from the sugar factory to the train station, work all day carrying heavy items, then walk back at night. I was trying to treat my injury with a cold wet wrap as much I could. The doctor sent me, along with 42 other ill forced labour workers, to have a further medical check. Next morning we walked to the army hospital, which was next to the Zagyva[17] river, guarded by some soldiers. As we arrived in the corridor of this brand new big hospital, l somehow managed to sit down on one of the few benches and some had to remain standing. We were waiting for the visit which would happen later in the day. I was deep in thought when I was interrupted by a lot of loud yelling. A short and stocky man in white cape was abusing our group. From the military stripes I was able to identify his rank. He was the Lieutenant-Colonel in charge of the hospital. "You dirty spies, you traitor communists, you fucking Jews!" He kept going on and on with his abuse. "All of you, stand up from the benches, you make them filthy just by even sitting on them," he yelled. His angry eyes were scanning us back and forth as we were standing in the hallway, which had become silent for a moment. Then his eyes stopped on me, he lifted his arm up and with his finger pointed at me said, "This is the only man who can sit down. Do not let anyone else from this useless bunch sit down," he ordered to the guard. I was astonished at hearing this statement from this wild and stormy man. I did not remember ever having met or had ever came across him in my life. When he left, all inmates wanted to find out the reason for his decision, but I could not answer them. Of course, not one of them believed my claim that I had never met this Lieutenant-Colonel before. Later on he maintained his positive discrimination of me, but as much as I thought about it, I was unable to find out the reason behind why he was sympathetic only towards me.

Each one of us from the group was sent to different departments in the hospital. I went to the orthopaedic ward on level one. A very tall captain doctor called me into the examination room, where there was no one else, only a range of different

---

[17] It is a river in Hungary near Szolnok

equipment. I was a bit scared by this huge man as I waited for the examination. I was very pleased when he asked about my problem in a very friendly voice.

He listened patiently as I became more and more open towards him when I was describing the symptoms of my knee. I do not deny that I was over-exaggerating a bit as I really wanted to be discharged and to go home. When I had finished, he called for an administrator with a typewriter and he dictated all my problems to her - word for word. It was difficult for me not to show my happiness as the captain handed over my prognosis after signing it. This was a 50% chance now of being discharged if this letter should end up in the hands of a reasonable professional. I said goodbye to this friendly huge doctor with gratitude, and he replied with warmth.

All of us inmates re-gathered at the same place we had arrived, but my inmates were returning very slowly - one by one. Some ended up having an examination in the internal medicine, neurology, or laryngology wards. They briefed each other in quiet whispers and I identified that not everyone had enjoyed such luck with the doctors as I had. There were some doctors who had been rude like the Lieutenant-Colonel who identified the patient as a malinger or as a hypochondriac.

It was late afternoon when everyone had finally returned, and we could hear the yelling of the Lieutenant-Colonel from far away as he was closing in towards us.

He was even worse with his swearing than in the morning. "The examination is not over just yet," he yelled. "You all have to come back tomorrow." Then his angry eyes scanned us one more time and again stopped on me and said to the guard, "This one doesn't have to come back for another visit".

The road from the sugar factory to the hospital was long so I was unhappy that I did have to walk the miles once more. But again, I did not understand the reason behind the privilege. I have never found out why only four of more than 40 men, including me, were discharged from the duty.

On the next forced labour call we ended up under the supervision of a strange company commander. He was a very young man, and he was responsible for more than 200 of us. He did not use the usual "funny jokes" on us. He did not allow the guards to be unkind towards us either. This was unnecessary because the guard group was also made up of kind men.

Our battalion's work territory was in Szolnok and when the new commander took over in Püspökladány we waited anxiously to see what kind of man he would be. He introduced himself in an unusual way. He ordered us to line up then he stated the following, "I will need everyone's full attention at all times. I will not allow any indiscipline. I will demand that you follow orders, and I do not want anyone to abuse or test my human nature." We listened to the next sentences with surprise. "I want any forced labourer who can tell me the biggest ever lie to step forward, because I will grant work-free days to reward the biggest liars." We looked at each other in astonishment. We did not think he was for real. The young commander was for real and he did encourage us to come forward. Based on my previous experiences, none of the battalion commanders had as much generosity that he would grant work-free days. In the past, none of them even took into consideration a dying family member.

Accordingly, our precaution and suspicion was understandable regarding this invitation. I thought to myself, "This world is made for the adventurous. Maybe the commander will live up to his words." I stepped out of the line with seven other inmates waiting for his questions. He called our attention one more time: "Whoever can obtain the best support of the 'audience' for the believability of the lie will be rewarded with a few days of rest." I stood at the end of the line while each of the others started their best performance. In my childhood I had been taught to create the best possible story. When it was my turn I started my monologue with stage fright. To be honest, I don't even remember the storyline of my few minutes of fame, but I waited in awe for my "audience's" reaction.
The commander indicated, "Your lie wasn't good enough."
I was upset. Then he said: "Your story was worth only two days off and a dismissal for two days".

I could not believe my ears when the order was handed to me and to the others as well. We all received two or three days off, except one man, whose performance had been worth five days off. I was pleased about my "prize" but I was a bit upset with myself that I could not create a bigger lie to get more days off. Our captain was in a good mood most of the time. We had an inmate who had grown a very big and long moustache. One morning the captain said to him during the line-up, "If you will shave off your moustache, I will grant you three days off." The inmate could not resist. He chose to see his family for three days instead of keeping his beloved facial hair.

We also had a very religious Rabbi with us, who prayed every morning and every evening. The captain did not disagree with this - completely the opposite. He wanted him to pray with more heart and enthusiasm for the souls of all in the battalion. One morning as we were performing our line-up, the commander ordered: "Rabbi, step out front of all these men and start praying." He had no choice. He had to put something together from memory on the spot. During his preaching the captain cut in a few times: "Not good enough!" or "Preach more from the heart!" or "Come on, no one is crying yet!" or "You need to preach about a much sadder event!". Poor Rabbi. He was sweating by the end and he could not get his preaching finished quickly enough.

The financial status of each inmate was very easy to identify from the quality of the clothes they wore. Some had backpacks and good quality pots and aluminium cups. I clearly belonged to the poor social economic section. As my father was a shoemaker, he could not let me go to the forced labour camps in very good clothing. My father had decided to sew a pillow into the inner side the back of my jacket before I left for this forced labour duty to help me against the cold.

This kept me warm but also gave me a lot of grief. I looked like the Humpback of Notre-Dame as the pillow had not been sewed in evenly and feathers were poking through my jacket. I was constantly trying to keep the fabric clean. Some inmates teased me for my "grotesque" look. Our commander had some sympathetic feelings towards the poorer labourers and often asked the cooks to give me bigger portions of lunch or dinner.

He also allowed me to do some extra jobs on the Sundays which were work-free days. I poured warm water in a big dish and washed the clothes for the richer ones for a few extra pennies, which I sent home to my family. Along with washing clothes I also took on cutting hair and shaving faces. I did not learn to become a barber, I knew only as much as I had seen at the salons. I had only a safety razor, a pair of scissors, and a comb. That was the selection of my tools. It was difficult to shave with my safety razor and I had to work hard for the few pennies I was charging. Poor "clients" also gave some painful noises until I finished both cheeks. Later, as I become more skilful, my clients became more satisfied. I also learned to click my scissors like a professional. I cut a lot of hair from the heads of my fellow inmates.

The news of my great work reached as far as the guards and one of my new clients was one of the guard soldiers. I placed a towel on his neck and started to click my scissors like a professional. I wanted to satisfy him. I was careful not to pull his hair by accident with the scissors because I did not want to get a kick in the stomach in return. The hair fell down from my cuts and I looked around with pride when I announced, "Done! We are finished." I did not receive any money in return from the soldier. He taught me his faith in me was good enough. I do not deny it was great propaganda for my private "business" because if our guards trusted my work, they might all trust me to provide their haircut and shave.

My barber business was going very well until one of the wealthy inmates gave friendly help that caused me some grief. He was a son of a businessman from Békescsaba[18]. He may have become sorry for me, or he was thinking about his own hair, so he presented me with a gift. Like presenting a ceremonial award, he handed over a brand new hand-held clipper machine with great pride. I pretended my happiness, but honestly, I opened the box with fear. I took the machine in my hand away from everyone's view and started to move it around for practice the way I had seen it done at the salon. I was just practising the movements without cutting any hair. Of course, the rest of the battalion found out about the "arrival" of my new professional clippers and many waited for me to put it into action. One of our long

---

[18] Békéscsaba is a city in Southeast Hungary, the capital of the Békés-county.

and thick haired inmates came and he looked with faith at my new machine and then at me. I placed the machine with great excitement on the back of his neck and started to move it upwards. I managed to cut a nice piece off, but my fear became reality. The hair became stuck inside the machine, not allowing me to open or close it. It clung onto his hair and I could not move the mechanism in or out. I tried every way to get the machine off his hair and neck, but it would not budge. My poor client hissed and he also tried to pull his hair out of the grip of the machine. In the meantime, I started to swear at the machine and its poor quality. I tried my best to blame my difficulty on my new gift. When we finally managed to free my mate from the grip of the machine he was sweating. I returned to using the comb and the scissors to finish up the job. I cleaned the machine, placed it back in its box and handed it back to its owner, pointing out all the possible defects it had.

For a bit of a change one of our captains decided to give us an important job. We had to clean the highway leading to Karcag[19]. We had to source our own brooms which we made from the branches of the trees along the road. The order stated as follows: *"A certain section of the road must be as clean as a white bedsheet!"* Water was poured on the road and we had to clean all the dust, dirt and tree leaves off it. As soon as one car had driven through, we had to start the job again. The warnings and the threats stayed and the guards questioned everyone who had dared to leave one small speck of dust on the road. They reminded us over and over about the importance of the job and our responsibility to perform it to our absolute best. The reason behind this was that the road was being used by high-ranking army personnel who deserved to drive on a clean road.
We could not ask questions. If we had been able, I would have asked why the Budapest–Debrecen 220 kilometre road had to be clean only on a few hundred metres for the high-ranking army personnel and, for the rest of their trip, they would not be disturbed by the dust and dirt on the road.

---

[19] Karcag is a large town in Jász-Nagykun-Szolnok county, in the Northern Great Plain region of central Hungary.

During my seven forced labour works I barely performed any useful jobs. We had incomprehensible orders. Some of them were just for the purpose of pure humiliation and for the entertainment of the soldiers.

At Szolnok-Alcsi we had the most brutal army crew. Having a yellow armband made us lesser human beings. We were more vulnerable than even the lowest-ranked army private.
One day, half of the battalion was ordered to lie down on the grass on their backs on the field outside the barracks and the other half had to lie on top of them. The order was to act like we were having sex.

On another occasion we were led to the banks of Tisza[20] river for a swim. No one asked if we could or could not swim - we were all pushed towards the water. All guards laughed as soon someone appeared to be about to drown - before they ordered a rescue operation.
On another cold winter morning, during the line-up, the guards poured cold water into the coat sleeves of each one of us.

We had a medical room which was known more as a place of infamy. We knew from first-hand experience it was more of a torture room then a treatment room. One morning I woke up with terrible tooth-ache so I reported it to my first officer Dévai who sarcastically said to me: "I'll be there when your tooth is pulled out because I know you are just faking it. I know you just want to have a day off work." I was escorted to a very unfriendly looking room where Dévai was already waiting for me with his hands on his hips. A man in a white cape showed me to a seat and they both looked sardonically at each other. The "white-caped man" asked a soldier to disinfect the tool with heat. Soon enough he returned, and I opened my mouth to show the aching tooth. The "white-caped man" pushed the smouldering tool to the corner of my lips. I jumped out of my seat from the burning pain which split my lips. Dévai asked me, "So, is your tooth still

---

[20] The Tisza or Tisa is one of the main rivers of Central and Eastern Europe. Once, it was called "the most Hungarian river" because it flowed entirely within the Kingdom of Hungary. Today, it crosses several national borders.

hurting?" Of course, it was, but now not only my tooth, but my burnt lips as well. Following my tormentor's witticism, I sat back in the chair. By now the tool, which seemed to me an ordinary pliers, had cooled off, so that did not hurt - but the pulling did - even more. I felt the iron on my sore tooth, and started to feel the pulling and twisting of it as I had not been given any painkiller. I was being lifted out of my seat by my tooth, but my guards shoved me back. A terrible pain, a cracking noise and only a broken piece was left in my mouth where my tooth used to be. I could not bear the torturing any longer, I jumped out of my seat and ran out the room leaving these "gentlemen" behind. They were not satisfied enough with my agony. Dévai shouted after me, "I will punish you for your pretending!"

I was heading back to work with my guard with barely any energy left in me from this event and I was dreaming of seeing a real dentist to help with my tooth ache. During the long walk, my pain started to ease from what was left of the half tooth in my mouth. It seemed to me that from the pulling and twisting my nerves had been damaged and I could not feel my tooth any longer. I had escaped from the toothache.

However my knee was very swollen from pushing the wheelbarrow. We had to take the sand down from the 'bullet-catcher' hillside in wheelbarrows and then carry it back up again. They did not care about the job being carried out with professionalism. Once again, a job with no purpose which would not help our nation during the war.   Other battalions had been performing the same job previously. Carrying the sand up and down the hillside was an extremely difficult physical job. On the way down the wheelbarrow ran with ease, but on the way up all muscles were tensed up from the strenuosity of the task. The guards pushed us for higher and higher performance with their yelling and many times I could not feel my legs and felt like my lungs would explode. Neither did the beatings disappear. They watched us closely without any mercy. By the end of the week my knee was swollen up badly, but my luck finally arrived.

The head of the guards called Mille was known as the most brutal of all. One Saturday morning he was sitting on the ground chewing on a piece of grass and as I was filling up the wheelbarrow with a shovel, I felt he was watching me. I was not happy about it. If this sadist was watching someone closely, it always ended up badly. I looked at him from time to time from the corner of my eyes and a few times our looks met. By now I was sure he wanted something from me, but I did not know what mistake I had made or what he would punish me for. Sure enough, he called my name, which was a positive thing instead of barking "hey you" at me. He turned to me with a very unusual request. "Show me some circus stuff! I heard you were a circus performer." I did not know where he got the information from, but I left him keep his belief and told him: "I'm unable to perform acrobatic skills right now and although my knee is very sore, I'm more than happy to give a short performance if that is something you would be keen to listen to." As I was in the drama group when I was younger, I still remembered some of the lines from various performances. Mille agreed with the change of plan and he made himself comfortable on the side of the sand wall and instructed me to start the "show". The inmates around me started to watch as well and had also became my audience. Mille did not yell at them so I managed to score a few minutes of break for my fellow members. I started my singing performance standing on the bullet-catcher sand dune. As I was singing, I started to notice my surroundings less and less. Soon I felt I was performing on a stage and the song went, "Lots of food has arrived to Debrecen,…".

I must have performed with success as my most distinguished guest in the audience, Senior Master Sergeant Mille was clapping with joy at the end. My fellow workmen were afraid to clap, but I saw the smiles on their faces too.

I had to conduct another performance but this time in front of all the guards, as Mille had decided to call all of them together for a break. Suddenly, I had been promoted to a well-known actor which had its positive side, as that night at dinner my pot was filled up to its maximum capacity with potato pasta[21]. As a result of my acting role, somehow the ruthless treatment of the guards eased and they looked at us now more as humans. I was happy for this change because, not only did it make my life easier, it did so for all the labour workers as well.

---

[21] Hungarian potato pasta is a simple dish made from pasta and potatoes and is seasoned with Hungarian paprika.

When I was discharged from the labour camp, I went home again and reported for work the next day at the Textile factory.

A few weeks later in February 1944 another call for duty arrived in the mail, but this time I reported my knee condition at the hospital. I spent close to three weeks there where more testing was done. The conditions there were not great. If we had to go to the toilet, a guard had to escort us there and back. We had two doctors there. One was called Dr Árvai and he was not performing his duty as a doctor with us. There was an elderly man with us in the same room who had a problem with his gall bladder, and he was in a lot of pain. When Dr Árvai came he asked him sarcastically: "Are you having a lot of pain? Good! Then you should suffer!", and he walked out of the room. The other doctor called Dr Kallós whom I knew from earlier, was a nice man and did his duty according to his medical vows. When he came he asked the patient how he was feeling. He then went out into the corridor, looked around to see if anyone was approaching or not, then quickly came back, injected a painkiller and walked out.

After three weeks of investigation about my knee I finally was given another statement, "Sándor Schwarcz has a meniscus tear in his knee which cannot be fixed, therefor he is dismissed from further forced labour duties."

By now we knew from the news about the big loss of the Hungarian-German army in the 40 below Celsius temperature at Stalingrad, Russia[22]. We knew Nazi Germany and its allies would lose the war, but we did not know what would happen to us Jews. I was brave enough to give my opinion, even at work. One of my "colleagues" warned me "If you don't stop telling everyone your opinion, I will report you to the authorities". We also had a Polish widow at work, and she warned us about the terrible treatment of the Jews. She also had a lot of information about the concentration camps. She told us to go,

---

[22] The Soviet Union announced that the 462-day Battle of Stalingrad had ended after the last of the German Sixth Army forces surrendered. Of the more than 250,000 German soldiers who had fought in the campaign, half were killed in battle, and the other half taken prisoners of war. Only 6,000 would survive to return home

leave the country and find some safe place to hide. However, we did not listen to her. We did not want to believe what she was telling us. On the other hand, my sixth sense told me that we would have difficult and catastrophic times soon. Still, we did not do anything, Some wealthy Jews were able to pay for their "freedom" and were either relocated or kept in a safe place.

I organized a group of six Jews (the Kurti brothers and others who moved to Canada after the war) to look after the elderly Jews in the city. We engaged in many fist fights with the young students from the University.

There was a man who was collecting Jew's long beards and long sideburns and paid good money for it. So, the elderly Jews were an easy target.

Windows of Jew's homes were broken, friends were de-friended and people were assaulted on the streets and at churches. The well-oiled Nazi propaganda had worked. By now, wounded soldiers had returned from the war and the news about the lost ones was arriving day after day. All these things were not helping us, the Jews, as we were the reason of their losses according to the propaganda, and the people believed it. The anti-Semitism was getting worse and worse. The loss of Stalingrad by the German army forced them to retreat. Like a cornered lion they became more and more blood-thirsty.

It is difficult to remember about every day of the four years and seven calls for forced labour, but what followed these events was much worse than I was expecting - ghetto, Auschwitz, Dachau, and so on.

After these four years a fifth one followed, but here, not only hundreds of thousands suffered, but millions disappeared and perished.

With great luck I was able to live through to my liberation to tell the truth.

Living with the Yellow Star…

By now from the Eastern and Western European countries (France, Belgium, Poland, Italy etc.) many Jews, Gypsies, gays, along with mentally or physically disabled people, had been transported by trains to the concentration camps where they were ordered to work to support the Nazi army, or killed on the spot.

On a Sunday afternoon March 19, 1944 [23] the rumbling of SS planes and vehicles was heard from the air and from the ground. Soon, armoured military vehicle troops arrived with skull badges on their hats. On this day, tens of thousands of SS armed soldiers occupied the most important stations and cities. The fascist troops quickly arrived at Debrecen as well. On this Sunday, not only were the main streets noisy from black uniformed soldiers speaking German, but the smaller backstreets were occupied too.

The occupying troops made themselves at home in no time. They moved around town like home-born citizens. They took over the pubs, rendezvoused with the ladies, and soon enough the sneaks and informers made contact with them with a pre-prepared list which included the names and addresses of the left-wing supporters. In minutes they arrived on the addresses of the wanted persons and transported them to the newly-established jail of the Gestapo. The underground cells on the Deak Ferenc Street building were filled up in a few hours with progressive and left-wing thinkers.

On this day, I was present at an event in the Arany János Street building of the local printing factory's culture room. We could hear the rumbling of the vehicles from outside and the news got to us very quickly. We stopped the event as no one was in the mood to celebrate. We all went home in the distracted city. I was upset too. I was assuming what the next few days would bring. We heard bad news about the SS soldiers' rampages and extreme behaviours. I knew I would be amongst the vulnerable citizens.

---

[23] 1944: Mar 18 - Nazi Germany occupies Hungary, Mar 31 - Hungary orders all Jews to wear yellow stars, May 16 - 1st of 180,000+ Hungarian Jews reach Auschwitz

Some citizens rushed to get home without seeing the SS soldiers and some started to befriend them.

When I entered our house at 60 Hatvan Street my mum, my dad and my little sister were waiting for me with alarmed looks on their faces. They understood the reality. There was no point ignoring the truth. There was no reason to say anything comforting. I went to bed very early. Maybe we would have a few more nights during which they would not come for us; they would not take us away. But I knew the fearful and dreadful days were coming; what the English radio was talking about; the ghettos, the gas chambers and the exterminations. The events rolled on very quickly. The arrests and the intimidations showed the presence of the Gestapo.

With the friendly cooperation of the Hungarian government officials, regulations which contained harsh and cruel instructions and which targeted the left-wing progressive thinkers, and the Jews even more, appeared one by one.

Billboards and signs had been placed everywhere notifying the Jew community to wear the David's Yellow Star from 6 am on the 5th of April. The details were clear – a 20 cm sized, five-pointed yellow star must be sewed on the left side of the jacket. The penalties were very brutal if someone did not follow the orders. Valuables had to be handed over also. Many had lost their businesses and homes, depending on their location.

I was born in the city of Debrecen. I believe I acted with integrity and humanity with all citizens. I worked at the textile factory on Bethlen Street, where I also tried to connect humanely with my colleagues. Nevertheless, I had to mark my clothes with plague-spot (blemish). I must be able to be recognised from far away so anyone who came face-to-face on the street would see it as a warning sign: '*I am an unwanted person here! Avoid me! Get out of my way or mock me; make jokes about the Jews until they are destroyed! Until then they must live with a distinguishing mark amongst us!*'

This was the reason of this measure.

I got myself a bright canary yellow star. My mother, my father and my sister had to have one as well. My sister sewed it on our clothes by hand. On this April day, I was the first one in the morning to wear this yellow star outside the family home. I had to be at work by 6am. I was particularly slow putting my clothes on, deliberately delaying the time. I was as frightened to put my clothes on as a patient getting ready for a big surgery. I looked at my coat, on which my sister had sewed the yellow star, which was waiting for me on the back of the chair, with humiliation. It was like my coat had tonnes of rocks in it. That is how difficult it was for me to put it on. I was ashamed in front of my parents and my sister in our Hatvan street home. I had to go. I said goodbye to my family with my head down. I was preparing for a big and difficult walk. I had to walk on the street of my birth-town with denunciation. I grew up around here, I made my first steps here as a baby, I sounded my first words here, and the first words I heard were in Hungarian. I was branded in my hometown with a yellow star. I had been turned into a stranger. I was ashamed of myself. I was ashamed of the Hungarian Government. I was ashamed to go onto the streets.

On this sunny April morning I stepped out of my home of 35 years with my eyes down, with my head down. The yellow star was screaming to be seen on my coat. I looked around and I was trying to avoid my first meeting with others on the street. I put my arm across my chest to hide the star. But this movement did not help; the edges could be seen from underneath the dark suit. There were already many people on the streets. The citizens knew about the new ruling. Many also knew me and they all looked curiously at me. I was trying to avoid eye contact. The people who made this new rule should have been the ones being ashamed of themselves as well as the ones who looked at my visible star without any sympathy. The rule was for everyone - kids, women, youngsters and elderly as well. Many elderly people had fought for their homeland in the first world war, and now instead of "medals of honour", they had to wear this new badge.
In Denmark, the king placed a yellow star on his coat, to express his solidarity with the hunted ones.
I did not meet with many who had any sympathy. The better case was when someone walked by without any expression. There were sarcastic looks and some made insulting comments. But there were some good examples too. Two university students came in the opposite direction to me. They had saluted

towards their special university hut. I could read the sympathy and regret. There were some comrades from my labour movement, who were brave enough to stop and talk to me. I had a friend Antal Pogácsás, who walked with me with arms crossed together as a demonstration of solidarity. He was not afraid of prosecution or the insults. He even invited me to his home. He and another friend, Gyula Rácz, asked me to join them to watch a football game. I told them it was not a great idea, but they insisted. So I went along, but it backfired as I had expected. I received a high number of verbal assaults during the game, which was what I had told them would happen. This was my last time to watch a football game and to go out into the general public. Even my supportive friends could not stop what was ahead of me and the other Jews.

When I arrived at the factory I took off my coat simply for comfort and to stay cool. The foreman who was always pleased with my work questioned me: "What do you think you are doing taking off your coat? You must wear the yellow star all the time!"

"It is very hot inside here and everyone here knows I'm a Jew. There is no need to wear a coat and a yellow star here inside the factory, I said.
"Then you should sew one on your shirt too. I do not allow the rules to be disregarded", he argued.
I saw from the faces of my colleagues how pleased they were that their group leader was being so strict. So, next day I came to work with two yellow stars. (After the war I ran into this foreman on the street and he apologised. He blamed the 25 years of education in the Horthy-system, and said he now knew it was all untruth and lies.)

One of our friends had a radio where we could listen to the English news. From there we knew about what was happening to the Jews in Europe. We knew about the concentration camps and the gas chambers. We knew how much the German army was losing ground. It was a terrible time to live through and to know what was coming. The majority of the public made us feel the discrimination even more.

The propaganda had changed its tactics. Now the news emphasized work camps. The Hungarian Jews were to be deported to German-held territory and would be working in labour camps to help the army's production in whatever way they could. The Nazis wanted to make deportation smooth - and it worked. We had wanted to believe that this would not happen to us as by now most of the allied countries and nations had turned against the Nazi regime. Only the Hungarian Government was loyal to Germany. Romania turned around; in Italy Mussolini had been jailed; and Tito had turned the Yugoslavian country around as well.

Without valuables

Five families were living in our courtyard, but only one was wealthy – Szentmihályiné (Szamuelyné). She had some valuables like silver cutlery sets, and she asked me if I could help her to hide them. I asked two of my colleagues if they could help to hide these for her. If Szentmihályiné could survive the war they agreed to return them to her, if not - then they could keep everything[24]. Hirippiné and Kis Sándorné agreed to the "terms". The SS and the Hungarian authorities searched every Jew's property. If they could not find anything, they would search the entire house/flat and if they assumed the person to be wealthy and were unable to find anything, the owner would be beaten up to surrender all valuables. Our neighbour, Szentmihályiné told the authorities during her search that I had helped to hide the valuables so I ended up in the same Deak Ferenc Street building as the progressive thinkers and the ones sympathetic to communism. I was beaten up for more than half a day, but I could not reveal our helpers as these women would have suffered badly because they were helpful to a Jew. I managed to survive the tortures and the beating, and I strongly denied I knew anything about Szentmihályiné's valuables. Late in the

---

[24] Her relatives have received every item after the war was over.

afternoon I was let go and managed to get home, but I was in bed for many days as the soles of my feet had taken most of the beating. It was hard to walk. Why was I not put in prison? They knew what was waiting for me - that I would have a much bigger prison soon - that I would face much bigger challenges I suppose.

In the small Ghetto

In the beginning of May 1944 we were advised, through announcements and posters on the walls, about the first day of moving into the located ghettos. It was Monday, the 15th of May[25]. A few days before I went to work as usual, and at the end of my last day no-one said goodbye, no-one cried for me, I was not wanted there anymore.

We had to move into the small ghetto which we could enter through a big gate at 39 Hatvan Street across the road from our house. The small ghetto was made out of the area located between Csokonai and Jókai Streets, and the big ghetto from the area between the Bajcsy-Zsilinszky and Simonfy utca.

In the morning I went for one more walk. It was a sunny day and I did not care about the people mocking me. I cared about the buildings which were bringing back many beautiful memories; the overhanging branches of the big trees, at which I used to jump up to practice my football header skills; my first dates; and many more things.

As I walked, deep in my thoughts, two young women came the opposite way on the street. I knew one of them and we used to talk a lot about the war. As I already had information about the ghettos, the gas chambers and the concentration camp, I used to tell her that I would end up like many other Jews in Europe. She did not believe in any of these "stories" and assured me if I needed any help, she would be there for me.

I did not know what to do as I was surprised to see her. I started to walk a bit faster and when I looked at her, she continued to laugh and walk with her friend. She did not stop and her eyes just acknowledged me but without any feelings. She did not even stop for one encouraging word, not for even one small handshake. I froze as she passed by but I did not say anything, I did not even look back, I just stood there for a bit. I did not care about my vanity, I had none by now, but this unfortunate experience of running into each other was a deep stab in the back after all the small wounds I had received here. My soul was deeply wounded and I knew that more would come. I could put

---

[25] 16th May – Railway siding which is located inside the camp is released for use. It permits deportees to be transported directly to Gas Chambers No 2 and 3 at Auschwitz 2-Birkenau. The start of deportation to Auschwitz of almost 438,000 Jews from Hungary.

up with all the beatings but stepping onto my soul was unbearable. I did not expect this from someone I had deeply cared about in the past. I decided to head home, where my family were waiting. They had already prepared a small wooden wheelbarrow to transport a few items across the road.

We could take only what we could carry - clothes, bedsheets and small items. The bigger items like furniture and kitchen appliances had to be left behind. On that Monday the 15th of May 1944, before 6 pm, we moved together to join one of our relatives who had a small home which consisted of a single bedroom, a kitchen and a living room allocated inside the ghetto area. There were already three families there, so there were not many spaces left for us at all. Later that day one more family arrived. The five families were squashed into this small home, all sixteen of us - mainly females. The men had gone - gone to the forced camps into the forever forgetfulness. That included all the young doctors and solicitors, my brother, my cousins, and many more whom I knew and many whom I did not.

As we moved into this house right on 6pm of this beautiful sunny day, the cabinet makers arrived and started to hammer wooden boards on the windows and on the big gate as well, to close down any access out of the selected area, the small ghetto. One climbed up on his ladder and looked inside the room through the window. I was not sure what was he looking for but there it was, one more sarcastic smile. He waved with his hammer and then someone handed him a wooden board up the ladder.

As each of the wooden boards was put up one by one, the room was becoming darker and darker. It felt like every nail which was getting hammered was targeting our hearts. They took away even the sunlight from us. Inside the dark room I could see only the outline of bodies - but not the faces anymore.

The big wooden gate was shut the same way as well. About a 20 centimetre gap remained underneath it. Here we sat in the dark, quietly next to each other, most of us on the floor. The room was quiet; only the noises of the hammering could be heard from close distance and from further away the cheerful conversations of all the workmen. Soon it was finished. All escape routes from the ghetto had been shut off. The room was still but instead of crickets I could hear something else - the quiet crying of many in the room - in the darkness. We stayed there until late. No one said anything. The younger ones fell asleep but many of us could not. It was also uncomfortable with no space at all. I laid there like this for most of the night. Many thoughts went through my mind until I was so tired that finally I fell asleep.

Close to 10,000 Jews were relocated by a government re-organisation in Debrecen city. It had been done in the matter of one day. I no longer cared what would happen to our home. I did not care who would move in and who would use our furniture or who would be sleeping in our beds that night. What I knew was that most of us had to sleep on the hard floor.

The next day the fence of our new living space was removed so we could go and walk around a bit. At the two ends of the ghetto, police officers stood and checked the documentation of everyone who was coming and going.
As we had nothing to do on the following days I just waited. I laid at the big gate for hours to see through the twenty-centimetre gap, what was happening outside the walls of our ghetto. To kill some time I also occupied myself walking around to find relatives and friends. I also got to know many new names. People had been believing in different 'fairy-tales'. Most were hoping that the allied forces would come and rescue us during the night with special commandos falling from the sky. They did not believe in the gas chambers and crematoriums. Maybe it was easier for them to survive the days ahead. Unfortunately, these hopes were very depressing for me, so I stopped these walks. I knew that the German army was moving back towards Berlin and, like a wounded lion, the SS soldiers had become more and more brutal and bloodthirsty. They did not even have to hunt for prey, we were all there in the ghettos, fenced in by walls - walls of our own homes. By now all we had left was each other and clothes. Anything which was worth something has been taken away from us.

There were a few police officers inside the ghetto to keep order. Soon, the members of the counter-espionage arrived and

collected all wealthy families. They were after the valuables of
these people. Many were tortured to find out the hiding place of
their items like jewellery, paintings, silver cutlery, and money.
The chief of police was Kovács. They gathered these items in big
boxes which were transported to the main train station and sent
to unknown locations. The costume police were going through
the homes as well and were looking for any remaining valuables.
They made a very selective list of the items so as to hide their
appropriation of the valuables for themselves. I told myself:
"Watch and remember. Watch everything that is happening here
because one day you may be the only witness to tell the tales of
how one human can act against another; how some friends can
ignore you just because the government decided to push us out
and downgrade us from citizens to non-citizens."

My friend Pogácsás did not forget about me. He managed to
"investigate" my whereabouts. One day a letter was slid under
the big gate. He wrote some outside news and a message that he
would be coming back the next night, and he would bring some
food for me. He must have known that we were extremely
hungry because the leaders of the city had forgotten to organize
food for all in the ghettos. As we had brought only a few small
belongings with us - whatever we were able to carry - we were
very hungry by now. We gave each other small portions of
potato, beans or cooked cornflour. It was only just enough to
survive.
I waited at the gate as soon as it had become dark. I was very
excited but also feared for my friend. There were many citizens
who were happy to see us being closed away from the rest of the
city. A few Jews had escaped from the ghettos, but with the help
of the citizens they were captured very quickly. There were
enough eyes that were watching our every move. I waited for a
very long time and whenever someone walked to the front of the
gate, I believed it was my friend. It was very late by now and I
was starting to think he would not come. Then I heard some
noises. My friend pushed a small packet and a letter under the
gate. It had two rolls of baked pasta in it. The letter was unsigned
and all it said was "I will bring some more food tomorrow, enjoy
this one". Of course, I shared the food with my relatives, even if
it was a small portion for even one person. It was not the food

which I was so pleased about. I got more energy from the humanitarian thinking and the caring of my friend. That gave me more energy than the few slices of "beigli[26]" which was my portion of the gift.

Ghetto entrance in Budapest. Picture from:
https://www.yadvashem.org/sites/default/files/jews_hungary6b.jpg

Moving into the Big Ghetto

Note: On the 15th May 1944 the first transportation of 14,000 Jews of Munkacs[27], Hungary left for Auschwitz. This was the first of more than 180,000 Hungarian Jews sent to this concentration camp.

The 2nd of June 1944 was a very sunny day. It was the same as any day since moving into the ghetto. Suddenly I could hear some

---

[26] Beigli is a traditional baked walnut or poppy seed roll of sweet yeast bread served as a special treat.
[27] Munkacs was the commercial capital of the Transcarpathian region of Ukraine. The town belonged to Hungary until 1920, to Czechoslovakia (1920–1938), and again to Hungary from 1938–1945. Munkacs had a very large Jewish population.

deep engine noises coming from far away. I looked towards this noise and soon I started to see some lights of many planes coming towards our city. More and more people started to emerge from the houses as the noise sounded as if hundreds of planes were heading towards us. As they got closer to the city the planes started to look bigger and bigger and the rumbling noise got so loud that I could feel it reverberating in my lungs. After the realization of the source of the noise and the loud noise of the siren, many people started to look for shelter. However, I decided to stay. I wanted to watch. I had nothing to lose anymore. If I got hit by a bomb at least it would be over quickly. It did not matter if the final stab came from the back or from above. We knew about the bombing of other cities, but the city of Debrecen had not yet lived through it first hand, until now. Small metal pieces left the belly of the planes and the sunshine made them look shiny. Rumbling followed their fall, and more and more bombs found their target. Smoke and dust followed them and the earth was shaking under my feet like in an earthquake. I could not see the planes anymore from the dust, but I could still hear them. Some ground-to-air cannons fired a few shots here and there but I just stood there on the street of the ghetto and forgot all about it.

The planes slowly flew off into the distance, only to turn around and deliver another series of rumbles, fire, smoke and dust. The unknown planes had delivered total chaos and death in the matter of few minutes by the
pushing of a few buttons. It did not discriminate between old or new buildings, young kids or elderly citizens. It felt like the fences of the ghetto had delivered some kind of protection.
The main targets were the central train station and its train tracks, and an army base which was holding many vehicles in a building a few blocks away.
Close to the train station, the houses where the gypsies lived were badly damaged. They would need new housing, so now we, as unwanted non-citizens, were ordered to pack up and move into the big ghetto. This was a quick move as not many of our possessions were left from our first move. We had used up all the food we had, so only our clothes had to be packed up.

We had another relative living in the big ghetto but we decided to search for another place to stay, as this location had become very crowded. As we were walking along Simonffy Street we came across a house in which many old and ill people were detained. Later we found out that all these people had been evacuated from the elderly persons' social homes and now without care and medication were suffering during their last days. A four-wheeled stretcher came there often to pick up the corpses.

After the long search we found a small wooden shed and decided to stay there to be close to my family. During the night I woke up to its smallness and to a weird feeling. I lit up my matches and was shocked to see hundreds of bugs crawling everywhere on the ground, and also on us. I jumped up and I woke my family. We ended up staying on the street for the rest of the night. Next day we asked our relative Sándor Liner to let us move into their home. There were already a few families there too, so we ended up on the floor again. However, it was better than sleeping with the bugs. We had no place to lay down so we slept sitting up every night.
In the big ghetto there was more to do. The local church was also part of the area. People were getting sick and they were taken outside to the doctor, and many others were taken for interrogation as well.

 The news from outside got to us inside the walls. The local public were blaming us for the bombing. One accusation was that a jeweller called Halász, who had a shop in the centre of the city, had given exact information to the allied forces about where to bomb. The other accusation was that our local church had a radio station and the Jews had directed the planes. Of course, these accusations were all made up stories, and nothing was true, but the public believed it. It was easier to blame us than the Nazis. The propaganda was working just as well as before, but now we started to feel its effect more and more.

The scrap cleaner

So, next day, 3rd of June 1944, as we stood on the streets of the ghetto, a policeman arrived and collected a few of us to help clean up the city from the bombing. We were taken outside the walls to a big pile of rubble where many shops, the Pannonia Hotel and a garage had previously stood.

This garage, which had been used by the German army as well, was brought to the ground by one large bomb.
Standing on top of the ruins, I did not realise that, 15 years later, I would be the director of a newly-built shopping-centre in the neighbourhood, close to this spot, laying the foundation stone.

We had to collect the bricks into another pile and the instruction was "Be careful, there might be some survivors under the wreckage."
Under the hot sun I was picking the bricks up quickly in a heavy sweat, as the policeman made us hurry. I was just about to pick up the next loose brick when my hand grabbed something soft. I speeded up my rescue effort and found a leg in a brown stocking. "There is a body here!" I yelled out loudly. Five or six of us helped to clear the body from the bricks under the 'supervision' of the policeman.

Soon we could see an old woman dressed in black with her fingers crossed. We could not see any wound on her. Probably the falling walls had squashed this small old lady to death. On her finger a wedding ring could be seen and this had been noticed by the policeman. He ordered us to pull it off her finger. It was not sliding off and we told him so. However, he did not care and he demanded it threateningly. He was disgusted to touch the corpse, but he was brave enough to have the jewellery. Until darkness we moved thousands of bricks, but we did not find any more bodies under the wreckage. This little old lady had become another victim of the madness, along with many others who were suffering because of this pointless Nazi ideology.

The news from outside, which was eagerly awaited by many inside the walls, arrived from day to day. The most sought-after news was about the retreat and losses of the German-Hungarian army. This gave hope for the finish of the war.

Some news was not as good. We heard about the crowded transport trains leaving from different cities and going to the German soil. The retreating Nazi dictatorship had accelerated the evacuation of the ghettos, but no one knew the end destination. It was questionable where this many people could be kept in an ever-narrowing Germany. The Nazi friendly Hungarian Horthy regime did not care. They left the SS hangman to deal with that. They even paid for us Jews to be transported out of the country. Many thought the trains had been sent to work camps. This was well believed as postcards were arriving from the camps. These postcards had been given from hand to hand. It made it easier to send millions to their death without major disruption. The Nazis had been well organized in terms of mass killing, but the ghetto in Debrecen still had to wait.

The baker man

Note: On May 16, 1944 the first transported group of a final total of more than 180,000 Hungarian Jews reached Auschwitz.

Since moving into the Ghetto in May 1944, many homes housed more than one family, and three generations had been squashed together. A fence closed us away from the outside world and we walked on the narrow streets up and down like a lion in its cage. The food which we could bring with us was meagre, just enough not to die from hunger and it was all gone by now. Potato, ground dry corn or beans were the menu from day to day. Finally, the gentlemen of the city hall came to their senses, and to avoid mass hunger or an epidemic disease, they decided to provide some food for the ghetto.

I walked up and down on the narrow streets all day, and I was eager to walk a bit outside the walls. One day an announcement came: "Looking for professional bakers, who will bake bread overnight for the people in the ghetto!" During the day the bakery was making bread for the rest of the city.

I was always an entrepreneur, so I thought I would put my hand up for this job hoping I would be needed, and that I would be able to fulfil the task. I had to do something. The ghetto felt like it had no air. The all-day idleness was driving me crazy. Even if I could do something for a few hours that would distract my attention from doing absolutely nothing, just waiting for our final days, would make these days easier.

There were only seven of us who applied for the baker's job. A note came and we had to be present at the gate of the ghetto late in the evening. As I was observing my "colleagues" I could tell they were all real bakers, and they all knew each other. There were not many bakers in the city, so they must have known all in this profession. But, thank God, they did not ask me any questions relating to the profession.

I was excited to leave the walls, so I presented myself quite early. Finally, a police officer arrived to follow us everywhere. Many "outsiders" were interested about the life in the ghetto so as we stepped outside the gate all eyes were looking at us with interest, somewhat like you would look at the performers and the animals in a circus arena.

I did not care about these curious looks anymore. I had dealt with many things in my head already. I was not so touchy like I had been in the first days. I did not look at the pedestrians and their staring eyes. I soaked up the well-known buildings on the sunny streets, and I got more exited as we headed towards my favourite place of the city, the Nagyerdő[28]. I was enjoying the many deep breaths I took as we walked towards this area. The gentle wind of May carried beautiful fresh air from the trees but the wonderful memories of this place reflected sorrow. I understood the reality when I was awoken from my dreams and I had to move faster at the instruction of the policeman.

---

[28] Located just north of the downtown is the 2280 hectare city park of which 100ha is a nature conservation area, with over 120 years old trees.

We arrived at the Nyil Street-based Schneider[29] bakery. He was a Swabian-Hungarian[30]. This was a well-equipped bakery, and though I had heard his name before I had never met him.
The policeman reported our arrival to Schneider, who started to get things organised. The introduction did not suggest anything good as he started to yell at us. "There is a room upstairs. You must go there and get changed immediately and get to work as soon as you are ready."

The policeman looked pleased. He was happy to notice a helper to whom he could leave us so he could relax. Accordingly, he did not come upstairs with us, about which we were happy. We became pleased when we arrived upstairs and had a look around. There were many baskets on the table. Each of them had different type of fine bakery in it, fresh from the afternoon baking. We did not waste any time. Like the hungry wolves we lunged towards the baskets and started to feast ourselves with pretzels, bread rolls and croissants.[31]   Only when we felt full did we realize that the yelling of Schneider was only a misleading act for the policeman. He knew for sure we were all hungry and he had sent us to have a treat. From here onwards, he kept up his "good cop – bad cop" act. When the policeman was present, he called us in different names in a loud voice, but as soon as he was out of sight, he treated us humanely. He helped us a lot. He gave us small baked goods which we could place into our pockets and at the end of the day we also received a fresh loaf of bread, to which the policeman did not object.

When we had eaten enough, we changed into our clothing for work, which was not too much - only a pair of long white pants. We worked half naked as it was very hot in the bakery. I looked like all the other bakers, but now as we started working would I

---

[29] After the war he opened his bakery in Malmö, Sweeden.

[30] Approximately 800 villages were founded in Hungary by German settlers from 1711 to 1750. Even though they came from various regions and spoke various dialects, the Hungarians called them Swabians, and the name came to be used in reference to all Germans who settled in the Danube valley. Although there had been German immigration to Hungary prior to 1711, the expulsion of the Turks resulted in an organized settlement program sponsored by the Habsburgs.

[31] Kifli is a traditional European yeast roll made into a crescent shape. The pastry is called kifli in Hungarian.

be detected as a fake baker? The oldest man took charge to send us to do different duties. I was sent to do the kneading and each of the others had his own job to do. I stood next to the big kneading tub and I started to pour some of its contents into it from a big bag. The older baker who was watching me he, recognised my lack of knowledge and knew I was not a real professional in this field.

I could no longer hide that I had no knowledge whatsoever in bakery, and I had not ever held even one baker's shovel in my hands. The old baker started to yell at me. He was furious that I had jeopardized their mission - their opportunity to help others in the ghetto - and also their safety. He swore that we would be punished because of me.

Schneider stepped in to smooth things out. "He can help here a lot. Someone needs to carry the bags, put water in the buckets and so on," he said. He made good use of me.

Later, my colleagues became satisfied with me and they benefitted from me. I did not avoid heavy physical work. I carried all the bags and buckets and then later they put me in charge of the ovens. I took the half-baked bread out from one oven and placed it into the another. Even though it was very unusual for me to work front of an extremely hot oven, I did my best.

After the bombing of our city, there in the bakery I was also a witness to another kind of abuse towards us. A man whose head was wrapped with bandages entered the shop. He started to yell at us, accusing and blaming us for the bombing. Schneider could not stop himself from throwing a few words back at him to defend us.

"Why are you blaming them? Just look at them! You cannot possibly think they had anything to do with the attack of the Americans? Just calm down. They have more problems than you can ever possibly can think of."

This quick defence made the accuser think for a moment and he stopped throwing his words at us.

Schneider also had some friends inside the ghetto, and he sent medications with us to them. He treated us humanely in every way.

Before this time, the inside of the bakery did not interest me at all. I did not rate this profession very highly though I love bread. But now, I watched it with the highest curiosity - how the white flour through kneading and forming and shaping of the dough came alive as beautiful crisped bread. I felt like I could work here for the rest of my life, but unfortunately the golden days lasted only for a very short time. The flour which had been allocated to the ghettos diminished in three weeks and the city did not provide any more for us. My bakery job did not last long and it was announced that we did not have to go out to bake any longer. I was sorry, not only to miss out on the evening walks towards the Nagyerdő, will also miss the beautiful smell of the freshly baked bread in the Schneider bakery.

After the night shifts it was hard to sleep at night in the fully crowded rooms where we could only sit down but not lay down, so I decided to wander around the streets.

I came across a big house which was owned by a landowner called Bayer who had many farms. He had left everything behind and run away because of the war. I walked into the big 4-bedroom house and it had many good quality clothes in the cupboards. I decided to get some fresh clothes for myself and also to take a few unopened shirts with me too. I was hoping one day I would be able to exchange them for food.

My next expedition was under the house at 30 Hatvan street. I walked down into the basement and ended up walking into a wine cellar. There were many barrels of quality wines there, all labelled. I picked up the sampling-tube and sucked up from one of the barrels which promised to have great quality homemade wine. I ended up becoming a bit drunk. Alcohol has a different effect on different people. I was not sad anymore. I was rather happy. I almost started to sing but decided to keep it quiet and just hummed along. I did not care about the difficult times any longer - the ghettos, the Nazis, the war - nothing. I managed to walk up from the basement and when I entered the streets I looked rather "out of context". Everyone around me had a sad face and a depressing mood, and on the other hand, I was singing by now - making jokes to the people who all looked at me with sympathy. "He must have lost his mind" (like many here) they said. Some were hoping that my good mood had something more behind it, like great news from outside the walls. Maybe the war had come to an end! People stopped me and asked "What is the reason of your good mood?"

"Wine! The best quality I have ever tasted! Would you like to have a glass with me?" I asked and started to invite friends and non-friends to the cellar. Soon, we had a happy corner there in the ghetto. We drank a great quantity of farmer's wine. We did not feel sorry to drink it as we had nobody from whom to ask permission. The house was empty, and our hearts finally felt happy for once. I was happy to share it with others.

As I was walking home again in the darkness that had closed in, two policemen stopped me. "Are you drunk?" they asked me.

"Yes, I am!" I said "dear officers, would you like to have a small glass too? It must have been a long day for you too."

"We don't seem to have a reason why not," they replied. So, off I went - back to the cellar to have some more fun. The cellar had a window which was a way out of the ghetto. The two policemen liked me and my gesture so much they pointed it out to me.

"When the day of the evacuation comes, use this window and escape from the deportation" they said. "You are a good man Sándor, you should live. We will help you to escape".

"I would not be able to go as a free man for long, there are many out there who would like us to disappear from the city and forever," I replied. "Besides, I have my family here and I don't have the heart to leave them here alone."

It was a great afternoon, but the next day was terrible. The realization of the truth hurt more than before. I had found the best medicine for depression, but unfortunately the healing did not last long.

The nurse

The feeling of depression was widespread and not everyone was strong enough to live with it. The citizens in the ghetto started to commit suicide.

In the middle of the Bajcsy-Zsilinszky Street there was a multi-story building which started to operate as a temporary hospital.

The doctor, who wanted to help the sick, had a big job to fulfil without nurses, medications, equipment and proper bedding. The majority of young men were away suffering on their forced labour or had already passed away. Dr Fejes was conscientiously trying to do his best but without great success. One day he asked me "Would you consider helping me as a nurse?"
"I cannot deal with the dead" I replied.
"You had better get used to being close to the dead as more will come your way soon," he said. So I decided to help him and those in need. However, it was more difficult than I expected. There was no medicine for the pain and for the groaning of the ill. One day a patient arrived with gastrointestinal bleeding. His entire body and clothes were wet with the cold sweat and he was constantly vomiting blood. Until he became unconscious, he begged us for some painkiller. Unfortunately, we could not provide such a mercy to him, so we had to watch his agony until he bled to death. He just lay there and his body was not moving any longer. I started to be jealous of him. He did not know anything about the events of the world anymore. He was over everything. I was just standing there gazing at the corpse. Dr Fejes looked at me and reminded me, "I told you there would be more dead coming your way. You must deal with it. Soon there will be more dead bodies around you than living ones." His words followed me along to the death camps where the thousands and tens of thousands of dead became a daily sight.

Unfortunately, more and more people decided to choose to take their lives as a way of ending this torture. Dr Fejes and I were called to the church of the ghetto. Under a blanket I recognized the couple hugging each other. It was Lukács the engineer, and his wife. They had chosen a painful death because they used strychnine[32] to poison themselves. Their faces had become distorted from the pain and it was clearly visible they had gone through lots of excruciating agony during their final hours. Later we were called to a doctor's family. Here the husband, the wife, the kids and the elderly mother had committed suicide. The

---

[32] Strychnine is a strong poison; only a small amount is needed to produce severe effects in people. Strychnine poisoning can cause extremely serious adverse health effects, including death. https://emergency.cdc.gov/agent/strychnine/basics/facts.asp

floor was strewn with ampules, from which this well-known orthopaedic surgeon, Dr Sarkadi had injected some kind of poison into all of his family members. We could save only the surgeon who passed away later during his deportation to Austria.

We were placed outside the law. This was proven again as no one from the authorities had questioned Dr Sarkadi for killing his family. We had been sentenced to death. Some of us had survived but with the suicides, our number was diminishing. This way, they would need fewer train wagons to deport the survivors. We were still on our home ground, yet we were losing a lot of our people already. There was no registration of the dead and there was no death certificate to be filled out as the leaders of the city knew there was no need to do it any longer.

Along with my nursing job, I also had to fulfil another position - grave digger. As the people were passing away, someone had to take them on their last journey. This was a sad and lonely "death march". I had to carry the bodies down the stairs from the upper level on my back, alone. I asked my friend Imre Fülöp to help me, but as soon he had one look at the number of corpses he just ran away. I placed these bodies on a two-wheeled wooden platform (like a big table made into a wheelbarrow) and pushed them out the gate of the ghetto, in the company of two policeman. No priest was present, nor was any family member allowed to walk with us to the graveyard at the Monostorapályi Street. Along the lonely walk I received a number of verbal assaults from the citizens of my birthplace. Occasionally rocks were thrown at me and the corpses. Many times, my face was split by a projectile. The two policemen kept a safe distance from me but at least their presence was enough to prevent me from being beaten to death. The Nazi propaganda accused us of being responsible for the continuing loss on the war fronts. Likewise, we were labelled as the direct reason for the lesser food supply inside the country.

How much had we been part of the Horthy regime when its supporters had decided to declare war on the Soviet-Union in June 1941? Not at all! We Jews had nothing to do with it.

Many citizens have been misled by all the lies. Well-dressed men and women and ordinary citizens of the city were standing on the side of the roads, shaking their fists towards me and the corpses. Many I had never seen in my life. Many others I recognised. They knew I would not even kill a fly, but still they would spit in my face. I could not react to their provocation as I did not even have the will. Later, after the war, I recognised many of the unknown faces, and many people asked for my forgiveness.

Upon arriving at the graveyard, I had to dig a hole with my shovel. When I had finished digging, I placed the corpse down the hole and began shovelling the soil back in right away. These "ceremonies" were quick and emotionless. There was no headstone and no number to mark the graves. I was trying to remember the location each one of them but managed to do that only for a few long days. Later on, I could not even remember their names as there were so many.

In the meantime, the morale was getting worse and worse. The news about the liquidation of the ghettos arrived from other cities day by day. We knew we had only a week, maybe just a few days left, before we would be deported as well.

Those who managed to get inside the ghetto with any kind of made-up reason were trying to get rich one way or the other. One day a policeman stood in the centre of the ghetto, pulled out a piece of paper, and started to read out loud, "I am hereby to collect any remaining jewellery which has not been handed over previously. This act is against the law and will be heavily punished if any item is found in anyone's possession!". He then took his hat off to hold any collectable items. It took only about 20 minutes and the hat was full, shining brightly in the sunlight. Who knows how many times he had done this previously? The ghetto had been robbed systematically, first by the law of the government, then by the costume guards, counter-intelligence workers, Gestapo, SS-soldiers, police officers, council workers and who knows who else or how many times they tried to get rich. The ones who handed over their valuables on the first call were the clever ones. The announcements and the news had been outlining the truth: "Leave everything behind as nothing will be needed where you are all going!" The ones who kept only their clothes had lost not only their valuables, but the need for further anxiety as well. The ones who returned home after the war never found their lost treasures.

I was now busy in the ghetto cleaning up wreckage, nursing the ill, digging the graves and burying the dead.

The evacuator

Note: On June 20, 1944, the Nazis began the mass extermination of Hungarian Jews at Auschwitz.

The next day started as all the other ones. There was a clear sky and shining sun. On the 21st of June 1944 horse carriages and two- and four-wheeled flat-bedded wheelbarrows had been arriving. I was with my parents inside the crowded house. Banging was heard on the big gate of the ghetto, then the sound of the key opening it was heard.

"Departing to the brick factory!" The final order had arrived.

This was the final collecting centre before deportation - a mirror-image of any other city. The evacuation had begun.
One of my other relatives had been living with us with her two young daughters. She pulled her hand containing some jewellery out of her jacket and showed it to me without saying anything. Her face was looking for an answer. I grabbed the items and ran inside the woodshed. I dug a small hole into the ground with my hand and the covered it up with some black charcoal powder. Unfortunately, she has passed away in Auschwitz with one of her daughters - but the father returned. We dug together at the exact same spot after the liberation, but the "modern day treasure hunters" had found it before us.

Two young policemen entered our permanent home. "Hand over all your valuables immediately to us. You will be deported onto

German soil into the labour camps. You will not be needing anything there".

As we had nothing to hand over, they searched the house followed by a personal body search. They did a comprehensive search but there was nothing left that they could take as everything had been taken beforehand by every possible department of the city.

I said goodbye to my family, and I reassured them I would see them soon in the brick factory. I had to stay behind to help with the elderly and the sick.

Only the most important personal belongings could be taken onto the vehicles. Even though we had almost nothing by now, we still managed to leave something behind for the joint forces of the Hungarian and German "federation". The motto was "They all get something and still some will remain". Many could not part from their luggage, and these were beaten up with a baton. The members of the counter-intelligence were searching for more treasures in the half empty ghetto. They did not give up easily, they knew where to look. The beaten up and tortured men and women could not bear the pain any longer and they handed over their last family jewelleries.

Those marching did not look back to their home town. Slowly walking with their heads down was the way of saying goodbye to their memories, to their houses, and walking towards the unknown final destination.

The walk was long to the brick factory on the Balmazújváros Street. The smaller bags were carried by carriages. Crying children were hanging onto their mothers and weak old men just managed to drag themselves along on the rocky brick roads. It looked like a funeral procession. All those who were departing were watched - watched by the citizens of the city. The Magyar Futár[33] trash magazine assisted to deliver the successful propaganda. Many believed that we were the enemy; that we were the reason of their suffering and for the ever-closer loss of this war. They were happy to see us going. There were no farewell words, only abuse.

---

[33] Vintage Hungarian WWII magazine - https://www.worthpoint.com/worthopedia/magyar-futar-vintage-hungarian-ww2-153542530

A few days later we received our order to move out of the ghetto also. The evacuation of the elderly and ill did not appear to be an easy task. Not even a proper stretcher was provided. It was left to us, to Dr Freedman and myself, to take people down the stairs. They were just like everyone in the ghetto and had received no proper meal for weeks. They had lost a great amount of weight. They did not weigh much but as I carried them down on my back I was sweating heavily. I had to carry about 20 people down. When we finished, we had to go to the Simmonffy Street house. Here they kept all the previous residents of the elderly social home. They all looked like living corpses as well. If they did not move, they looked like they were dead. "We need to go ...." I started to say but the rest of my announcement got stuck inside of me "….. to labour camps on German soil!" It did not seem appropriate to finish the sentence. They might have smiled at me if they still would have had the strength to do so.

Each of them had to be carried in our arms. We placed most of these people onto a horse carriage, but three bodies had to be placed onto the flat wheelbarrow as that remained the only empty place. This had exhausted me but it was not everything, someone had to push them too. I caught up with the other carriages and asked to have these old men carried with the rest, but there was no more room left. The 'bodies' were on top of each other already, but I needed to continue along the long road. The empty houses and empty streets looked rather depressing. It looked like a ghost town.

As we exited through the big gate of the ghetto, we had the same human walls on each side on the road as in previous days, all happy to see us going. The atrocities began right away. They were mocking us, small rocks were flying towards us, so was the spitting, just like when I used to deliver the corpses to the graveyard. I had no desire to respond to any of these once again. None of us did. We just kept marching. I just kept pushing my human load.

As I looked back, I could see about 60 people remaining inside the walls of the ghetto. Later I found out these were the "chosen ones". These people had great connections with the Germans and had enough money to buy their freedom through the Gestapo.

The road to the brick factory was an old-fashioned rocky road. I was as careful as possible with the three old men on my wheelbarrow, but it was impossible to avoid every big crack or dip. Unfortunately, one of the old men's hat fell off and he was desperate to get it back. I stopped and handed it back to him. It was probably the last of his remaining valuables - a black, hard rounded-top cylinder.

I was extremely tired by now, even though the three old men probably weighted less than the actual barrow itself. We did not know who would be lucky enough to return home. Would it be anyone at all? We knew our destiny was death. All of us had been sentenced to die.

By helping out with the evacuation against my will I had become an important link in the Nazi mechanism.

I could barely walk by the time we ended up at the brick factory. I picked up the old men and placed them under a roof. I could not carry them any longer. As they ended up on the third transport which was going straight to Auschwitz, I'm sure they ended up being executed by getting sent to the gas chambers. I had done as much as I could for them but now, I wanted to find my family.

Here in the brick factory, there were a lot of people. All ended up there from the ghettos. The work of the factory was on hold. I am sure the bombed city and its homeless people needed the produce of this place more than at any other time, but still, our deportation and our execution was more important for some.

I looked everywhere to find my relatives, but I had no luck. I asked around with everyone I knew, but no one had seen them. They had spent the last three days here on the factory floor ground, sleeping on the red slag. I had not seen them since I said goodbye to them in the ghetto.

The first transport load was waiting to leave the train station. This was the first of three trains, each of them carrying between 3,200 and 3,500 Jews to their final destination. My parents were probably on this train. I tried to get close to the train and I yelled out their names, but there were plenty of police officers and SS-soldiers around the train guarding them. I did that from a safe distance, although I knew they were on the train, somewhere. I decided to embark on one of the stock-cars as the sliding doors were still open, but an SS soldier saw me and only by running fast could I avoid a beating. I had no luck. I had to accept that I might see them at the other end of the trip, but I did not know that for sure.

The wagon doors were shut, and they remained so for hours in the hot sun before the train started to roll out slowly towards the unknown destination. Tears rolled down my cheeks with a slow speed - just like the speed of the train. This is how I had to say goodbye to my parents - no hugs, no kisses, no good wishes.

I had to look for somewhere to sleep for the coming night. There were no places left under the roof and everywhere I looked I could see the rooster feathered hats of the gendarmes. There were no walls, only roof. I managed to find a place and was hoping it would not rain. I was not lucky this time. In the middle of the night the rain came, and I had to lie down on top of other people. Still, the water found its way down and under us. I was wet from underneath, but I could not do anything about it, just to curse the summer rain.

Next morning, I had to find a place where I could urinate. There were some bigger holes which had been used as a toilet by males and females. There was no difference between us anymore, we were outsiders.

As I was closing toward one of these dips, I could see another hat with rooster feathers. I was curious what the officer was doing there. There was no toilet paper provided for us, so even those who had managed to hide some paper money could not see the point keeping it any longer. They started to use it to wipe their bums. This officer was collecting these and wiping the faeces off them. They say "the money does not stink" [34]! I bet this was!
He shoved the paper notes into his pocket after wiping them. The opportunity to make money was here. I also found a roll of 100 Pengő[35] notes near some bricks. I hid it between the bricks, but I did not know who the lucky one was who ended up finding it.

My clothes had dried and I was just lying down under the sky. As I looked up it was just like any other summer day before the

---

[34] In Latin: Pecunia non olet
[35] Hungarian currency during WWII

war. Looking up, I could not see the rooster feathers, the gendarme officers. I fell asleep but not for long, as a very familiar noise awakened me. It was the familiar deep rumbling noise of the planes. I looked towards the noise and I could see them flying towards the city. The air attack sirens had gone off, but I did not move. I was tired. I was over it. I was ready to die. The Nazi propaganda and the war had done it for me. It had fulfilled its message. I was not interested anymore and I did not care about the future. As I lay there I looked around and not one person was looking for shelter. It was bizarre. We all stayed and just looked at the sky, hoping for the quick ending - not the officers though. They all managed to disappear and hide somewhere. I guess it was the same outside of the brick factory too. I guess all the citizens were trying to save their lives, but not us. We remained still. I was looking at the belly of the planes from which the shiny objects would deliver the final end for so many when they fell. However, they did not come, they did not fall. The planes just passed by over the city towards another target, so we had to keep waiting for the unknown destiny.

As it became quiet again, I could hear something else - my stomach. I was hungry, always hungry. I could not find enough to eat to get rid of the pain inside of me. I detected some appetising smell - the smell of onion. I got up as my nose had become my best radar and I was heading towards the source of the smell. A few women were making onion and potato soup in a big bathtub. Someone had a bath a few weeks ago in the same tub and now we were using it to cook in, to survive. I filled up my small pot but when I had finished, I was even hungrier than before. I felt like I needed to eat for an entire day to get rid of the hunger. I had to start from scratch. I had to look for more to eat but there was nothing to find.

The list for the next transport had been announced. Another 3,500 had been pushed into the stock-wagons, and after half a day waiting in the sun, finally they also rolled out. That left only us, the last 3,500, the last "load" of human outlaws.

The SS officer's travel book had only two lines in it:
Place of delivery: Destruction camp
Passenger's fate: Gasification

Between Ghetto Walls

They locked me behind wooden planks
Women and children, and men of no ranks
Both the street ends enclosed by fencing
Locked are the gates at both of their endings.
Scared looks on all faces on each narrow street
To be transported soon without a heartbeat.

Families are cluttered in small, tiny nooks
Seven, eight people per room just like books,
Helpless fathers, wailing mothers, grandparents
Weak babies feeding on empty, soggy breasts.
Without optimism there is no solace,
Yellow stars are shining on all jackets,
Marked us not to be mistaken with another citizen
To be seen from far away who are Israel's children.

What is waiting for us, what will be the Final Solution?
Surely there will be no blessing - in their resolution.
Some cannot wait for the tomorrow,
Some bit on poison in a vial and let go.
They have no suffering anymore, helped too,
Less to carry for the hangman, in a day or two.

Food barely given, hungry looks on many faces,
Whoever has bread gets envy looks at every places.
Money, value, jewellery all been seized,
In return, surely a bit of food can be squeezed.
But their concerns are greater than carrying,
It does not hurt them seeing us suffering.
For them this is celebration, and they are very happy,
They empty their glasses merrily, drunkenly.

For us suffering, torment, remembrance
Nowhere to appeal for the death sentence.

Even God turned away from his chosen People,
For the SS-guards, gendarmes we are vulnerable.
Prison guards are those where there is no law bill
Without the legislation - they can beat and they can kill.

The human mercy is unknown, their mind is narrow
Unlimited owner of the people here in the ghetto.
No head count, no list, not even a memo
No registrar kept of the people in the ghetto
Hundreds of empty wagons are ready to go.

The ghetto emptied, the residents are taken
New owners in their homes when mornings awaken.
The righteous owners are awaited by the gas chambers
Then there is nothing more for them, no traces.
Mothers and their children have become smoke
Their new place is Heaven, as one they will revoke.

The passenger

29th June 1944.[36]
Our day had come. In the early morning we had to gather our
remaining items and line up. A long line of gendarmes
conducted another final body search. We had barely anything
left, but still they were searching for more. They did an extensive
search in our luggage. They dug in it and threw everything
around willy-nilly. Many of them managed to put together a
fortune this way during the war. They were looking for more
hidden treasures.

My last contact on my home ground with a Hungarian citizen
was with a red-faced officer of the law who looked very sly. He
looked at me and for some reason he just let me pass through

---

[36] **Jun 29, 1944 -** US 7th army corps conquers Cherbourg - German counter attack at Caen - Nazi
Paul Touvier shoots 7 Jews dead - Rommel & von Rundstedt travel to Berchtesgaden - Soviet
Armies join in Bobroesjk

without any search. He did not look too happy as he knew he would not find anything in my pockets or small bag, but my heart was pleased to see his disappointment. I could keep my clothes for only another few more days.

After the body search has been completed, we could not return to the factory ground. We had to settle down next to the train tracks which were watched closely by the young SS soldiers and the Hungarian gendarme officers.

The train arrived around noon. The order was given "Into the wagons!" A young SS soldier waving his baton started to shout in German: "Los, los" (go, go)! To speed up the movement, we received some "encouragement" with the baton without any mercy towards the elderly, towards the women or towards the children. They hit whoever they could, like we were not humans, like we needed to be in a hurry.

This entire evacuation process was closely watched by Adolf Eichmann[37] and he showed no mercy either.

---

[37] Otto Adolf Eichmann was a German-Austrian SS-Obersturmbannführer and one of the major organisers of the Holocaust—the "Final Solution to the Jewish Question" in Nazi terminology. He was tasked by SS-Obergruppenführer Reinhard Heydrich with facilitating and managing the logistics involved in the mass deportation of Jews to ghettos and extermination camps in Nazi-occupied Eastern Europe during World War II. https://www.britannica.com/biography/Adolf-Eichmann

A young girl was calling out: "Mum, Dad, where are you?"
"We are here, this way" the father replied.
One gendarme officer shouted "There is no need to look for
places! Faster, get up or I will shoot into the crowd! You do not
need to travel in comfort. Do not worry, at the other end of the
trip no one will be looking at your clothes to see if they are well
ironed or wrinkled. You are traveling for free at the cost of the
Hungarian government. They provided wagons for you, but we
could not give you first class; and do not even think about
escaping! Come on! Move in further - all the way to the back!
Now, we will lock the sliding doors, and if people try to force
them open, we will shoot them in the head!"
About 80 people were pushed and shoved into each wagon,
children, men and women. There was hardly any place to sit.
Everyone was standing close to each other. It was about 2pm by
the time we were all inside. It was summer, it was hot outside,
but inside it was even hotter. There was only a few about 20cm x
25m wide windows with bars where some air was coming in.
The air did not reach the ones inside the wagon very well. They
had very little oxygen and they started taking off their clothes to
ease their body heat.
I ended up at the window with my friend Friedman, who was an
engineer. I had also seen my friend Béla Bláyer. There were
many of the sick and infirm whom I had been looking after back
in the ghettos. They had no energy to stand, so they sat or laid on
top of each other. There was no room at all to sit down, but if
you were sitting, there would be less air down there.

Friedman said, "The murderers have locked us in without food
and water. This heat is already unbearable. It is only half past
two and I am thirstier than hungry. It would be great to have a
glass of cold water."

I replied, "I am thirsty too. My tongue has already stuck to the
top of my mouth. All our jewellery and valuables were
insufficient to pay for a little water and bread? Where are they

taking us? I counted about 40 wagons. Must be between 3,200 and 3,500 of us on this train alone. I felt betrayed. I did not think that what the gendarme officer told us in the factory, that we would be transported to Germany for work, was true. None of these old and ill men and women could do too much in any factory."

Friedman said quietly to me, "Before the ghetto, I was able to listen to the English radio. They talked not only about the war and the position of the ever-changing front, but also what had happened with the prisoners of the war from the German occupied territories - Jews from the Soviet, Polish, Czechoslovakia, Italy and other European war prisoners, communists, Nazi opposition thinkers and the Jews. They have all been transported to crematoriums which have been built in Poland. Do you think that is true and that is our destiny too?"

"I believe our trip is heading towards the gas chambers as well. The officers and SS soldiers did not treat us like workers in recent days. They have taken most of our belongings away and did not provide us with food and water. If you wanted someone to work, wouldn't you treat them differently? We have had barely nothing to eat for weeks now," I replied.

Friedman: "This heat is killing me. I feel like I will suffocate soon. This roof is just pushing down the heat of the sun. How long will they keep us here waiting? I must take my shirt off, and you should do it too. I can see the sweat just running down on your face."

Me: "Yes, good idea, I am very hot too. I will take it off as well," and I removed my shirt. "Now, that is better! I can see that everyone is following our move. Everyone is taking off their clothes, even the women. Today is the first day of the traditional harvesting, Péter-Pál day[38]. We have not had much heat yet this year. It must be about 30 Celsius outside, and in here, I have no idea."

---

[38] Péter-Pál day was the start of the harvesting in Hungary. The Sun is over the Orion-constellation and it brings very hot days.

Friedman: "There is no place to sit. It is very tiring to stand here but at least we have some air coming in through this small window."

A woman to Friedman: "How long we will be here standing on the same place? This heat in unbearable!"

Friedman to the woman: "I can see some officers walking up and down, I will try to find out for you." He called out through the window: "Sorry, dear officer, would you be able to tell us when will be leaving from here? It is very hot here inside. Would you be able to bring some water for the children at least?"

The officer replied, "There is no schedule here. Your travel is non-urgent to us. Just get comfortable and get lazy, get friendly with each other, and do not think for a second that anyone will run and get some water for a Jew! You just embarked on the train and you are already thirsty? The caravans can go for days in the Sahara without water! This friendly world does not exist for you anymore. When you get to Germany you can apply again with your requests, but be careful, maybe your needs might backfire with the Germans. I'm finished, no more discussion!"

The woman: "Dear officer! I have two young children with me, if you know God, do not let them suffer and die from thirst. Give us some water or shoot them in the head! Why are you torturing us? My husband is on forced labour-work in the Soviet front, serving our country. I deserve a cup of water!"

Officer: "Stop quacking so much! Shout your mouth! You all can have a drink in Germany."

Woman crying to officer: "Be cursed for your cruelty!" To us she continues: "These soldiers are not human! They have stone in their chest where the heart should be! What should I do? How can I help my suffering children?"

Me: "I wish we would leave now. When the train is in motion, we should have more air and it would at least cool the wagon and that would help us to put up with our thirst. It is already getting dark outside and we are still here at the brick factory."

Friedman: "I can hear the hissing of a steam train, hopefully we will be leaving soon." The train jolts a bit. "Did you feel it? They just connected it to the wagons." We can see a lot of movement amongst the SS and the police officers too.
We heard the whistle of the locomotive and the train slowly started moving.

Me: "Thanks' God we are moving! At last, we are moving somewhere!"
I was looking outside the window; "I know this place very well. We are moving towards the city, and the opposite direction of this road leads to Hortobágy.[39] I was there a few years ago on a big folk-fest. It was great to see so many happy people. I tasted some fantastic beef made on open fire-grill, some lángos[40] and drank a big jug of cold beer after that. No one asked me then who I was and what I was doing there. How great it was! It was not even so long ago. I was home in just about two hours, and I could rest after that great weekend. Now, I am a prisoner. But what kind exactly? A non-guilty prisoner who cannot even have a mouthful of water. Even really guilty prisoners who have been sentenced to death, are asked, what is your last wish? We do not even get that! We are non-registered citizens; we are outside the law. We are not counted by anyone and no one is accountable for us.
The leaders of the city have sent close to 11,000 of us on our way, guarded by SS solders and gendarme officers. We have been compressed into wagons; they have not provided anything for us - no cup of water, no mouthful of bread - and they have dumped us onto a hard wooden floor without even straw on it."

Friedman: "I am glad it is dark now. At least all the female passengers can take off their clothes without shame to cool down a bit. They cannot bear the heat as much as we do."

---

[39] Hortobágy is an 800 km² national park in eastern Hungary, rich with folklore and cultural history.
[40] Lángos is a Hungarian food speciality, a deep-fried dough.

Me: "Look we have arrived at the small train station. I was born around this area and if you peek out you can see straight into our Hatvan Street. This is where I grew up. What a coincidence we have stopped right here. Can you see those big trees? When I was a little boy, I wanted to become a professional football player. Many times, I pretended that the lower branches were a passing ball, and I used to jump up to all of them to practice my header skills and used to kick a homemade rug-ball around here too.

Will I ever see our house again, our city and our scattered family? Many of us have been sent away to many places.

Look, there are some young couples hugging and kissing like everything is "ok". What a terrible day this is. At least I can say goodbye to my street. I may never see this street or these houses ever again."

I said these words with my eyes filled with tears, but I wiped them off before they were ready to roll down my cheek.

Friedman: "Finally, we have left the city. I'm glad. I did live around this area too, almost for 20 years. My two sons were born here in Debrecen too. Both of them have been taken for forced labour work to God knows where. We have not heard from them or their whereabouts for months and my wife is stuck somewhere at the back of this wagon - sadly by herself."

Me: "Look how fast this train is taking us! Looks like our trip is very urgent. Everywhere on the war front the fascists are losing ground and retreating, but they could still find transport for our deportation. Looks like Hitler would like to destroy the 'unwanted race' before they are all destroyed too!"

An old lady to us: "There is no toilet here and they have not supplied even a bucket to satisfy our most human needs into it. What should I do? I cannot hold it any longer."

Friedman: "Pick any dish from your luggage, use it and give it to us and we will try to pour it out through the grid"

The woman did so and gave a small metal cup to the people next to her to pass it over their heads as there was no room pass it any other way. The people were as close to each other as sardines in a tin can. As the train moved her pee started spilling out from the cup and people started to complain to each other, "It spilled on my head"; "Can't you be more careful"; "I will not hold onto that waste by-product". Finally, the cup reaches Friedman and me at the window.

Me: "I do not think I can empty it like this, but I'll try my best". Unfortunately, almost the whole contents poured on my clothes and whatever I could tip out into the driving wind was blown back inside the wagon.
"I think this is an unimportant issue," I said to Friedman. "Have you noticed the smell? No one can hold their needs back and they cannot go outside either".

Friedman: "They have planned our trip in the most evil way possible. They compressed 80 of us into this wagon and they have not even thought about our most human needs. It is clear they do not care about how many of us will survive by the end of this trip. Look at those elderly people you have been looking after for weeks. Some have not moved for hours. Do you think some are already dead?"

Me: "I am not sure. I have been watching them as well. How ironic. I was trying to keep them alive, and for what? It would have been better for them if I had not done my job so well and let them pass away.
"We are stopping for some reason, but it is so dark out there I cannot see the sign clearly. It must be a very small station as there is no street lighting."
From the back of the wagon there was a woman who had been getting more and more loud on the trip, but by now she was hysterical. From outside, an SS officer yelled and a Hungarian officer translated, "Make that women shut up, or I will fire inside through the grid!"
The people next to her are trying to calm her down, but she gets louder; she screams even more.

Officer from outside: "Shut that women up, or we will fire immediately."

People from the wagon next to her: "Keep it quite would you, you are putting all of us into danger! Be quiet!"
After this, the very loud yelling suddenly becomes very quiet.

Me – turning back to others: "Did you guys manage to calm her down?"

A voice from the back: "We did, but only by covering her mouth with a scarf."

A young female voice screaming hysterically from the back: "She was my mother; you are all wretched; you killed my mother; you suffocated her!"

Friedman: "Poor lady, she had probably gone crazy. No wonder in this hell. What else is waiting for us? She is the most envied of the 80 of us. She is over everything now."

Me: "This smell is getting unbearable, and now we have a dead body in this small place as well. If we travel much longer, we will end up dead too, or we will go insane. Let us tell the officer down there that we have a dead body amongst us. Maybe we could put it out of the wagon," I suggested.

Friedman to the gendarme officer outside at the train station: "We have a dead body here. Open the door so we can move her from here."
Gendarme officer: "The locks have been sealed. The door can be opened only at your final destination. No one is allowed to break the seal or open any doors. No need to be so fastidious, we allow you to use some Kölnisch water[41].

We could hear a quiet conversation outside the wagon, then the gendarme officer called out to us," The passengers of every wagon must hand over a few items. This wagon must present

---

[41] Eau de Cologne: a type of perfume made in Köln, Germany

86

four watches! Collect them quickly and then through the wire-fenced windows pass them down. You have 10 minutes otherwise we will fire one bullet into the wagon for each missing watch. You can hand them over and be rest assured you will not need them where you are heading. Give it to us instead the Germans. They will take them away from you anyway."

Inside the wagon there is a loud discussion going on right away: "I will not give this away. I may will need it later!" one person replies to the request.

"I need to receive something in exchange for this watch," another said.

"I do not have a watch, so do not wait up, the minutes will be over soon," someone else says.

"Come on, take off your watch now. They will fire on us without mercy," says another.

"Is that bloody watch more important than your life?" another asks from the back of the wagon.

"We have nothing left. They have already taken everything from us, slowly, piece by piece, in the ghetto!" says someone else.

"Do not worry about your watches. It is not worth using to keep track of the passing of the time here. We will not be late here for anything," says someone.

The gendarme officer yells again: "Come on people! Your 10 minutes are almost up. Our guns are loaded. You people up there are very stubborn. From the other wagons we have received our desired stuff much quicker."

There is loud argument inside the wagon. One very firm voice said, "Whoever has a watch, take it off immediately and hand it over! Do not risk a human life for a lousy watch!"

A women voice, "I have my children here with me. If they fire inside, they could hit them too. Why are they so stubborn? We already lost everything. They already have taken our homes, furniture and clothes. Come on, give them four watches."

Friedman: "I have a watch. To be true, it is not a wrist watch, it is a pocket-watch. I will give it to them. I got it from my father, so it holds a great level of memory for me. It has always been reliable.

I have always had it with me and even at night it was on my bedside table. It was also my good luck mascot. I have always felt that if I do not have it with me misfortune will come on me. Now that I give it away the misfortune will come for sure." Finally, the four watches were collected.

Officer from outside: "So, what is happening?"

Friedman to the officer: "We have the watches. Hang on a minute until I stretch the wires on the window out a bit. Here you go. One of the watches is a pocket-watch but please accept it. It was mine. It is a perfectly reliable watch. With this one you will be lucky."

Officer: "Give it to me?! Ok, I will accept it. How about money? Did you collect any?"

Friedman: "No, we could not."

Officer: "For God's sake, this wagon has the most money-grabbers of all. The other wagons have more decent passengers than this one. They even gave us gold watches. Hang tight, we may require other things."

Me: "Bastards! This officer says that we are 'travelling'. It is brazen-faced to call this 'travelling'. The animals are receiving better treatment than we are."

Finally, the train left this dark place and rolled on into the morning.

Me to Friedman: "Look, the sun has come up. I better pee quickly before it gets bright. I cannot hold it anymore." I watch as my piss floating down the side of the wagon. "Maybe it's better we have no food, otherwise I have no idea how we would do our 'big job'," I say as I do my 'little job'. "There, it feels better now."

I could not sleep for one second. There are people who can sleep while standing. When a friend of mine was in the army he said he could sleep standing when he was placed into guard duty. He used to pride himself and say, "I can hear steps coming towards me from 50 paces away, so I could greet the commander awake".

Friedman: "We are approaching a much bigger station. Would be good to figure it out which way we are heading. Looks like we will stop because we are slowing down. I know this city! I have been here many, many times. This is Kassa[42]. One of my relatives lives here, so I used to come and visit him. Every time I came, he used to greet me at the station. There. On that exact spot," and he pointed out through the small window. "That is where he greeted me last time as well. Possibly he has already been taken away. It hurts to arrive to Kassa again like this."

Me: "Looks like they have no intention of opening the doors again. I am ashamed of myself, but I cannot control my bowel movement any longer. I do have a small cup but no matter which way I turn there are women and children everywhere and unfortunately, I am forced to complete my need in front of my friend.

As the train is standing on the station, lots of people were yelling out and begging for some water to drink:
"Give us a little bit of water!"
"Have mercy on my children with water!"
"I'm dying from thirst, give us a little water!" But there is no one out there who would help.

Me: "I think it was in the summer of 1942, I saw a train just like this one carrying deported ones at the Central train station in Debrecen. It was a hot day, just like this one. The SS guards did not allow anyone to get close to the train. They used their long truncheons to hit all the arms and hands which were reaching out through the window grids for help. The people who were locked in were begging for something in a different language. I did not understand what they were saying. Now I know - they were begging for water. I felt very sorry for them. Never in my mind have I thought that one day I would be transported the

---

[42] Slovak: "Kosice"; German: "Kaschau" has been Ceded to Czechoslovakia from the Hungarian Kingdom after WWI and again after WWII: http://hungaria.org/vadasz/1848-49/kassa.html

same way, in an animal-carrying wagon, with locked doors and windows with a grid on them. I believe they were Italian Jews and now we are probably getting deported to the same place, all 3,500 of us. I also remember, during that afternoon walk I went to a pub and asked for ice-cold soda water. While I was drinking it, I completely forgot about the deported people on the train, which was standing by very closely. I am sure any of them would have given their soul for a cup of water then."
The train left from Kassa.

Friedman: "The train is going very fast now. We did not stand long at the border. I could not see any more gendarme officers with their rooster feathers on their kepi hats. I could see only SS officers. We are officially in the hands of the Nazis. We are travelling on Czechoslovakian land without any passport check - who knows where to? This Hitler must have a great level of power. We are traveling outside of our country without any official documents."

Me: "If we had been wiser and braver, we would have never ended up in here. In the factory where I was working, we had an old lady who escaped from Poland. Her entire family had been killed, but somehow, she had managed to flee to Hungary. This woman called me aside one day and warned me: "You must escape to somewhere. You must hide, because we will be made homeless and we will be deported too" – but I did not listen to her.

Friedman: "We are traveling so fast I could not read the name of this station. I do not know this place. I do not even know if we are in Slovakia or Poland. One thing is sure, we are not traveling west. We are heading east. Unfortunately, this is not a good sign. We will go through a very heavy ordeal.

Me: "A doctor friend of mine put his entire family and his mother 'to sleep' with an injection in the ghetto. They have all escaped from the torments and from the suffering which still waits for us. This doctor's family did not believe any fairy-tale of the ghettos."

Friedman: "There was even some kind of breaking news that with the cooperation of the Swedish ambassador [43] (Raoul Wallenberg) we would be deported to an island which is not affected by the war."

Me: "I too have heard many different kinds of made-up stories, but the doctor in the ghetto disillusioned me. He asked me to help him to nurse the sick and feeble in the ghetto. I told him I disliked the dead. I even turned my head away when I saw a dead body. Many people committed suicide in the ghetto, and I had to deal with their bodies. I was trying to avoid these corpses but the doctor noticed this and he scolded me and said: 'You must get used to these mute humans. You will have enough to do with them'. I think he will prove to be right soon."

Friedman: "The Polish Jews kept their dignity in a much braver way then us. In the Warsaw ghetto,[44] more than 400,000 faced the Nazis, who were armoured with tanks. They fought for weeks for every inch of the ghetto. Their motto was: 'If they must die, before we do, we want to kill as many Nazi as many possible'. I was well aware of their braveness from the English radio. What did we do on the other hand? We waited for our destiny by sitting with arms crossed. To be true, we had a much more difficult situation. The Warsaw ghetto fight was backed up by the best of the Polish resistance fighters, and we did not receive any help. Also, the Hungarian ghettos did not have strong men anymore, only elderly men and women, and children. Most of the strong men were killed during their forced labour work on the Russian front. History will remember about the Polish heroes, but what will they say about our story?"

Me: "You now, I am a very likable man. Everyone liked me at work and at the football club. I was always helpful towards others. I never thought that one day a man like myself would be taken away like this, like an animal."

---

[43] Raoul Wallenberg - http://www.raoulwallenberg.net/wallenberg/testimonie/stories/andrew-fuchs-my-savior-raoul/
[44] https://www.history.com/topics/world-war-ii/warsaw-ghetto-uprising

The train was just running fast towards the north-west.

Me: "Pay attention, another station is coming up. It has a very weird name; I cannot even pronounce it."

Friedman expressed his hopes in vain: "This is a name of a Polish location. We are in Poland and somewhere a gas chamber is waiting for us. Let us avoid the panic. Let us not tell the rest of the poor passengers that we are on Polish land. There are many more here who were listening to the British radio and they all know what it means to arrive to Poland. We are all sentenced to death, just like the Germans decreed. We are unwanted persons, who have been wiped out from the citizens' records. No-one counts us and no-one cares about us. They can do whatever they want with us."

Me: "The land of a foreign country will be our cemetery. If we end up in the gas chambers and the crematoriums, we will become ashes without a grave. Our ashes and smoke will be carried away by the winds towards five continents. Hopefully, these ashes will warn future humanity not to let this ever happen again. I am so thirsty by now that speaking is becoming very difficult and tiring. They are very cruel to us. So many valuables have been taken away from us. Surely, we deserve a few buckets of water. These Nazis have managed to destroy our deepest human feelings. To endure the suffering, we have been well trained so far. We should be thankful to our hangman for all the tortures and excruciating miseries as the view of a quick death does not sounds as horrid any longer."

Friedman: "It has become dark again. We have been locked in here for a day and a half, and by now we have been travelling more than 24 hours. During this time we have not been given even as much as one mouthful of water. These poor suffering children cannot even cry now. They just hugging on their mothers who feel helpless and cannot ease their needs. My heart is hurting just looking at them. We must watch their suffering helplessly. It would be good to escape from this hell. If we travel much longer, I will go crazy."

Me: "Since we left Kassia we have been travelling at high speed and have not even stopped for one second. We must be hundreds of kilometres from home. We should be deep inside Polish land by now. I said goodbye to my parents and my sister inside the ghetto while I was still helping with the evacuation of the hospital as the doctor's assistant. Will we see each other ever again? Maybe they travelled on the same train tracks a few days ago."

Friedman: "I'm more worried about my wife then about myself, but if we have to die, I would love to die with her by my side. I hope we can ask for that much as our last wish from the Nazis."

Me: "The nights are the shortest during this part of the summer. The sun sets for a few hours. I can see the red colour of the rising sun in the distance. This is our second night without sleep, food, or water, I don't think we can handle this any longer as humans. I hope their intention is not to make us die here in the wagons. In this unbearable condition we can live a maximum of another day, then we all will smell the roses from underneath one by one."

A few hours went by and we just stood and looked out the window into the dark distance.

Friedman: "Can you feel it? The train is slowing down. Look over there. I can see huge smoking chimneys. Looks like there are factories in the far distance. Maybe they did not lie to us after all. Maybe they will make the stronger women and men work here, and they will not separate the families from each other."

Me: "It is hard to see in the morning dawn, but now I can also see the chimneys and the red brick factory-looking buildings. The barracks are also visible now. Lots of them, but all divided by barb-wire fences. There are also high watch towers everywhere. The train is going very slowly now. Looks like this huge factory might is our final destination. This scene looks very positive. Not sure what are they making here. This smoke is very dark and has a smell which I have never smelled before. I think we can tell everyone else that we have finally arrived. We will have water, food and hopefully we can rest from this long trip in a normal bed."

Freidman reported to his wife and the rest of the people at the back of the wagon: "We can see big factories, smoking chimneys and lots and lots of barracks. Looks like the Germans did not lie to us. We will be working in these big factories after all. I can see lots of people between the barracks. There are many of them. Thank God, we will not be executed after all. Where there are factories there are workers needed."

Me: "Look, there is a big sign says: "ARBEIT MACHT FREI[45]". We are almost at the train station and the train is coming to a stop. It will be delightful to step out of this wagon and lay down on the grass. Finally, we have arrived. I can see the sign with the name of the place, Auschwitz. We have arrived at Auschwitz. I have never heard of this place."

Picture from: https://listverse.com/wp-content/uploads/2016/01/auschwitz.jpg - The main gate of Auschwitz camp

Now, everyone knows that this place was the worst place in world history and has become the graveyard of the greatest number of destroyed lives ever. It is only a few square kilometres but more than 2,500,000 people vanished from here. There is no

---

[45] Work makes free

battleground in the world on which more lives per square kilometre were lost than here.

Through the window I could see a long "ramp" made of yellow gravel and looking very organized. Our train, which was made up of 40-45 wagons, was able to fit alongside the ramp. We could hear the clattering of many wooden shoes and human voices even before the doors had been opened. As I looked out I was surprised at the look of these people. They all wore grey and blue striped "uniforms" which were complemented with a similarly striped hat with no sun visor. On the left side of their uniform there was a white tag with numbers on it. They were running around and getting organized. They seemed like they were trying to look well organized to get ready to greet our arrival. They were all young but skinny males, and they all looked up towards the windows with rigid, blank, tired and emotionless eyes. We were trying to guess who these people were. We found out later that they were mostly Polish, and that they belonged to the forced labour groups. Most of them had been working here for a month, or maybe longer.

These men were trained slaves from the lager. They worked there and helped the Nazis to speed up the product of this factory – this DEATH FACTORY. The final product of the contract was set out clearly by the "Final Solution" agreement. This contract was "agreed" only by one of the parties, the German side. Labour workers had no right to sign the contract. These young and strong men worked on the conveyor belt of this factory for about three months directing millions, selected in front of one man, then they all ended up in the gas chambers themselves. Millions arrived there, and there were enough to supply replacement.

The command has been announced: "Open the doors!

All doors slid open at once, like it had been rehearsed for years – and so it was.
The workmen all jumped up onto the wagons and started pushing and shoving everyone down off the train. We did not

even have time to pick up our belongings. They did not act with any more care towards the elderly either. This was their job.

Picture from:
https://www.scrapbookpages.com/AuschwitzScrapbook/AuschwitzAlbum/Platform.jpg - Arrival to Auschwitz

Picture from:
https://furtherglory.files.wordpress.com/2015/07/auschwitzarrival1.jpg -
Auschwitz arrival on the ramp

Picture from:
http://s3.amazonaws.com/s3.timetoast.com/public/uploads/photos/4182966
/67842-004-727F1906.jpg?1474687108 – Disembarking the wagons on the
Auschwitz ramp

We stood in front of the train - husbands with wives, kids with
mothers, brothers with brothers, friends with friends. We all
tried to stay with someone we knew.
Me: "This is the real welcome. Thank God no one has got injured
in the wrestling."

Friedman: "Who knows why they are in such a hurry? Maybe
they are waiting for another transport and must empty the
ramps beforehand."

Someone else: "Look, all our suitcases, travel bags and backpacks
are getting thrown into a big pile. They are all getting mixed up.
How on earth will we find our belongings now?" Everyone who
heard this turned their attention towards the pile. Many started

crying for their valuables which, until now, they had managed to keep secure.

Picture from:
https://static.timesofisrael.com/www/uploads/2016/04/RetrieveAsset-640x400.jpg

The luggage left behind after disembarking the trains at Auschwitz
Pictures are: http://www.whale.to/b/auschwitz_p.html - Collected luggage
on the Auschwitz ramp after arrival. More pictures on the link.

Suddenly big trucks arrived and stopped at the wagons. Many
had lost their lives during the three-day travel without food or

water, so the loaders started throwing all the corpses and they did this without showing any sign of humanity. Their movements were very mechanical because they had been doing this for a long time. The corpses were dumped onto the trucks, on top of each other like bags of potatoes. When one truck was filled, the SS guards gave instructions for the vehicle to drive away. They headed towards the big red-brick factory looking building.

Soon after, another SS yelled his instructions and all the striped uniformed "workers" started to organize us into two groups. They were doing their "job" without hesitation. They knew the smallest mistake would be repaid with the biggest prize.

Splitting of the remaining less than 3,000 of us into groups was accomplished in a short amount of time.

The group on the right had the younger and also the stronger males. The group on the left had all the younger kids, their mothers, the elderly ones, and the sick "travellers".

Picture from: https://isurvived.org/Pictures_iSurvived-4/auschwitz-peron.GIF - After the selection process at Auschwitz ramp

I ended up in the group to the right, but I felt a bit sad as I could see a few relatives and many friends in the left group, including Samu Liener, Erzsebet Fuchs, and Mrs Gellg Miksa. I did not speak any German so I could not ask anyone to put me with my friends. I started edging across to the left but an SS officer saw this and pushed me back into the group on the right.

Mother before the gas chamber

The wagon door opens, wind blows the hair,
The faces touched by black smoky air.
Pushing, shoving down the scared ones,
Clinging into each other with daughters and sons.
Cruel reception for everyone at the ramp,
Selected for destruction or work camp.
The SS breaks decades of family ties,
Crying child, helpless father, young one and the wise.
Only the mother looks with anger at the executioner,
Who did not break by the ghetto mould either?
With the little ones they move her aside,
Grabbing their clothes, her joy and pride.
The mother is not a hero, yet she is the strongest,
Holding all children from tallest to shortest.
Calming them from all the cruel faces,
With her worn dress, her body embraces.
She gave birth to them, she has the right to march along,
Towards the Red Brick Crematorium, she is that strong.
She already knows that this is the end,
Like iron brace she grasps their hand.
Only after the death can they be separated,
From the child she carried and created.

"Gehen" sounded the instruction in German and they started pushing us forward. The two lines walked side by side and they did not even make us hurry. I saw mothers with two and sometimes with three children. Another friend of mine, who was a tree lopper, was limping in front of me as one of his legs was shorter than the other.

Soon we arrived at a crossing where a tall officer about 30 years old stood.

"Halt!" he called out loudly and lifted his hand up. Not many of us spoke the language but the hand sign was clear. We all stopped. He smiled at us, which brought hope to many of us. I was looking at his clean black and grey uniform and his spotless shiny black shoes.

"Who is this man?"

"Who is this?" many of us started asking ourselves.

Dr. Josef Mengele, Rudolf Hoess and Josef Kramer (left to right) - Picture from:
http://www.whale.to/b/auschwitz_p.html

He stepped towards the left group and he signalled towards them to continue walking the same way.

This man was the notorious Dr Mengele, the chief medical doctor of the lager. This was how he sent millions and millions of Jews to death without causing any panic - one signal with his arm. That was it! Everyone on the left had been sent into the gas chambers. They had only less than one hour of their lives left - if that.

The selection process has been done. Left or right – To die or to live - Picture from: http://i.ytimg.com/vi/ubZH1j_zDMk/hqdefault.jpg

Then he stepped over to us. He spent a bit more time with our group. He looked at each of us, one by one, then he signalled to the left or to the right. I waited about 15 minutes before it was my turn. He looked at my friend next to me and he signalled him to move to the right. As he walked away Mengele looked back and saw him limping. He told the guards to move him over to the left group. Then he stepped in front of me. I corrected my posture and pulled myself up straight. I was about a half a head taller than him. He looked at me from head to toe about twice, then he started squishing my arm muscles. He clearly liked what he saw and then he sent me to the right.

Hundreds and hundreds got a closer look from him and they are all got a decision - left or right.

We had no idea what it meant so we were just standing there waiting. Only about 150 to 160 of us were standing on the right side. Everyone else was on the left. We still did not know who this man was, but he did his job with German precision. There were about 40 men and the rest were young women. Most of the strong men had already passed away in the war, digging in the Siberian winter or from other causes during their forced labour work.

The Auschwitz ramp - Picture from:
https://www.yadvashem.org/yv/en/exhibitions/album_Auschwitz/images/arrival/268_3.jpg

We were finally getting to move and were walking towards the barracks so we could have a look around - barb-wire fences, dry soil (no grass at all), dirt, black smoke, guards with beating sticks, guard dogs. We were all scared but we could not show any weakness. As I looked back to the other selected group on the left, I could see two of my young nephews, Tomi (Tamás) and Jancsi (János). They were 5 and 6 years old, and they were hugging my aunt's legs from each side. This was the last time I saw them and their mother, my mother's sister. They were lost in the Holocaust with about 50 of our family members.

We were directed towards a big brick building which had a big sign in Hungarian over the entrance: FERTőTLENÍTő (DESINFECTATNT). We all stripped naked. There were workers shaving every bit of hair from our bodies without any brotherly touches, They were very rough. They were all Polish workers who were also prisoners of this place. They cut our skin here and there but there was no mercy - no pardon or excuse from them. Then we all got wiped with pure petroleum which stung our skin, especially our small cuts. We then received our new "uniform"- the same blue and grey striped clothes. Some had a few sizes too big, some had a few sizes too small, but we could not ask for the right fit. No one cared how we looked. Some workers were collecting our old clothes and putting them up on an arrival truck.

"Bewegen, Loss, Reihen," (move, come on, line up) shouted one of the guards.

"I can't keep up with this fast pace," said a young boy. He was about 16-17 years old and still half naked after the disinfection and shaving processes. Why were they pushing us at this insane tempo?

We were commanded to our next "station" which was a huge barracks, painted green. This building swallowed all 160 of us easily. We were all happy to sit down and take our place on the dirty floor next to the wooden walls. We were all tired from the three days of travel and the last few hours had been a huge shock to us too. We still had not received any water or food. Most of us just sat and stared straight in front of us and wondered what else would come. Soon, two SS officers stepped into the barracks and everyone's eyes looked at them. They looked with disgust at us lying on the ground, then one of them cleared his throat and started speaking in German. They had their personal translator with them (in the same striped uniform as us) who started translating:

"Stand up! Line up!" he yelled. We all jumped up and stood straight. Then he continued with the translation, "I am bringing to your attention that you are in the death camp of Auschwitz – in fact in its side-lager called Birkenau. This is not a health recovery sanatorium; from here there is only one way out, through the chimney. Until your final day arrives you will be working here. You must perform your work to your best ability. The only things authorized are what we order. What we do not command is forbidden and will be heavily punished. Whoever does not like it, you can run into the high voltage electric fence now. The road is clear for everyone."

Then they walked out of the barracks. These few words destroyed the last hope in everyone. My heart broke even more as I looked at the faces. The day was not over yet. It was only about midday.

We had just briefly met the SS officers there, but we hated them already, and now some new ones entered the barracks. These were just as fearsome as the others. Probably these would tell us what our duties would be, we all thought, but something else happened first.

The Football Player

Two SS officers stepped inside the barracks: "Stand up! Line up!" the translator yelled out. "Hands out!" came the next order and one officer started going around to check everyone's hands to see what kind of job they should be selected for. The other SS officer was swinging back and forth from his heels to his toes a few times. Everyone looked at him with scared eyes. The room was very quiet. We could hear the cracking noise of his leather boots.

"Can anyone play football?" he asked. Silence in the room.

"Is there anyone here who is a professional football player?" He shouted again, and the translator translated him. We heard some mumbling noises as everyone looked at each other with surprise. The officer was looking at the faces searchingly.

"Come on now? No one has ever played football?" Suddenly I step forward with three other men at the same time. I had never been a professional player, but I trusted my football talent, even though I had not played since my first forced labour camp about three years ago. We were all still in good physical condition. I was hoping to have a much more privileged life if I was selected. Someone next to me said, "Don't step out! Look, we are all going into factories to work. They are checking our hands to see what the best work would be for each of us. Step back, can't you hear me?"

"No" I whispered back to him. "I'm a football player and I must see this out."

"Follow me," the officer ordered, and we all formed a straight line and followed him out of the barracks onto a small field. There was no grass there. Nothing could survive the conditions. The soil was as hard as a rock and we were all wearing shoes with wooden soles that were a good two to three sizes bigger than our feet. It was even hard to walk in them. There were eight Nazi officers, a capo[46] and a short-haired prisoner waiting there for us. I recognized the man in the grey-blue striped uniform. It was Dezső Steinberger Solti [47] from Balmazújváros[48]. "Why was he here along with the Nazis? Why was he not shaved bald? Many questions that I would have liked to have asked him came into my mind but he did not look at me. He clearly ignored me. "Here are the players," the officer announced on our arrival and we lined up front of the "Selection committee".

They all started looking at us and the investigation began. I felt like a race horse. They all started touching and squeezing our ankles, knees, and thighs. We had to perform a few deep breaths (in and out), to fill our chest up with air so they could have a look at how much our chest would expand. They all showed great interest in me, but not much in the others. They had a quick meeting amongst themselves, then one of the officers stepped in front of us. His name was Heinz, and Steinberger started the translation.

"In what team have you played?"

"In the Team Bocskai in Debrecen," I replied, but I started sweating and felt my face becoming pale. Steinberger looked deeply into my eyes as he knew I had never played in the first league, but he turned around and translated back to Heinz. He had not revealed our secret. It ran through my mind that I would thank him at the first possible occasion for this.

"In what position did you play?" comes the next question.

---

[46] Capo (Kapo), trustee, an SS appointed prisoner who was the head of the labour squad. He or she retained this privileged position by terrorizing subordinate prisoners.
www.holocaustsurvivors.org

[47] Dezső Steinberger (Solti) also know as Desiderio Solti – (1912-1993, Balmazújváros) Hungarian born. Played In Balmazújváros SC. His family owned the Reiner-Mill factory, so he also managed the club. After the war he moved to Italy where he become the director and manager of the Milan Internazionale (Football Club Internazionale Milano, commonly referred to as Internazionale or simply Inter and colloquially known as Inter Milan outside Italy,) in the 1960's.
www.futbaltortenet.blog.hu

[48] Balmazújváros – is a town in Hajdú-Bihar county, in the Northern Great Plain region of eastern Hungary.

"I played for years as the right-wing defender, but then I was moved to the right front as a striker. My coach's explanation was that he needed my speed and my quick decision-making at the front more than…"

Heinz cuts into my story: "How fast can you sprint 100m?" He was clearly looking for short answers.

"Less than 12 seconds," I stated "and after training I used to run 5 to 6 kilometres every…."

Heinz cut in again: "What was the quality of the games you played?"

"We did not have one easy game in any season," I replied as I stretched my posture. "We always scored in every game, we played strongly till the end and we always had full …"

"Enough! Step aside!" ordered Heinz

He moved on to the next volunteer player with the same questions. His steel face did not show any emotion and I could not read anything from it. We did not know whether he liked or disliked any of us.

Heinz finished his interview which felt more like an interrogation: "Now, we will see if you really are a great player, or whether you just have a big mouth," Heinz said with sarcasm. This was the first human feeling he showed since meeting with us.

Suddenly a ball showed up - a proper ball made of leather with the stiches on the side. I had never seen such a great quality ball since the start of my football career. We all looked at each other with raised eyebrows with surprize.

They called me first for the test which was still unexplained. This was predictable. If the Germans set up a precise system and if it works, they will not change it.

I was not happy as I had to perform for them first so I did not have time to analyse the situation.

"Go onto the field! You have to head the ball back exactly into the hands of the capo," Heinz explained my first test.

I was anxious, so I prepared myself for the worst. Heinz was not nice at all. The ball flew at me with great speed. "What a jerk" I whispered to myself, but I headed the ball straight back in the hands of the capo. I couldn't believe it. The officers started to smile on my great ball return.

"Now, you have to pass the ball back with your feet," came the next order from Heinz.

"Ok, this is the end, I'm done," I said to myself as I looked down at the wooden shoes which clearly did not fit me. "Come on Sándor, you can do it," I said trying to inspire myself, but the ball was already flying towards me. This time it came with less power and only at mid-body height. I squeezed my toes in the wooden shoes to try to make them remain on my feet, and I used the inside of my sole to pass the ball back towards the capo. And once again, the ball went straight into his hands.

"Now, you have to take the ball down," stated Heinz. The capo threw the ball up about 6 metres into the air. I ran under the ball, pulled up the pants a bit on my thigh, reached under the ball and with great gentleness I tried to slow the ball down with my feet as it fell. Due to the wooden shoes, it bounced off a bit, but then I stopped the ball by stepping on it, like it was meant to happen. I did not give away my small mistake with any facial expression. I showed clear success. All the officers were happy for my performance and they asked me to step aside. My test was finished.

The other prisoners did their best but did not do as well as I did. The Nazis formed a small circle discussion group for about 2 to 3 minutes then they all looked at us and then let Steinberger speak. "Schwarz, you made the team." I looked down onto my feet so no one could read my happiness. I was 32 years old and I still had it. The other inmates were not as happy.

"You have a game tomorrow," stated Heinz. Then the capo led us back to the barracks. The building had been emptied. No one was there. Everyone had been taken away during our football test. Soon someone arrived and took the other three man who had not passed the test. I was alone in this big building for a few minutes then my friend Dezső arrived. Finally, now he smiled at me, he pulled me off the ground and hugged me. He acted like a totally different person.

"Come, let's find you some better place to stay," he said, "this building will be your new permanent accommodation, the Birkenau 9th barrack. I have lived here too for five weeks now. I came in May with one of the first transportation of 10,000 Hungarians. You will have 10 more players with you, and I am the team manager. You will be playing with the Gipsy lager team." Dezső just talked and talked. He did not stop, and I did not ask. Everything he said interested me. He was clearly very happy.

"The tall, wide shouldered SS officer who did your test - his name is Heinz. He and a few of his friends are passionate football fans. They have been looking for weeks now to find two men for the team. They already found one last week, a Hungarian as well. His name is Weigner, and now you are the 11th player. Weigner was a professional player in the Kis-Pesti team[49].

Steinberger stopped for a second, cleared his throat, and continued as we walked along.

"The capo, who was there at the test, is Polish. He was the person appointed by the SS officers. He looks after the team. Tonight he will provide you with proper football shoes, shin guards, underwear, and a jersey. I advise you to put them on immediately and do not ever take them off, not even during the night. If they see you in those clothes, it will give you protection, even in the lager. The officers and the capos will not be cruel towards the players. Of course, you cannot trust anyone. On your first game tomorrow you must do your best, play your heart out just like the others, because here you cannot loose. Losing the game will be deadly to all of you because the gentle football fans will turn into bloodthirsty animals. Be safe and do not get injured. Don't get into any hard tackles because there is no place or need for a limping or injured player. According to the SS officers, these players belong in the gas chambers."

---

[49] **Budapest Honvéd FC -** is a Hungarian sports club based in Kispest. Originally formed as *Kispest AC*, they became *Kispest FC* in 1926 before reverting to their original name in 1944. The team enjoyed a golden age during the 1950s when it was renamed *Budapesti Honvéd SE* and became the Hungarian Army team. The club's top players from this era, Ferenc Puskás, Sándor Kocsis, József Bozsik, Zoltán Czibor, and Gyula Grosics formed the nucleus of the legendary Hungarian team known as the *Mighty Magyars* and helped the club win the Hungarian League four times during the 1950s. *Honved* means the Homeland Defence.

I memorized everything until the last word then I started asking questions. "Do you know anything about two transports which should have arrived here three days ago from Debrecen? My parents were on the first train. And tell me, what kind of gypsies are the ones we have been placed with? How did they get here? Will we get enough food and will I be able to keep my condition?" I fired all my questions on him at once.

"For a few days the railways were shut and no trains arrived here," Steinberger replied. "What I have heard is that all trains have been sent to some place in Austria, but I am not 100 per cent sure. I could be wrong. Yes, the gypsies," he continued, "I did ask, but I cannot tell you much about them. They have been living here more than a year now, with their families, here in Birkenau. They live opposite us and next to us. There are about 800 families stationed there. They are the same kind of deported race, just like us, from all over Europe, but because they are Germans, they think they are a higher race. You should not trust them."

We were now in the barracks and Dezső continued to educate me about the life there. "In the morning the prisoners receive same sort of a coffee substitute or some tea made of different grasses. For lunch they make a soup from one kilogram of potato and from a few dried cattle turnips in a huge pot to feed almost an entire barracks. For dinner a quarter of a chunk of bread, which is 350 gram, a small (about one-tenth portion of margarine), and twice a week one spoonful of carrot jam. This is the usual menu, but do not worry, as a football player you will receive some extra food. The food is distributed here in this barracks for the whole Birkenau lager, and the people living with us in this barracks are responsible for the portioning. Make sure you become good friends with them, and you could get some extra portions too. And one more thing," says Steinberger with his eyes glued to the ground, "I did not want to tell you but you must know. Your debut as a football player here in Auschwitz will be at the same time as everyone from your train is to be executed by gas and their corpses will be placed into the crematoriums to burn to ashes." Then he put his hand on the back of my neck and pulled me close to give me a big hug as he can see tears rolling down my cheeks.

During our chat it became dark outside and all the people were coming back from work. I introduced myself to my inmates, but who knows where they could have been until now. They all welcomed me with friendliness, especially Weigner. Soon it was dinner time. I ate super fast as I had not eaten for three days - since the deportation in Debrecen.

The capo, just like Steinberger said, arrived with the jersey, pitch-black leather football boots (brand new), pitch-black shin guards (brand new), pitch-black shorts and pitch-black jersey-shirt, both made from first class quality silk. As I put these on, I looked like a grieving man. I was wearing the world's most expensive and blackest jersey made by the best craftsman of the world who had been deported there. They were sewn out of the clothes of the deportees executed in the gas chambers.
I agonized on these facts. I fought with my conscience. Was I not committing an offense against the dead by wearing these garments? Then I sent these thoughts away. There was no place for sentimentality in Birkenau. I started
thinking about tomorrow. What would happen? What would the conditions be? Where were we going to play? I hoped to go outside of the electric-wired fences - outside onto the green fresh grass, into the fresh air where the smell of the crematoriums would not reach us. Who would be the opponent? Would I be able to play the two 45 minutes of play time? I started counting the ones I knew from our transport - whispering each and everyone's name. I could see their faces in front of my closed eyes. I reached about 50 then finally fell asleep.

Meeting the team

Next morning I woke to loud talking and conversations. I lay there for a few minutes before I realized where I was. I rolled up onto my elbow as I still felt very tired from the last few days of travel without any water and food. I had ended up sleeping on a stack of straw which was more comfortable than the wooden bunk beds.

The wooden barracks of Birkenau. Picture from: http://i0.wp.com/minoritynomad.com/wp-content/uploads/2015/01/Auschwitz-Birkenau-Concentration-Camp-Prisoner-Barracks.jpg

Inside the barracks. Picture from:https://imgix.ranker.com/list_og_img/125/2490370/original/everyday-life-in-concentration-camps-u6?w=817&h=427&fm=jpg&q=50&fit=crop

I lay a bit longer and the barracks became empty. I looked around the huge empty space (this place is only for briefing and final selection for work) but it was where we stayed overnight.

Then I saw Weigner. He was around 37 years old but looked very skinny from the month he had been here already. He was putting on his black football shoes.

"Do we need to get ready?" I asked.

"I was just about to wake you up," he replied. "It is 10 minutes to 7o'clock", he said "and at 7 o'clock the entire team and the capo will be here in these barracks for meet and greet, and we will have our first briefing as a team as well."

"Why so early?" I asked, then I realized I must get ready too, so I jumped out of "bed" and started putting on my black jersey as well.

"I think the officers are available only this time of the day, or maybe the opposition team cannot come at any other time," Weigner said.

"If you had the game later during the day you would be cooking yourself in the sun anyway" says Steinberger, who was leaning against the doorframe and was listening to our conversation. Then he stepped in front of me and repeated his yesterday's instructions.

Weigner added: "The rules of the game are the same as outside in the free world. There is offside. Touching the ball by hand will be punished and you will be sent off for deliberate or intentional harsh play. Minor offenses are awarded with free kicks."

As soon as he finished the door opened and we all looked outside. The gypsies were coming and they all gathered in the centre of the barracks. The last one who entered the building was the Polish capo.

You were not allowed to leave the barracks without permission or without the presence of your capo.

Weigner and Steinberger greeted them all, but I stepped back and just watched them. I realized, with quite a surprise, that all the gypsies were about 25 to 35 years old. All of them had thick black hair and had not shaved. Steinberger said they had been living there for more than a year but all were in great physical condition. Some of them looked almost overweight with the jerseys stretched across their chests.

"This man will be your eleventh player. He was a professional player, and he has a great ball-handling skill," said the capo and pointed at me.

I could not see any positive or negative expressions on their faces as they listened to him. Then they all started coming towards me to shake my hand and introduce themselves, and this time I could see some smiles on their faces.

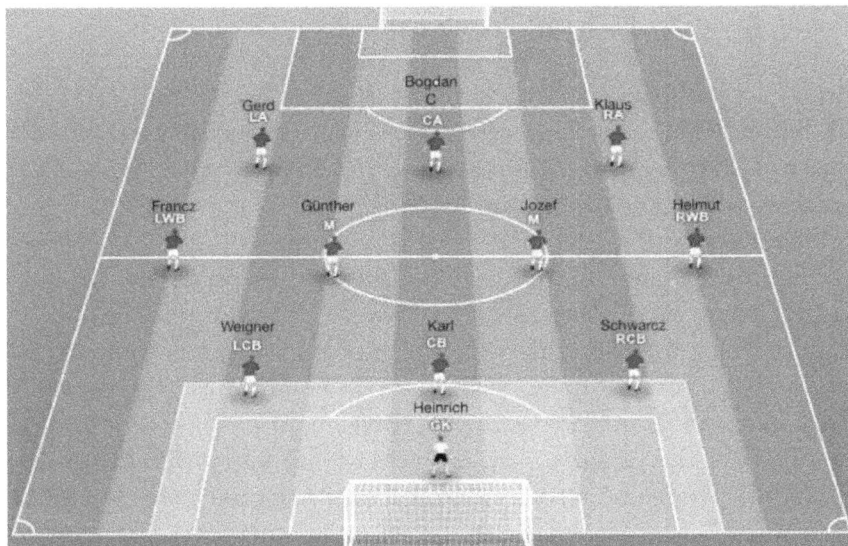

Reproduction of the players position on the field.

"Henrich, I'm the goalkeeper" – he was a very stocky looking, huge person. (GK)

"Karl, I'm the centre-back" – he had long legs. (CB)

"Josef, I'm the inside right" – he was very skinny and tall. (M – midfield)

"Francz, I'm the left defender" – he was about 2m tall. (LWB - Left wing back)

"Helmuth, I'm the right defender" – he had very dark skin compared to the others. (RWB – Right wing back)

"Günther, I'm the inside left" – he looked very pale but very friendly and even tapped my shoulder. (M)

"Gerd, I'm the left outsider" – he had big shoulders like a professional wrestler and gave me a huge smile. (LA – Left attack)

115

"Klaus, I'm the right wingman" – he was the shortest of all the players. (RA -Right attack)

"Bogdan, I'm the centre player and the team captain" – he even said a few welcoming words. (CA – Centre attack).

I was a bit sceptical at first because Steinberger had said the day before that these German gypsies may consider themselves superior to the Jew prisoners, but now I was starting to warm to these guys.

"Free activity" – announced the capo unexpectedly.

The gypsies started talking to each other in a bunch and I started talking to Weigner and Steinberger. The capo decided to come to our smaller group. "Translate," he says to Steinberger "I need to say a few things to the rookie".

I looked him in the eye with interest.

"The game will start in half an hour and your opposition will be a team from one of the nearby subcamps. You will play in the right fullback position, but this does not mean you cannot move forward, all the way to the goal if necessary. During the game you can communicate only to your own team members. If you try to talk to the players from the other team you will be heavily punished. The game will be refereed by a prisoner, who was a professional referee. Whatever decision he makes, you cannot express yourself in any way. Only the team captain has authority to do so and he will appoint the player to take the freekick or penalty kicks too."

At 10 minutes past 7, an officer stepped inside the barrack and told us to move. The capo lined us up – Bogdan the captain stood in the front, Weigner in front of me, and I was last in the line.

"Is the field far away?" I ask Weigner.

"Shut up!" yelled the SS at me and of course Weigner did not say a word. He did not even turn towards me.

Aerial view of the camp of Auschwitz and the position of the football field.
Picture from:
https://holocaustdeprogrammingcourse.files.wordpress.com/2014/01/ausch
witz-football-pitch.jpg

The first game

We all got up and walked out towards the gypsy barracks. We
left the gypsy lager behind us through a gate then turned right
not far from there and we walked through another gate. On one
side there was the gypsy barracks and on the other side very
close by there was the crematorium with its chimneys. At the
other end, opposite the gate, were some low-set brick buildings
and a high watch tower. The grass field was a proper-sized
football field with all the exact field markings on it in white, but
in many places we could see dry soil which looked very hard as
well. The grass had been burnt by the sun. The goals were made
from wooden boards but looked like the proper size. The net had
been handmade, probably by the prisoners there, but they
looked very strong. We were between the electric wired fence

and the guard towers. We did not have any spectators, only the guards from above. I felt like I was walking out onto a proper football pitch, but the heavy smoke and the terrible smell brought me back to the reality.

I asked the skinny Weigner about the building at the back. "They keep all the twin children there. Mengele[50] is conducting cruel scientific experiments with them," he said.
"Like what? I asked.
"Nobody knows for sure, but he is searching for the answer of how to develop twins for the "Clean race" to speed up their multiplication process. Also, he is experimenting to see if they feel the same level of pain during torture. He is amputating limbs without anaesthetics and many more terrible things."
I looked over there and I saw the kids running out of the building to their little playground and they saw us. Some came to the fence to watch.

Picture from:
https://www.history.com/.image/t_share/MTY1MzM4NDk5NDU5OTE3MDgw/holocaust-twins-gettyimages-89277106.jpg
Holocaust twins

---

[50] For more information on the experiments visit: https://www.dw.com/en/skeletons-in-the-closet-of-german-science/a-1587766-1, https://www.chicagotribune.com/news/ct-xpm-1985-06-30-8502120086-story.html https://en.wikipedia.org/wiki/Josef_Mengele

win survivals. Picture from:
https://i.pinimg.com/originals/b9/22/74/b922749ae334f87583fa2781f71891d7.jpg
Watch a video of the twin survivals:
https://www.youtube.com/watch?v=MWJyjAYyF8E

"What is this? Come on, let's go, warm up!" called out the capo.
"You were a trainer?" He turns towards Weigner,"You, conduct
the warm-up," he ordered.
Weigner looked surprised. "Jogging - one circle," called out
Weigner with his little German knowledge, and we all started
jogging around the field. We jogged close to the crematorium
and as I looked over the fence I could see people marching into a
long building. One mother was holding an infant and two of her
other kids were holding her skirt. There was a big sign over the
entrance just like ours had - FERTőTLENÍTő (DESINFECTANT).
I asked Weigner again about them: "That is the gas chamber," he
replied.

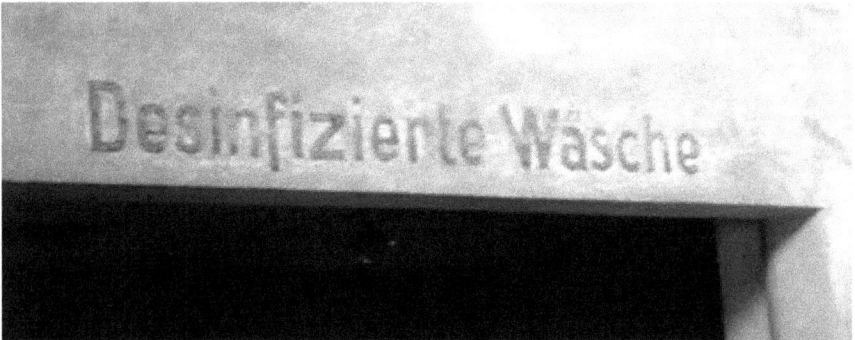

Picture from:
http://www.scrapbookpages.com/AuschwitzScrapbook/2005Photos/Disinfec
tionSign.jpg - Sign over the entrance of the gas chamber - Disinfection

"I don't understand!", I said and I stopped my jogging. Weigner
came back and grabbed my arm and pulled me back to jogging
speed. "Don't stop, otherwise the Capo will hit you," he said.
"That is the gas chamber. People walk in there without any
panic. They keep changing the sign to whatever language the
arrivals speak. If they are from Italy, then the sign says
DESINFECTANT in Italian. If they are from Serbia, then it is in
Serbian, and so on. People believe everything here. No one ever
thinks that what is actually happening is going to happen to
them. It is unbelievable to think they are marching to their
death."
"And then what?", I asked.

"Then all the workers in their striped prisoner uniforms lock the doors behind them. Inside its looks like a big shower. Then they are all get killed with a toxic gas through the shower heads."

"And what happens with all these bodies?" I continued to ask. "Can we yell out and warn them not to enter in the building? Can we not do something?"

"The workers pull them out and put them into the crematorium. They are all getting burned. The chimneys have been smoking for days. They are in operation now as well. Thousands are leaving us every day. If you think you want to die right now, then you can start shouting over the fence, but you will get shot instantly and you may put us into danger as well."

"I see," I said with deep sorrow," "I will be quiet, but you know, all these people are from my city – the ones I arrived with. I know many of them. I even had cousins there as well," I said as I looked over to the black smoking chimneys as we still jogged around the field.

"So, these chimneys do not belong to any real factory then?" I asked.

"Yes, they are. They are called the DEATH FACTORY," he replied, and continued. "When the gassing has finished the prisoners get sent in to check everyone's teeth and see if they can find any golden fillings. They still get to search for the last remaining jewels or any valuables. Then they must hand anything they find over to the SS officers in charge. The gold gets melted into gold bars and gets taken away somewhere." Weigner stopped as we had finished our one circle run.

"Ball passes, 20 times," called out Weigner for the next exercise. When we had finished we did some more stretching, and Weigner continued. "The death factory workers are also prisoners. They are 'contracted' for a three-month period, then the next group from amongst the new arrivals takes over and the previous crew gets executed by gas and their bodies are loaded into the crematoriums also."

The SS officers arrived. Our team "manager and owner", Heinz, arrived with them too. He was happy to see the warm-up session had been conducted. He looked proud, but he was unhappy to see that the opposition team was not yet there.

"That's ok," said one officer, "we can make our bets until they arrive", and the betting started.

Bogdan started to draw some tactics into the dirt. Finally, the opposition team showed up with three SS officers.

Their jersey was black shoes, black socks, light green shorts and T-shirt. It looked like Auschwitz had different campsites, and the SS officers formed their own teams for their own pleasure. They were all around 20 to 25 years old but they all looked very tired and worn out. The players looked surprised to see the crematorium from this close. One of the players just froze and tears ran down his cheeks. He saw the hundreds marching towards the buildings.

"Sorry, we are late," said one of their officers to Heinz. "We had an urgent job to do".

"That's ok," replies Heinz, and the "disagreement" was quickly over. They were very lenient towards each other.

The opposition team's "manager" was happy to skip their warm-up and the game was on its way.

Heinz, at the moment the match started, looked like any ordinary football fan, but during the game we would see his real self. He walked up and down on the sideline waving his gun and shouting something in German. I understood - he wanted us to win, otherwise we could be killed.

In the outside free world, the players get cheered by thousands of fans. If they win, they get paid well and get names like "HEROES" and "STARS". This day, we were running and playing an international game to stay alive, to hopefully receive a bit more food than the other prisoners. There was no place for unfair play. There was no place for a mistake or to get injured. There was no place for someone not giving their absolute best. The motto of the game was, "Play well to stay alive!"

From the first moment until the last I could not take my eyes off the smoking chimneys of the crematorium. As soon as I had no possession of the ball, something forced me to look there. This was the closest I had ever been to a place like that. The entire place had been built by the prisoners. The train-tracks has been laid by them as were the barracks, the barbed-wire fences, and the crematoriums. With a new workforce arriving on the endless trains carrying more than 3,000 people each, a total of more than 2.5 million had soon been reached. There was one thing in my mind, if we lost or if I got injured, would I end up there too? They would not even have to take me far away, just over the fence.

We started the game and our attack was towards the crematoriums, but we lost the ball in the defence line. The green team was moving forward very slowly. They were passing the ball to each other with great precision, then as they reached the half-way line, they started moving faster. In the second minute a well passed ball flew over to my side. The front wingman ran into me, but I managed to kick the ball back inside the field with my first touch.

"That's it! Well done!" shouted Heinz and the others were clapping as well.

I felt relieved, my debut had started well. I gained some confidence and from then on I played with more positive feelings about myself.

The game was well balanced but there had been no goal yet. When we were in the 10th minute the ball flew to the opposition midfielder who handled the ball well then, with a great trick, he dodged Karl and with great power he kicked the ball into the net beside our diving goalkeeper, Heinrich. They celebrated, and we froze like statues. We did not want to look towards our officers but we could hear them well enough. They were not pleased. I peeked towards Heinz and I saw him pulling his pistol out from its case again and started to wave it over his head with some unrecognisable words. I was glad I did not speak German.

Weigner runs to me. "Come on Schwarcz, we must win, otherwise this will be our end," and he taps my back. The gypsy boys were encouraging each other as well. Bogdan said a few words to the team and placed the ball down in the middle. This was useful. We ran more and we took the possession of the ball for most of the time, but without any results.

In the 22nd minute Gerd tricked his way through four players and faced the goalkeeper. Unfortunately he missed the goalpost by a few centimetres.

The next great occasion was a corner kick from Klaus. It flew towards the tall Franz, but he headed it into the goalpost.

Josef got a great pass and he targeted the left top corner, but the goalkeeper leapt into the air and saved the kick.

We were in the 44th minute when Klaus, the right front-wing man, took a fantastic and powerful kick. The goalkeeper looked surprised but he could only punch the ball out right front of Bogdan, who finally scored the equalizer.

Half time. We all received half a lemon. It took a few minutes rest before our breathing calmed down and we managed to squeeze the juice of the sour lemon into our mouths. Our T-shirts held more water than we could get from this half piece of fruit. The SS officers were yelling around us, all of them had their pistols in their hands. Luckily, there were only 11 of us. If they wanted to see the game through, they could not eliminate anyone.

We had only 10 minutes break before we started the second half with the usual change of ends.

The game was very balanced but an opposition team forward had a great run towards our goal. I took the ball, but all I could hear was Heinrich yelling something in German. I had absolutely no idea what he wanted. All I could guess was that he wanted the ball. So I passed it to him, but he ran out of the goal and luckily the ball rolled just a few centimetres past the post. If I had caused an own goal I may not have lived past the game. The swearing in German was just flying from everyone's mouth, and I was lucky I could not understand any of the words.

In the 18th minute of the second half I pushed forward and the only way the "greens" could stop me was with a foul. It was about 18 metres away from the goal. I stood behind the ball with courage and Bogdan let me take the free kick.

There was no defence wall and I placed the ball inside the net easily.

Everyone was cheering and Heinz smiled and shook his fist in the air with happiness. The other SS officers were jumping and hugging each other.

It took only 2 minutes when the "greens' pushed forward and Karl, our defender could stop him only with poor sportsmanship. They received a well-deserved penalty kick. Our goalkeeper moved towards the right direction, but unfortunately the ball had been placed well – low, with power, and very close to the post. They celebrated and we dragged ourselves back to our end of the field while we looked at Heinz, who had almost lost his voice from yelling by now. He had his revolver in his hand again and we knew what he meant by shaking it, even if we did not speak any German. The message was very clear – we must win, or we would lose our lives.

There were no more goals until almost the end of the game. I am not a very religious man but I quickly said a prayer. The wind changed direction and the smoke from the chimneys brought an unbearable smell. It was very difficult to breath in this smoke. There was only two minutes left and we could end up as smoke soon as well. Klaus, our right wingman, took possession of the ball at the half-way mark and he set off. No one could stop him, not even with a foul. "I want to live, I don't want to die," (this goes on in his mind). He took the shot and scored. We won, 3-2, and we received our prize – our lives. Heinz placed his handgun back into its side pocket. There was no chanting fan club, no fireworks, just the heavy smoke from the crematoriums. We could not celebrate as we knew what was coming for our opponents. Heinz collected his money over the win but the SS officers with the other team were not happy, their faces were asking for blood. The "greens" left the field first, just dragging their bodies off, and I almost start to cry as I felt the choking in my throat.

The capo led us back to our 9th barracks. "You must win again next time." Heinz ordered. "You are to have some rest and you will receive a well-deserved dinner," and he walked off. That was it. The dinner was far away – it was still only lunch time. I still had nothing to eat since leaving Debrecen, only the little soup last night and a half of a lemon. I do not know how I managed to play two halves of 45 minutes of a game. I could not wait until dinner. My stomach was hurting very much by now. I kept my black jersey on for the rest of the day as had been suggested on the first day and that gave me a bit of a protection. I felt proud for once in there. I decided to have a look around. Stepping out of the barracks gate I saw what real life was like there. A man whose back was hunched from the few months living inside, and from the 12-hour working days, receiving the bare minimum of food, was walking somewhere. A capo, without any reason, just started to beat him in the most brutal way. There was no reason, and there was no mercy, just anger.

Most likely he was a criminal, and now he had managed to move up in rank with his brutality to be a capo. When he had finished the beating, he just walked away. The poor man just lay there; he could not move alone. Someone came a few minutes later to help him up and get him moving. I decided to pull back into the safety of our barracks instead.

I started getting a bit bored so I asked Steinberger to help me make some contact with the team who was responsible for the portioning of the foods. They were living in the same big, almost empty looking "selection" barracks with us. Only one of them could speak a bit of German, so it took a while to double translate. The three Polish men had been there for almost six months and this conversation brought back bad memories for them. When they arrived, just like with any other transport, their family members had been "selected" right before their eyes. Now they knew they had been murdered after being "escorted" into the gas chambers by the Germans on the same day as their arrival.

"The Nazis told the lie that they had to take a shower before taking on various work duties there in the camp," one of them said with tears in his eyes.

"It was winter, and during the selection one SS officer told my wife to pull her coat together, so she didn't catch a cold," tells another, "what a terrible people they are."

"This Schwarzhuber[51] is a monster. He sends thousands to death every day," says the third one. "I just want to kill him!" he shouts.

Steinberger translated all these testimonies with sincere condolence on his face, and I listening to him with horror. Now I knew for sure that I had lost all my relatives and friends. I felt ill. The conversation had stopped. The three Polish inmates had returned to their work, and I returned to my wooden bed. I just lay there looking at the ceiling, then I turned my head and started to look at the wall. I realized there were gaps between the wooden pallets on the wall. As I looked closer, I could see two SS

---

[51] Johann Schwarzhuber (29 August 1904 Tutzing, German Empire – 3 May 1947 Hameln) was a German *SS-Obersturmführer*, who was in charge of various concentration sub-camps during World War II. His positions included the *Schutzhaftlagerführer* of the Auschwitz-Birkenau men's-camp, where he oversaw the selection process for the gassing of thousands of detainees.

officers outside. They were having a conversation, then they burst out in laughter. I turned away with hate and waited for dinner time. I did not want to go outside to see the suffering of the prisoners.

A few hours must have gone by and it must have been around 3pm when I heard lots of movement outside. SS officers were moving quickly and "escorting" prisoner groups towards the lager's gate.
"Looks like there is a new group arriving," says Steinberger. "You see, the loading team is going too. These guys have the best work in the lager. When they move the luggage of the new arrivals they always slip a few valuable items into their own pocket." Steinberger was right. Soon, freshly shaved and frightened prisoners walked into our barracks.
"Is their selection to take place here?" I ask Dezső.
"Yes, every time," he replies, and we moved to the far end of the building.
As I looked at the faces of the group, I knew how tired, thirsty and hungry they were. I had been there yesterday and I had barely eaten last night. I had even played a quick football game too. But I froze, and my eyes opened widely as I was in a shock as I recognized a face, even with the shaved head. It was my cousin, László Köves from Szombathely. I had not seen him for years and now we had to meet up in this death camp. I did not say anything as the Nazis could arrive at any time. However, I could not hold myself longer than a minute and I called out his name, "Laci, Köves Laci!"
He did not move. He just looked at me. He clearly had no idea why I was in a black football jersey. We were about to move towards each other when two SS officers arrived. They greeted the new group with the same few words about the death camp. They looked at each and everyone's hand, they split them up, and they were all gone in less than 15 minutes. I had no clue where Laci had gone. This pain in my stomach was not getting better. It was an awful feeling to see my loved ones come and go so quickly.
I walked out to see if I could find him somewhere but the roads were empty except for one person who was moving fast. He was coming towards our barracks. But hang on. I know this guy! I

moved towards this 23-year young man fast. I grabbed his arm and I pulled him inside the building.

"Emerich, what are you doing here?" I asked him as I gave him a hug.

"Someone, a common friend of ours, told me he saw you here when he was here to pick up food for the SS for lunch. I had to find you. I cannot bear the hunger anymore. I need to eat something. Can you give me a piece of bread or something to eat?" he begged.

I could not say a word, I was so shocked. "I will find something for you, I promise," I said when I could finally say something back to him. He thanked me in advance, then he continued, "We are doing a terrible and difficult job. We are building and renovating buildings. The wheelbarrows are loaded fully with bricks to such a degree that every time I am unable to pick it up - but I must move it because the capos hit hard with their sticks. I cannot bear it any longer. After the big day I cannot even have some rest at night. The barracks are stinky, there is no air inside for everyone. The lower-level beds have hay on them. They are now full of mud from the walkways. It is releasing a terrible smell. The roof is full of mould which is peeling off as well," he explained.

What could I say in this situation to anyone? I just gave him a hug and sent him back to his barracks with "have a safe return" message.

Finally, it was dinner time. For our win we received a "special portion". Potato soup, which actually had some potato in it, and a few small pieces of meat. I ate fast as I'd had nearly no food for the past four days, but I suffered for my impatient quick eating. My stomach was aching from the hot and quick feasting. It took me a long hour to digest and get rid of the pain. I did not know what tomorrow would bring but I wanted to live. I knew it would be a miracle, but I believed in it. I wanted to see my family again. These were the last few wishes in my mind before I fell asleep. I dreamt about my hometown. I was sitting with my family in our home at the dinner table. When I woke up, the reality hurt me even more. I was disappointed with myself. Why had I dreamt about something which was so unreal, so far away, and besides, my family was dead.

I smelled coffee. I sat up and I saw Weigner and Steinberger with hot cups in their hands. I got up to join them. It was about 7 o'clock. They were talking about the capo, cursing him, and calling him in all sorts of names. They are so much into it they did not even realise he had entered the building. As he stood front of us we all froze, but then we realized, there was nothing to be afraid of – he did not speak Hungarian.

The officers decided that the team had to train every morning until our next game. We started at 8am. "Weigner," said the capo, "you will be the team coach. Stop having breakfast and start putting together a training program for a two-hour session immediately." He turned around and there were a few people standing behind him. "These men are your training partners," and he walked off.

"Can you guys help me?" asks Weigner, looking at us. We agreed with a simple nod of heads and then we stood up and introduced ourselves to the newcomers. They had just arrived the day before with the latest transport from Hungary. One of them was called Gyula Hecskovits. Later we managed to transfer his older brother into the training team too. His duty was cleaning the barracks.

We were just about finishing up the plan when the rest of the team arrived led by the capo. We moved out to the field. "Line up!" yells the capo, "Weigner will lead the training. I will be watching and if I see anyone being lazy - he will be punished - understood?"

"Yes" we all replied together.

"Good, now let's start" – he says.

During our training I could see the latest transport getting lined up and getting moved towards the building labelled "shower and disinfect". By now I knew where they were going. I knew most of them would not be alive by the end of our training session. This was very depressing. They looked at us with interest. They could not understand what was going on. What was a football team doing here. This might have made them even calmer if they all believed the big lie that this was just a factory and they all were getting a big shower after their few days' long trip in the animal-carrier train wagons.

I stopped for a second and I wanted to scream "RUN, run away, it is trap, you are all going to be locked into the shower and they will throw in Zyclon-B gas!". Weigner could see my internal battle and he dragged me back into training once again. I could not believe I was playing football a few meters away from all the people soon to be murdered. It was something very difficult to just walk by and to feel absolutely helpless.

The training was well planned. We had included ball passing and handling skills, upper and lower-body strength, core exercises, short sprints and, towards the end, my favourite – header exercises and competition. At the end of this block we finished up with a four-lap jog around the field. We had a small "fan club" made up of the twins at the back. As we passed by they all started to cheer and encouraged us: "Came on! Faster! Hurry!" We were surprised that these kids spoke Hungarian.

"Fifteen minutes break," called out Weigner and we sat close to the fence. The gypsies walked back to the other side of the field. It was forbidden to talk to anyone on the other side of the fence or from the opposition team. The capo was on the other side as well so we were very quiet.
One of the boys told me he was from Szatmárnémeti[52]; he was a 14-year-old who had just arrived yesterday with his family and twin brother. I asked him if he could get me a piece of rug, more like a textile handkerchief. He promised he would bring one the next day.

"The break is over," yelled out the capo. We all put our T-shirts, which we had put out in the sun to dry, back on. For the rest of the training we played a game against the training-partner team. Towards the end of the game an officer unfamiliar to us walked up to the capo with an elderly prisoner. They waited for us to walk off the field then the capo stated, "Attention, this person will be your team masseur. Heinz ordered him to be part of the team. If anyone needs a massage after the training or after a game just let him know." A bit of confusion started amongst us. We were not sure if this was a trap or was it real? If we stepped

---

[52] A city which was part of the Hungarian Kingdom, now part of Romania called Satu Mare.

forward, we might get recognized as an injured player. We were hesitant of what to do or say. We could not trust the Nazis any longer. It was unbelievable that we would have a team masseur here in the "death factory". I decided to step forward and a few followed. The masseur waved his arm showing us to follow him towards the showers. We didn't speak the same language. As I was the first one to step out, he indicated to me to take off my clothes and lie down on my front onto a wooden bench, which he had decided to use as a massage table. I undressed and did what he asked me to do by lying down. He used some water from an aluminium can and poured it on me, then he pulled out a square looking cake of soap.

We had all heard how this kind of soap was being made. According to the camp citizens, who had been living there for more than a year by now, these had been made from the fat of the burnt bodies in the crematoriums. The Germans had developed a technique of how to capture and process it.

It had a greyish-green colour with a RIF mark on it[53].

---

[53] Germany did not have enough fats to make soap during World War II. Because of this, the government took control of making soap. "RIF" stood for *Reichsstelle für Industrielle Fettversorgung.* This was the German government agency in charge of making and giving out soap and washing products during the war. (In English, the agency's name was the "National Center for Industrial Fat Provisioning.") RIF soap was not very good and did not have any kind of fat, not even human fat as some suggested it.

Picture from: http://www.malcolmwagner.co.uk/wp-content/uploads/2017/06/DSC00270-1024x768.jpg - The greenish-grey soap

The soap of Auschwitz

Small square, like a toy cube you play with,
Greenish-grey the colour of it.
Made of human fat, unscented,
Burning humans, dripped down, and invented.
German chemists made a special blend,
An Auschwitz product for family and friend.
Made for the son from the fat of his mother,
Cooked for the daughter from the flesh of his father.
The parents were pressed into a cube,
Shaped into toiletries for to use.
Stroking it, we lift it to our hearts,
Parents in soap without body-parts.
Fearing it from water, we put it in an ornamental urn,
Buried it with honour, and to heaven they return.
In the infinity of time the dust comes together,

And will rest with the Martyrs forever.

September 1966, Debrecen, Hungary

He covered my body with it then he started massaging my back,
legs and arms, then he leant a bit forward and in a very quiet
whispering voice he introduced himself. "I'm Statek." I opened
my eyes and, with the little German I had managed to learn in
two days, I replied, "I'm Sándor, I'm Hungarian".
My body felt refreshed after the massage. It was the first relaxing
20 minutes since the start of my first labour work. It was about
noon when we returned to the barracks. The rest of the day went
slowly with conservation until dinner time. I was happy to know
there was no new transport that day.

Next day the program was the same. Breakfast, training,
massage, shower. I could not complain, knowing what the others
were going through day by day or knowing how many had been,
and would be, marched to death.
We again had our own small fan club watching us, the TWINS.
During the break I went over to the fence and asked the same
boy if he had managed to bring me a piece of clothes or
handkerchief?
"I did not promise anything for you. I do not even know who
you are!" he said and walked back from the fence.
I was a bit surprised with his behaviour as he had been so nice
yesterday.
A few days later I saw him at the fence again and he waved me
over to the fence. "I have the rug you asked for. I am so sorry for
the delay but I was unwell from the experiment Mengele did to
me," he said.
"Are you feeling better?" I asked him.
"Yes, much better," he replied. I must have looked weird as he
asked me if I was ok?
"Yes," I said slowly, looking behind him like there is a ghost
there. He looked back also. "Ah, yes! He is my identical twin
brother," he said. There was a boy there who looked just like him
– same everything. Mengele had chosen them for his
"experiments".

Later I had the opportunity to see other identical twins there. Little ones and older ones too. They were mirror images of each other.

I was unable to talk to the workers from the crematoriums, also known as The Sondercommando[54]. They were not allowed to come to the fence. The Nazis were afraid that the mystery of the gas chambers and the crematoriums would be told to others in the camp, so all the workers were kept under the tightest security.

But unfortunately, the secret was not a secret at all. Every "one day old" prisoner knew of the death factory's function and they also knew that all of their relatives had been destroyed there. Heinz did not always come to see our training, but if he had some time he showed up and he followed our movements with great interest. He must have been a busy man. He must have had a great part in the genocide. Thousands were killed there every day in this "automated" death factory and these persons were pushing the buttons for it. These hangmen needed some sort of relaxation too during the mass killings.

I never ended up finding out what the duty of our officer was there in the camp but he must have had a high rank if he could organize his own football team.

The tiring training was always followed by a hot shower and massage.

One day Bogdan did not pay enough attention in training, so the capo took his dinner away. Bogdan was not happy, but now even the German gipsies knew there was no excuse for laziness. It was simple, you either trained hard or you did not get dinner, which was not much anyway. I had already noticed that I was losing weight.

During my football career back in Hungary I had never had a massage. I had to become an international football player in Auschwitz to have a massage. They had a cheap workforce here. Everything was possible.

---

[54] The Sonderkommandos were a group of Jewish prisoners forced to perform a variety of duties in the gas chambers and crematoriums of the Nazi camp system. They worked primarily in the Nazi killing centres, such as Auschwitz, but they were also used on other killing sites to dispose of the corpses of victims.

After our first training our capo pulled out a green bottle of snaps.[55] "You will receive half a bottle of snaps to last until your next game. This is a present from Heinz for your win."

We handed the bottle to each other, and each of us had a mouthful of it. Most of us started coughing as we were not used to the strong alcoholic beverage. It was not common for an athlete to drink alcohol, but being consistent with the contradictions of habit manifested by so many facts, they no longer surprised us.

The huge amount of lunch on the day of the game had not been repeated. The daily menu was as average and as poor a quality as for the rest of the prisoners of the camp. However there was more in quantity. The soup was made out of who knows what kind of grass or weed, very little bread, some fake jam or margarine and sometimes a piece of cattle-turnip. It was not high in calories, and the soup was mainly water, but I could fill up my stomach with a few litres of it and feel satiated. With the addition of the members of the reserve team, we received an additional barrel of grass-soup – which contained no calories.

Accordingly, I could guzzle as much as three to four litres of this muddy soup. I felt full because my stomach was satisfied. I could access such a great amount of soup as would feed six to eight men from Debrecen.

These people sneaked into our barracks, risking their lives, but they had a strong will to survive, somehow.

One of them was my friend Emerich. It is possible that he is alive in some part of the world today.

The quality of food got better only when we played games - and if we won there was some bonus too.

It was only a week ago since the work had "made me free", but it felt much longer than that. My knee started to inflame. Although I could use the handkerchief from the twins and make a wet compression with it, it did not get much better during the nights. I hoped it would get better, otherwise the only way they could cure it was in the gas chambers. I hoped to be able to avoid that.

---

[55] Snaps is a Danish and Swedish word for a small shot of a strong distillate alcoholic beverage - 40 % alcohol content or more. Widely used drink in Europe.

The second game[56]

We had 10 days of training. These days had become routine – training in the morning, rest during the afternoon, dinner at night. The highlight of the training was to see the twins lining up at the fence. But one day I had a "surprise visitor" – my dear old friend and travel companion from Debrecen, Sándor Friedman. He was standing on the other side of the fence. It was against the rules to talk to anyone from the "Sondercommando", but we managed to have a quick chat. He told me briefly how terrible his work was.

"The ones escorted into the shower-looking gas chambers are hoping to receive water from the shower heads, but instead of water there is Cyan gas coming down on them," my friend tells me. "When all the screaming and yelling stops, one capo looks inside the gas chamber through a small window. Then, we must ventilate fresh air into the chambers and pull all the dead bodies out into another chamber. Another team washes the concrete floor by spraying water on it. We have to work very fast as the next group of people are already waiting outside. The SS-officers make sure we are doing our job with speed and precision. Another group is looking through the dead bodies and searching for any more jewellery or gold teeth. These are getting pulled out and collected and then we have to hand them over to the officers. Unfortunately, I have recognised many friends and family members, but I cannot recall each and every one's name because there are far too many. We are getting enough food, but I do not have any hunger or feeling to eat because of the depression this job is causing to me. We are working in two shifts.
Unfortunately, the trains are arriving one after the other. I know, my 'contract' with the death factory will be only a short one, about three months.

---

[56]*Writer's note: 1944, Jul 12 - Theresienstadt Family camp disbands, with 4,000 people being gassed.*

"But Sándor, if you ever make it out of here alive, and by some miracle you will make it home, please tell my parents that I love them, and please, under no circumstances, tell them what inhuman job I had to do here during my final weeks."

Picture from: http://cdn.history.com/sites/2/2014/01/auschwitz-ovens-P.jpeg - Auschwitz – Ovens

Removed wedding rings after gassing of the Jews
Picture from: https://i0.wp.com/www.worldwar2facts.org/wp-content/uploads/2016/12/wedding-rings-from-concentration-camps.jpg?resize=625%2C480

The Gas chambers…

Many metal made shower heads,
Expecting water from it with lips spread,
Under the shower together the family
All naked among each other shyly.
Crowding and begging for water
Lifesaving mother lifting up daughter.
Water, lifesaving and also cools,
The airtight doors sealed by the cruels.
Why? "Just hiding us from prying eyes,
They are not malicious" – The wise ones advise.
All clothes hanged up nicely, no coincidence,
Little children with us, all innocent.
Why would they kill them?
No more air here! Windows! Open them!
There is none here! Shower without windows!?
Where is the sunlight, the life giving, the luminous?
Cannot be seen in the concrete square,
Only the shower heads can give us air.
The water delivering perforated metal,
All of them next to each other settle.
Its pipe system will provide safe water,
The sweat glows as it thickens the air.
"Turn it on! Open the door!" they yell,
"Oh my God! What is this nauseating smell?"
"This isn't water!" White mist breath the air.
It suffocates with his angry taste, beware!
Yellowing faces, dishevelling breath,
Declining and decomposing death,
Carving the flesh with clinging nails,
Covering the little ones still conscious females,
Trample on each other, the weak on the ground,
Growl torn from the throats all around.
No more time to shout a last curse,
The crowd is quiet, left this Universe.
All waited for the water but mountain of dead,
Gas, Cyan gas poison killed instead.
Sprinkled it on mothers and fathers,
Four million killed like this by executioners.
The executioners in fascist uniform,
As the Final Solution, Hitler's brainstorm.

September 1966, Debrecen, Hungary

On the morning of 13th July 1944, the capo announced our second game which would this time be in the afternoon.

When the opposition arrived on time, we could not have felt more sorry for them. None of them looked healthy and strong - weak legs, skinny arms, baggy eyes, yellow skin colour. Their jersey was light blue, which drew more attention to their unhealthy look. They wanted to win just like us. Maybe their reward was also a big portion of dinner and staying alive. Not one of them was Hungarian. They sounded more like Italians and French. Possibly they had to work besides training and did not have the privilege, like we had, of only having to train. One of them, their left wingman, was an especially skinny and broken young man. I attacked him carefully, paying attention not to kick him in the slightest way. I noticed from his gaze that he recognized my intention and when he was next to me, he spoke softly and quietly to me. I did not understand what he said but from his tone I felt some kind of thank you. As previously, we had been warned not to talk to the opposing team members so I avoided more talk, and besides, I only spoke Hungarian.

This had also caused a communication problem within my team. This deficiency was particularly detrimental to me because I did not understand what the gipsy boys wanted of me in the heat of the game. Maybe I did not pass the ball on a number of occasions to their wishes, or they had disagreed with my placement on the field.

I detected this once or twice when I received angry looks from the gypsy boys, or maybe they were somewhat reserved towards me because I was not a master of the German language. I do not deny I was a bit ashamed when I met these angry looks. During training their "independence" was more visible, and loneliness stuck on me. Sometimes I could talk to Steinberger or Weigner, or from time to time to the Hungarian twins.

Our second game was against a different team. We all stuck to our positions but the other team did not really look like they had a game plan. They did not keep their structure during the game and they just ran wherever the ball was. "We need to use our ball-handling skills," called out Weigner, "they are not a well-trained team."

First, Klaus heads the ball into the net, then suddenly we hear gunshots.

"What was that?" we asked each other.

"No need to worry, it is only Heinz and the officers celebrating our first goal," says Bogdan.

A few minutes later Günther scores. The officers on our side are very happy, but not the other side.

Bogdan sends out a short message to our team, "We need to take it back a notch, we are too strong a team for these guys." No one disagrees. The opposition team noticed the change in the pace, and they showed their gratefulness with gestures. Luckily the officers are too busy drinking and betting to notice any change.

Soon, Bogdan took possession of the ball and scored another goal. The opposition's SS officers complained because they believed Bogdan was offside. Thankfully, Heinz was a higher ranked officer, so the argument had to stop.

A few minutes later it was our corner kick. Helmut stood behind the ball and curved it high over to the other side of the 5-metre box and the arriving Günther scores. It is half time and the score is 4:0.

We received half a lemon each just as before, but there was nothing refreshing for the opposition team.

The 10 minute break was over, we changed sides, and the second half was on its way.

After a few minutes of a fast game the opposition team's right front-wingman, who was a very skinny guy, charged forward along the sideline. He showed great speed but suddenly collapsed. There was no one near him so we did not understand what had happened to him. His team-mates picked him up and carried him off the field.

Heinz shouts from the sideline, "We are in overdrive. I want goal!" However, we continued to play with the greatest care.

It took more than 10 minutes before the skinny guy got up and joined back into the game. He had just run out of energy. His system had shut down.

But then something extraordinary happened. The Sondercommando team had been watching us and one of the members from the opposition team must have recognized one of them, probably a family member. He just left the field and ran towards the fence to greet him. The crematorium worker handed a small package over to him. One of the escorting SS officers had seen what had happened. They were a bit drunk by now but they were still watching the game, even though their team had been losing. One officer made a quick move towards the fence, took possession of the package, and dragged the player back to the sideline where all the officers were standing. There was some discussion and then the player returned to the game. We do not know what happened to him after the game, but we know this move of his would not have had a nice result.

The game continued and, as expected, our physical condition was better than that of the "skinny team". We took possession of the ball for the rest of the game. Gerd took control of the ball and charged towards the goal. Unfortunately, he ran into one of the defenders.

"I should have looked up earlier," he yells to himself and started to walk back, but the referee blew his whistle and pointed to the penalty spot. Everyone was a bit surprised by this, especially the opposition team and their escorting officers. They were very drunk and they started running onto the field.

"We did not even touch him!" yelled one defender.

"This is not true!" yelled one other player.

The officers arrived too. "What do you think you doing?" and one officer grabs the referee's attire.

"I'll kill you," threatened the other officer; and they started to punch him from both sides. One punch ended up on the back of the referee's head and he lost balance. He fell on the ground but the officers did not stop there. They kept assaulting him kicking. The poor man was just getting kicked and kicked until the officers got tired of it. None of the other officers or our players tried to stop them. We could not interfere at all if we wanted to live. When the beating had finished, the referee was unconscious. He had blood everywhere on his head and the soil stuck in his blood as well. He looked awful. The team had to carry him off the field. Everyone was shocked what we had just witnessed.

Heinz called the line referee closer to him. "You will be the new referee and you will continue to run this game. Understood?" asked Heinz.

This poor man was shaking from fear, he turned pale and looked like he would faint any minute. He walked over to the penalty spot and we could see his hands were shaking as he pointed to it, but his eyes looked at the officers with fear.

Franz delivered the ball into the net. Heinz yelled out, "5:0," and threw his hands up into the air.

We were not as happy as him. We all looked out to see how the first referee was doing as we walked back to our end of the field. He still had not moved.

This incident had made a mark on the new referee's decision-making as well. His calls were all against us.

The game was getting close to the end and Bogdan took possession of the ball. He almost got past the right half back of the opposition team who could only stop him with a foul. Bogdan got up quickly and kicked into the defender. The referee gave him a red card and sent him off the field. Bogdan did not look very happy, but the decision was correct. Heinz started yelling at him as he walked towards them to leave the field, then he and the capo started pushing and shoving him as he got off the field. They were questioning him for his unsportsmanlike behaviour. Luckily, we were leading in the game and we were in a better physical condition compared to the opposition team. Soon after this the opposition team tried their last attack using their last resources of energy. They got inside the 16- metre box, but their centre player fell. The referee blew his whistle and pointed at the penalty spot. It was not a bad foul but not one of us wanted to argue, not after what had happened earlier. Heinz did not look angry. He was not mad at all. We all looked surprised as we did not know how this team managed to get so much energy together from soup made from grass that we were all receiving under the name of a "meal".

Their centre player scored from the penalty. Their officers were happy and celebrated with more drinking. They were getting very loud and they were clapping. Now they looked like ordinary football fans.

But this was not the end. Gerd took possession of the ball and he delivered a strong, bomb-like goal from about 20 metres out. Heinz was very happy. He looked like a proud football club owner.

This was the end of the game and we won 6:1. We did not think about the extra premium dinner, about the potato and maybe a small amount of meat. We were still in shock from had what happened to the first referee. He had to be carried away, still unable to stand up. As we walked back towards the barracks, the 90 minutes of running had made me hungry. My stomach was rumbling and aching from hunger.

The dinner arrived and that was when we all got surprised. There was no extra potato and meat.

"The opposition team was very weak. It was an easy win," the capo said. "No extra dinner," he said and walked away. We did get a bit of extra margarine and some jam which was better than the grass soup. I was just not sure how I would be able to share this with the other prisoners. They were sneaking in every night now for a bit of extra food, with my regular "guests" Emerich. I ended up eating only just a little so that I could keep my promise to him.

During the dinner they delivered sad news for us. The first referee of our game has passed away from his injuries from the beating.

That night it was hard to get to sleep again. There was always something dramatic which kept us awake during the nights.

Just a number

For the next few weeks we just trained. Morning session for two hours, shower, massage, then rest. I know it sounds boring, especially in Birkenau. There was nothing else I could talk about with Steinberger nor with Weigner anymore.

One day I decided I would go for a tour and have a look at what everybody else was up to. I knew my black football jersey would keep me safe.

I did not say a word to anyone, I just walked out of the barracks. The internal streets and the internal roads were empty as most of the prisoners had left for work. Suddenly I saw a tall blond capo with his yellow armband walking towards me pushing an empty wheelbarrow. He looked at me, stopped, then started talking to me in a foreign language which I did not understand. I looked at him and said in Hungarian that I did not understand what he was saying to me. He lost his temper and flicked the wheelbarrow towards me. I had to react quickly and jump out of the way to avoid the flying object. It almost landed on my leg. He pointed at the wheelbarrow and yelled to me in his language. Finally, I managed to say a word in German, and pointed at my chest: "Fussballmann" (football player). His reaction to this was to take a huge swing of his beating-stick across my chest. I was struggling to breathe. My chest was hurting so much that I bent over. Next there was a big hit across my back which made me stand back up. I could see him swinging his stick again, but I was quick to pick up the wheelbarrow and started to run so that he could not hit me again.

We arrived at a group of prisoners who were building a road. "Looks like we are expanding the camp," I think to myself. "Put as much as possible into his wheelbarrow," says the capo to another worker, who looked at me with great interest when he saw my black jersey. But it wasn't only him. Suddenly I saw everyone stop briefly and gaze at me until the capo yelled out, "Back to work!"

My wheelbarrow was so full I could barely lift it up. I was thinking right away about Emerich, who had told me how hard he was working all day, and how much weaker and skinnier he was than me.

I cursed myself for this tour. I should have stayed at the barracks. I walked back and forth pushing the sand or the bricks, whatever was getting put into my new work appliance. The capo was smiling every time as I walked past him.

Another capo came about two hours later. I was exhausted by then. "I need 20 men to dig up a new mass grave at the crematorium," he said to the other. Our capo made the selections and he made sure to place me into this group, knowing how strenuous it was to dig into this hard ground. He was still not satisfied with me. Probably not many prisoners have told him off lately.

We walked towards our barracks as we were going next to the crematorium. I saw familiar faces outside the barracks and I was in luck - I could see our capo as well. I started waving at him slowly and hoped he would notice me. He did. He looked up with consternation on his face then he ran out and stopped our group.

"Stop," he put his hand up.

"Why are you stopping us," asked the group-escorting capo?

"That man in the black jersey," and he points at me, "he cannot go with you?"

"But I need 20 man to dig up a new mass grave at the crematorium" the other capo replies.

"I don't care - you will be taking 19. He is a football player. He cannot work!" says our capo then he pulls me out of the group and into the barracks. The other capo realizes there is no need to get into an argument over one prisoner, so he gets the group moving.

"Danke, danke!" (Thank you, thank you) I repeated to our capo, but he did not look very pleased over my expedition. He dragged me all the way into our barracks and he just started shouting and pointing his finger at me. I did not understand a lot but, like previously, I was able to understand the gestures. He wasn't happy about my trip out of the barracks.

Steinberger and Weigner were asking all sorts of questions after the capo had gone back outside.

"Where did you go?"

"What were you thinking?"

"Did anything happen to you?" they bombarded me with their questions.

I answered all their questions then I started using my wet handkerchief that I got from the twin boy to ease the pain on my chest. I hoped I would be able to train properly tomorrow.

The training was painful in many ways for the following days. Not just my chest and back hurt, but my knee was getting worse too. It was swollen, despite the cold and wet bandaging I was applying on it, but I could not let anyone know as there was only one way for recovery - through the chimneys.

Late one morning high ranked SS-officers arrived at the camp. Kramer[57], the camp commander, led the team and was explaining something to them with great interest, using a lot of gestures and hand movement.

There was a man in the group who looked very much like an Arabian. I am sure they thought it was a bit strange to see football players in black jerseys amongst the striped uniformed prisoners, but these people were used to seeing specialities. They must have been happy with what they saw as they laughed happily. I was trying to avoid their sight as you could never be sure in which way the SS-officers were trying to satisfy their visitors.

Next morning we noticed some sort of restlessness in the camp. The daily schedule of the camp was out of order. The usual head count was at a different time and the officers had been calling orders which were against the orders of the others. Some working groups had not been escorted out for work and the delivery of the breakfast was late by hours. The well-informed inmates found out the reason behind this - an assassination attempt against Hitler in Berlin.

We were happily running up and down in the barracks, even though we did not know if the assassination was successful or not. We all gathered, formed a circle hugging each other, and hoped for the best. We were excited about the news which gave us hope for the survival.

The rest of the day for all of us was dreaming about our hometown, to see our family again, to walk on the streets with freedom. That night we went to bed relatively late and we all fell fast asleep.

Next morning July 21, 1944, we received the bad news. Adolf Hitler had survived an assassination attempt led by German army officer Claus Von Stauffenberg[58]. The treatment from the officers became stricter, the portion of the foods became smaller.

---

[57] **Josef Kramer** (10 November 1906 – 13 December 1945) was the Commandant of Auschwitz-Birkenau (from 8 May 1944 to 25 November 1944) and of the Bergen-Belsen concentration camp (from December 1944 to its liberation, April 15, 1945).

[58] The 6th attempt to assassinate Hitler. Stauffenberg put the plan into action on July 20, 1944, after he and several other Nazi officials were called to a conference with Hitler at the Wolf's Lair. https://www.history.com/news/6-assassination-attempts-on-adolf-hitler

That resulted in more deaths in the camps, but the hope was there - even some German army officers were not happy and satisfied with Hitler's strict regime.

The camp was still out of order. An unknown capo came to our barracks: "Steinberger, Schwarcz, Weigner," he yelled. "Here!" we all stood up and presented ourselves. "Come with me," he ordered. We looked back to the others in the barracks, and we feared the worst.
We followed him to a brick building in front of which was a huge number of people waiting outside. He pushed us into the crowd. We could hear a few Hungarian farewell words but other than that we did not really pay attention.
The metal door on the building opened. "Inside!" sounded the order, "Came on! Move! Faster!"
When we were inside we were relieved to see that we had not gathered there to get executed. We were there to get our name taken away - in return for which we would receive a number.
First our dignity, then our citizenship, then our home country, and now our name. It would all be replaced with a number, just like the horses and cows.
"Your left arm," called out a Polish worker. I showed my arm then he grabbed me and pulled me forward so hard that I could feel my shoulder joint almost getting dislocated.
He dipped his device into blue ink and started marking my arm with it. He was not gentle, and he dug deep into my flesh. At one point he dipped the needle so deep into my arm I pulled it back from reflex. In return, he punched my jaw and pulled my arm back onto the table.
"A Siebzehntausend-achthundert-vierundfünfzig," he yelled out and the SS-officer behind him put this number on a small pink sheet of paper. The next person handed me two small "nametags" with the numbers on them, "Here and here," he said and pointed at his left chest and his left hip. Preceding the number there was a colour code as well. The Jews got a red and yellow star, the Polish prisoners red, the Russian captured prisoners had black and the German prisoners also had their own colour.[59] The Soviet prisoners helped each other and the

---

[59] *Zigeunerlager* (Gypsy camp) were given a separate number series preceded with the letter Z

ones in need. The SS officers and the capos did not treat them as badly as they did the Jews. We were the lowest ranked prisoners and vulnerable to everyone.

I stepped out of the building and I started learning my new "name" – A-17854, and I rubbed my jaw which was still hurting. "Line up!" called out one SS and we quickly got into line. The same capo who had escorted us there also escorted us back to the barracks. Everyone was happy to see us alive.

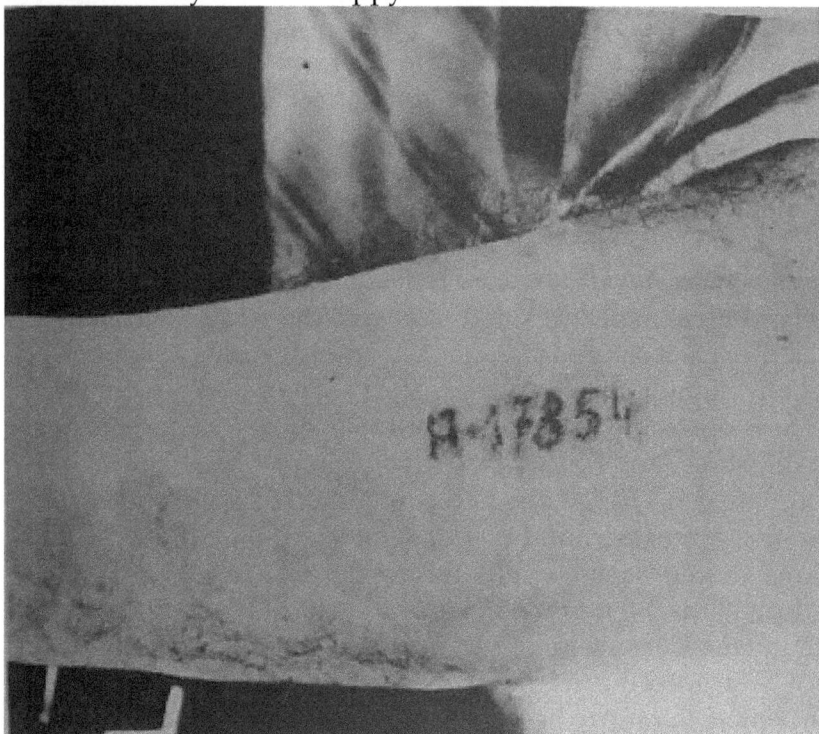

The tattooed number on the left forearm of Sándor Schwarcz – Picture from personal collection

At lunch time our football team, which had been kept together, went out to train as we were preparing for our next game, once again against an unknown team.

After training as we were resting in the barracks, a clerk came in with a bunch of postcards.

(Zigeuner). Correctional prisoners *(Erziehungshäftlinge)*, chiefly Poles, were marked with the letter "E". Auschwitz was for them a type of replacement correctional labour camp *(Arbeiterziehungslager – AEL)*. Soviet prisoners of war (POW) had black marking.

"Who speaks German?" he asked. Steinberger and a few more stepped forward. "Translate!" he ordered.

The clerk handed over postcards to me and said (Steinberger translated) "Write to your relatives back at home; write to them that you are well; you are playing football and that you are enjoying yourself at Waldsee[60] in the work-camp."

"But I don't have anyone left at home. Some died in Siberia during forced labour work, the others have been deported into concentration camps," I said to him.

"I do not care," he said, "you will do it now, understood? In fact, here are two more. You have five minutes to finish!" he ordered and stayed next to me until I finished.

So, I put on a made-up address, something that never existed. I did not want to be any part of the Nazi false propaganda.

(The point of this was to make it easier for the relatives and the Jewish community who were still at home to be taken away without violence, without force and, to mislead the public. The British radio had started to talk about concentration camps and a few escaped prisoners had been warning the Allied forces about the purpose of these camps. There was still no explanation why there had been no direct attack against these camps which were visible from to spy photographs that had been taken from the air.)

I handed back the written postcards. "You see. I'm sure they will be happy to receive your mail," the clerk said with a grin on his face.

When he left, we turned towards each other. "Where is Waldsee? Are we not in Birkenau?"

During the night I felt lucky. I had been lucky because I was still alive. I was only just a number now, but still alive. Some inmates received a "B" and some like me a letter "A" before their "new name." I tried to make a quick head count. According to these numbers and what I knew, millions had lost their lives and only about 40,000 strong men and women had been kept alive, at least for a while, until their ribs started to show from the hard work and from being underfed. The estimated 40,000 "selected ones" had regularly undergone the "Mengele style" selection method.

---

[60] Waldsee is a municipality in the Rhein-Pfalz-Kreis, in Rhineland-Palatinate, Germany. It is situated approximately 3 km north of Speyer.

Not even a great work ethic could keep you alive. My friends, whose lives had been spared, had been spread far away from me in the camp and only occasionally had I run into someone from my hometown.

Nameless Auschwitzers

The registrars are prestigious SS-officers,
Who do not write birth date or home address.
Marking us with numbers, using purple paint,
Puncturing with needles under the skin without pain.
Humiliation can be felt only under the skin,
No one feels guilt, no one is responsible for this sin.

The numbers on the left arm are no need to be erased,
The fire of the crematorium deals with the human "Waste".
There is no one responsible for this offence,
Working in cohesion they hope for innocence.
But the remaining numbers are looking for the killer in hide,
Even after ten and twenty years later, with enormous pride.

Despite every effort to hide it in the dark,
Shines like a reflector in the deepest night,
They run, they race, they are the sinners,
Taking no responsibility for the "Numbers".
All deny: "Not me! He did it!
Pushed crying baby in it!
I was not the selector of the mothers,
We did not destroy the fathers,
Only took the dead arrivals
And placed them into the fires!"

The number – Seventeen thousand,
Eight hundred and fifty-four is blaming,
Only the coffin will make this ink and limb fading.
But in the meantime, he is looking, searching

For the owner of the needle, he is researching.

The third game

Our capo arrived in the morning. "Game day," he announced.
"Good morning to you too," I mumbled to myself.
We got ready quickly and were taken out towards the field
which had a surprise for us. There was an audience this time,
about 60 of them. It was a mixture of SS-officers and higher and
lower ranked capos.
"Look, they are sharing snaps with each other and smoking
cigarettes too." I turned to Weigner.
"It doesn't look like we are in Birkenau. They are having great
laughs as well which proves the 'friendly' relationship between
them," he replies.
"After all, the capos are the ones executing the orders with a
great level of aggression on behalf of the SS - but where is the
opposition team?" I asked Weigner as Steinberger was talking to
Heinz.
"I'm not sure. Looks like they are not here yet. None of them
have jerseys on."
"Look at that big capo in the middle. He is the one who beat me
and made me to join the work with the wheelbarrow," I said to
Weigner with anger. "How can I get even with him?"
"Don't worry. Let it go," Weigner replied. "There is nothing you
can do here in the camp. Maybe one day when we are free."
"That would be good," I said. "I could show him what I'm really
made of."

Heinz and Steinberger walked towards us onto the middle of the
field with an officer we had not seen before.
"Attention," calls out Heinz, "We will take a few pictures of my
team".
"What? Pictures! For whom?" I asked Weigner quietly.
"Into his photo album," he replied with sarcasm and he also
winked at me. That brought smiles onto our faces.

The SS, with a modern camera, stepped forward.

Heinz: "The goalkeeper, the three defenders and the two midfielders into the back line, the rest in the front on their knees," he ordered.

"Smile!" the "photographer called out.

"What a misleading comedy," I whispered to Weigner.

"Come on, bigger smile, like you are alive," he called out again and took a few shots.

"It will be ready by the afternoon and you can have a look at it," said the photographer to Heinz.

The opposition team arrived. They were in black and white striped jerseys and they all looked very well fed. As they ran onto the field, the audience became louder. They all clapped and yelled for the team, like on a real-world game.

"Now I understand," I turned towards Weigner, "this team is made up from the capos".

The gypsy boys also realized who the opposition team was made up of.

"What do we do?" asked Weigner.

"How do we play against this team?" I asked as well.

"Do we try to score and win or let them win?" asked Weigner again.

"Just play gently and we will see what the game brings" said Bogdan, our team captain.

The first attack was led by the team of capos. They had already lost the ball at the second pass, and they ran back to defend. We, like a slow-moving team, attacked. Heinz could see what was going on. "Come on! What is going on? Move forward! Faster!" he yelled from the sideline. We had to obey him, and we hoped he would stand up for us if we won. We hoped the capos would not try to get even if they lost, by beating us at any given opportunity.

Klaus moved forward and almost scored. We looked around like a group of scared mice, and were happy to see there was no punishment. It looked like a win for the capos was not as important as it was for us. They would get their dinner anyway.

A few minutes later there was a side throw-in for the capos. However, before they executed the throw, a few of them ran out to the supporting fan club and inhaled a few deep breaths from the cigarettes and drank a few mouthfuls of snaps. This was a clear message for us. This was just a friendly game. We could play hard and win without punishment.

It was about 20 minutes into the game when I kicked the ball forward to Josef on the right side and he moved up and inside towards the goal, then he lifted the ball over the keeper and we scored our first goal.
The "fan club" became quiet on the sideline for a moment, but then they became even louder than before, "Come on, let's go! You must score an equalizer!"
The opposition team did not really push hard, they did not run after lost ball, they did not run for any longer passes, so the game was controlled by us most of the time. Soon Gerd headed the ball in and we were leading 2:0. Heinz and the officers surrounding him were happy for our lead and that was the important to us. We reached the half-time break of the game with this score.

After the break they started playing a bit harder than in the first half. "Team capo" was executing their side throw-in, and two players jumped up. One was our centre back Karl and other was their centre front. Accidently they headed each other. The centre front jumped up and attacked the rising Karl. Suddenly, he slapped him on the face and Karl fell back onto the ground. But, thank God, the rest of the capo players were not in their violent mood and they pulled their player back to calm him down.
The game became a bit physical too. The "Team capo" started using their bodies a bit stronger. This style was really to their liking.
During one pass and block, the ball flew off the field and hit one of the SS-officers who was watching the game very close to the sideline. The Nazi became very angry, and he pulled out his revolver and shot the ball flat. The officers around him tried to calm him down while the referee looked for another ball.
The team captains used these few minutes to have a tactical meeting.

The "Team capo" had become more and more nervous. They started yelling at each other realizing that they could not keep up with the "International team of Birkenau". Josef scored one more goal towards the end and the final score was 3:0 to us.
We were happy that we could in some way take revenge on the aggressive "Team capo".

We impatiently waited for the dinner. We were hoping for some extra portions as this was our third win in a row. The dinner was porridge and some meat. I was once again happy to share my dinner with the Emerich boys and some other men from my hometown. This was against the rules there. I made small bite-sized pieces and gave them away. Unfortunately, the barracks' commander, a Slovakian Jew capo, entered the building and when he saw the "feast" he became very angry. He started yelling at me, "What do you think you are doing? Do you think this is a charity dinner? You are getting the extra food to keep yourself in a good physical condition as a football player, and what do you do? You are giving it away. If I see this one more time I will report you to your capo - understood?"
"Yes, of course," I replied, because I knew he was right, but I just could not help myself supporting others in much need.

Before going to bed I realized my football jersey had gotten very loose on me despite the extra portions of dinner. I also noticed my knee was getting much worse. It was very swollen and it was even painful to walk, but I could not report this to anyone. I hoped for an easy next day when I could rest my body.
During the last few days, train had followed train; transport followed transport. The Hungarian Jews were "delivered" in lots of about 3,000 each time. They were from the East side of Hungary, beyond the Danube River. The crematoriums had been burning day and night, non-stop.

In my dream I was home again walking among the big trees of the "Big Forest" of Debrecen. Awaking from this was again brutal. I could not believe I was here in the hell and another day would start again with its unknown end. My knee was swollen and did not get better during the night, but we had to get ready for another training session. I could not tell anyone about my knee as I knew what had happened with my limping friend on the first day during selection. I knew I would be gone, so I had to put up with the pain as much as possible. I was about to take off my bandage when Weigner saw it. He came to me and asked, "What is wrong with your knee?"

"Nothing!" I replied quickly.

"Let me see," he says, "I had to deal with a few injuries when I was playing and coaching in Budapest. "It is very swollen," he says, "You must have ligament damage.

"I had a meniscus and ACL tear in my knee during a football game earlier in my career, but my parents did not have the money to pay for the surgery and not one surgeon was able to do that kind of surgery anyway. In some ways I am lucky and thankful for my injury. Without it I would be most likely dead by now. I received a discharge document from the forced labour work because of my knee."

"Why did you not tell me about this earlier?" Weigner asked me.

"Because I know how they treat people here with this kind of injury."

"Ok! Here is what we are going to do. I'll put together an easier training program," he offered.

"That is very kind of you, but now even the running is hurting, and we both know there is no football training without running," I replied. "What if I get out of this team and get some work here instead?"

"I don't think there is any reasonable way they would let you out of this team. Remember, we waited a month for someone like you, with a skill set like yours, so Heinz could form a team of 11 players for his pleasure."

"What if I hid or tried to escape?" I asked.

"People have tried to escape with very little success. Besides, they have dogs, and the dogs would find you in a matter of just an hour, then you would definitely be executed," he reasoned, "Promise me you will not do that."

"I promise," I replied.

Weigner was right. There was no way I could escape or hide there. Our barracks was a distribution place as well. People had come and gone - some in a few hours, some in a few days. It was the only place which had no system.

It all depended on the war. If the Germans had to retreat, they would send all the "chosen ones" into the gas chambers as well.

The training had begun once again, and the smoke was very thick, almost frighteningly black and smelly. It hurt the eyes but it hurt the soul even more.

My knee was very painful. I tried not to limp because the capo watched us very closely. Suddenly I felt a very sharp pain during a stop and turn. I started to cry, but I kept going. I had to. My life was at stake if I did not continue. The capo had seen it and he called me over, "What is wrong with you? Looks like you are crying, "he said.

First, I did not know what to say, so I quickly replied, "Nothing".

"But I saw you crying, Schwarcz".

I had to make up something. "It is just the smoke. It makes my eyes watery. Besides, I'm sorry for all those people who are from my country and they are lining up to be sent to their death."

"Schwarcz, I have had enough of you. First you go on a walkabout, then you give your food away, and now you are crying. This is not the place for mercy and sensibility. Now, wipe your tears off and get back to training," he said with no gentleness in his voice.

I returned to training. The pain was unbearable but somehow I managed to push myself through.

This time I used a cold shower to keep the inflammation down. Unfortunately, we did not have our masseur anymore so I could not ask for his opinion nor for his healing hands.

As we arrived back at the barracks Weigner came to me, "So, how is your knee?" he asked.

"Very bad and painful," I replied.

Steinberger came too. I showed my swollen knee to them.

"I don't think I can go on any longer with this. The capo is already keeping his eyes on me. He will see on the next training that I'm limping," I say to them.

"I'll plan a stretching session for tomorrow then," says Weigner.

My dreams took me home again but the morning brought me back to the painful reality. Thousands had been executed again during the night and the crematoriums had been burning nonstop. The smell from the smoke was unmistakable, unlike any other smell I had ever experienced during my life

I was stressing about the training day, but for whatever reason, our capo left us after he had escorted us to the field. We were doing the stretches that Weigner had planned for the day's session as he had promised, but even that was hurting. Luckily, I could relax for the rest of the day and use the wet bandaging.

It was late afternoon when the capo came to our barracks. "You will have a game tomorrow," he announced, then he left.
The heat ran through my veins. I knew this was the end for me.
"I am done. I will be in the gas chambers this time tomorrow," I said to the boys.
"Remember how weak the last camp team was against us? We won 5-1 - just try to stand as much as possible."
"But I will not be able to do my defending job if there is be an attack from the opposition strikers," I replied.
 "You know, sometimes the training is harder than a game if the opposition team isn't physically strong," Weigner encouraging me.

That night, I could not share my dinner with the Emerich boys. There was not much for dinner. It was some kind of soup from some kind of grass again - enough to fill the stomach, but only for a short time.

Next morning after we got ready we walked out to the field. The chimneys were releasing the thick smoke as always.
The opposition team arrived on time. They were dressed in light blue jersey. Their skinny bodies did not suit this coloured football jersey at all. The scene was grotesque.
The players were well skilled and if they had been in good physical condition they would beaten us for sure. But this was not the case. They must have been there a long while, performing heavy physical work for 12 hours a day. Even the strongest body would lose weight there with the grass soup provided in the name of food. There was close to no carbohydrate, maybe some

in the 350 grams of bran bread. Everyone was grossly underfed there.

This decided the fate of the match. The ball was mainly on the other half of the field, so I could rest my knee. At half time we were leading 1-0. During the second half we kept possession of the ball.

Heinz saw we were keeping a slow pace but he did not say anything as his team was winning. We scored five more goals during the second half. The game was close to its end when our left wingman Gerd moved forward after receiving a long pass and collided with the opposition team's defender who slid into him to stop him. We heard the snapping sound of bone and a painful scream. We all raced to see what had happened. Unfortunately, the defender had hurt his ankle. He was unable to stand up and every time he moved his leg he was in excruciating pain. We had to carry him off the field where he remained for the rest of the game. We were certain he had broken his leg and we all knew the devastating end for him by the end of the day. This made us play even more carefully, but we still ended up winning 6-0.

It was the 2nd of August. We had one more training session after the win. I could barely move. Weigner was nice to everyone and he planned an easy session, but even this was painful for me. Our capo was not in present. He had been called away for an urgent meeting, so he left us on the training field.

When training had finished we walked back to the barracks by ourselves although this was against the rules of the camp. However, there was no capo to be seen, anywhere. It was very bizarre but, in a way, normal. All the working groups were out of the camp in the nearby factories and the capos were having their rest time.

We were all resting when all the working groups marched back into the camp. The so-called dinner should have been coming soon, but instead the doors got locked on us from outside. "It is a LOCKDOWN!" called out Weigner.

"What is a lockdown," I ask?

"There will be a mass execution of the camp workers. Usually an entire barrack," he replied "and we don't know beforehand which barracks it will be."

"Can it be us," I asked?

"That is possible," he replies.

We heard the dogs, the orders of the SS officers, and soon we could hear the defensive yelling of men, women, and children. We moved closer to the wall to find some gaps in it to see what was happening but our view was still blocked by bits of the wall. We rolled into our beds and tried to cover our ears so as not to hear all the drama. There were some gunshots, dogs barking, yelling and screaming - it was unbearable. The noise continued all afternoon and all night. It became quiet only in the morning. Someone opened the lock on the gate of our barracks, but did not come in. They just left. We slowly got up and moved towards the gate. We slowly opened it and all we could see across from our building was an empty barracks - - the one which had held the gypsy families including their children. It had been their "home" for more than a year. They also had been part of our football team – nine of them. Not even they had been spared. All of them had been executed in a name of a better world. [61]

We were just standing and looking at the empty barracks when Weigner started to bring up some memories about our fantastic team's players - Bogdan, Klaus, Gerd…, and we mentioned something nice about each player as a way to say goodbye to them and to our privileged International football team of Auschwitz-Birkenau. We did not speak to each other much, but we had become a team during the trainings and the games. We had fought together to win each match, to win a bit more food, to win to stay alive. Not even Heinz had been able to save them, but of course we did not know if he tried at all. The officers used us not just for free work, but to live out their darkest sides, to torture us, to use us as human experiments and many more things, but also to entertain themselves.

"What will happen to us now," I asked Weigner?

---

[61] Aug 3 1944 - Auschwitz-Birkenau concentration camp gases 2897 gypsies (writers note). - https://www.onthisday.com/date/1944/august/3

"We don't know, but at least we are alive," he replied "And you don't need to worry about your knee any longer. There will be no more training and games, nor extra food for dinner."

Birkenau Aerial picture from:
https://www.globalsecurity.org/intell/library/imint/images/auschwitz19-12.jpg

The locksmith

The Slovak barrack commander capo arrived. "Take off your football jerseys and put on your uniform," he ordered.
We all started undressing and I looked at myself. I must have lost about 10 kilograms since arriving here about four weeks ago.
The capo picked up our football gear and left.
We were all waiting to see what would happen to us. We could hear some German words which were getting stronger and

stronger and soon three SS-officers stepped into our building. We had not seen any of these faces before.

"Line up," one of them ordered.

"We need a locksmith. Is any of you one?" one of them asks straight forward.

We were not sure what to make out of this.

I slowly stepped forward. I was the only one. Everyone else was a bit surprised as they knew I had worked in the textile factory as a loader. However, I had learned a lot about this profession when I was in Szolnok during one of my forced-labour duty when Veres, the group leader of the railway locksmith team, had taken me under his protective wing.

"Where did you work?" came the question from one of the SS.

"In Szolnok, Hungary with the railway mechanics team," translates Steinberger for me.

"Follow us," one of the SS orders. I followed them and I looked back to say goodbye to my remaining team mates and some friends (Steinberger, the Emerich brothers, and some more). Weigner had already been taken away earlier back to where he had been before the team had been formed.

We walked back to the main Auschwitz camp. Between two barracks there were already a lot of people waiting for selection. Three engineers from the factory were there asking technical questions from the applicants. I recognized one of the prisoners in the selected group from my hometown. He knew I had no clue about the locksmith profession. The applicants had to use and set a slide calipers[62]. He tried to teach me quickly, but of course it was an impossible task.

There were about 40 to 50 selected locksmiths already in one group. I was trying to figure out a way how to get into that group.

Earlier I had seen selections which were built on lies and people had been sent to death instead to work, but this time I was sure these people would be sent to real work.

---

[62] Slide caliper can be used for measuring outside and inside dimensions. Graduations are in inches, fractions, or millimeters. The Slide caliper is made as a separate rule or it is incorporated in a folding rule like the extension on a extension rule.

The three engineers waited for an important answer from a candidate and they were deeply occupied when I decided to use this moment and sneak into the selected group.

The process had been going on until each candidate had his chance to prove his knowledge of the profession. Now there were about 85 to 90 of us in the selected locksmith group.

Soon an SS-officer arrived, had a long talk to the engineers, then we got the order, "Bewegen (move)!"

We were escorted into an empty barracks.

"You will all stay here for 10 days. The quarantine will decide who is healthy to work," stated the officer and then he left.

The days were very long. We could not leave the barracks. The side of the building was exactly two steps away from a high voltage electric fence. There was no grass there, just dirt and dust. I did not talk too much to anyone. There were only a few Hungarians there. Most of the others were Czechs, Polish and Dutch.

We had some visitors - doctors. Firstly, they checked our entire body to see if we had any skin problems. The other area of interest was our throat. This was checked for a long period of time and almost daily. In their opinion these illnesses were the most dangerous and most contagious. Of course they did not care about us, more likely about the SS-guards who would be amongst us in the factory.

The hiring factory was called "Krupp Ammunition Factory[63]" and they had been provided with an endless workforce for almost nothing - only a few pots of grass soup. Whoever became too weak for work or was injured, had been gassed. It was that simple. The trains had been delivering the finest European professionals daily.

We did not receive much food and there was not much air inside. We all started to lose weight rapidly and we all started to look pale. Every time I stepped outside into the small corridor-like space all I could see was the crematorium. It was right in front of me. Even when I did not want to look that way, for some reason I always ended up watching the ever-smoking chimneys. It was

---

[63] Krupp was one of the largest industrial combines in Germany and a recipient of slave labour from Auschwitz during the war. https://www.globalsecurity.org/military/world/europe/krupp-08.htm

very depressing to know that my family and friends were getting killed and burnt there daily.

I tried to divert my attention to something else but every time I caught myself looking at the smoke. I decided to try to look at the sky and see the ever-changing clouds, but in the heat of the August summer, I could not even enjoy that.

I decided to look for birds. I wanted to see how free they were. I wanted to listen to their twittering and the beauty of their movements in the air. Birds which could fly freely. There was no high voltage fence in front of them. There were no SS-guards in the watchtower with machine-guns to stop them either.

I waited for these little creatures in vain. They did not come. As far as I could see there was nothing in the air of the camp, only the smoke.

I realized that even the birds were avoiding this terrible place. Their sense of direction had changed and they avoided this realm of death. Maybe they could sense the smell of the smoke from far away. They did not smell the usual city smoke of the chimneys, but a special smell, the burnt human bodies which made the air stink.

They could fly far away from the hell of Auschwitz, but for us, many lines of protective zone separated us from our freedom.

Even the birds avoided it

Barracks, treeless and grassless roads,
Dirt, garbage, scourge, and capos,
Polluted, damp and smelly air,
Mixed with crematorium smoke in the atmosphere.
Children crying, adults screaming,
Wild bloodhounds loudly howling.
Rough chase, wild roar commanding:
"Schnell! Los!" – with intimidation pounding.
The mooning of the ill, the last breath of the dying,
Mourning of the loss of wife with children are terrifying.
Rattling bones, thigh chests and wheezing,

Infected blisters, wounds, the odours are displeasing.
Sweats smelling, rotten faeces stinking,
The filthy mixture covers everything.
Living, half dead, cold corpses,
Resting peacefully within frozen bodies.
An entire army of dead-transporters with their cargo,
In three shifts carrying bodies to the ovens below.
The Sun hides behind the human smoke,
Falling ashes are covering the pine and the oak.
Far, far away a flock of birds flying,
"Avoid Auschwitz!" – Their singing sounds crying.
They shall not nest in the haughty land of wickedness,
This Empire is home to horrors and viciousness.
The infinity of the sky in vain we spy,
Leaving us alone to await until we die.
If our luck were favourable and we were to survive,
We would pet every bird with love, peace and strive.

10th August 1967, Debrecen, Hungary

Finally, my eyes became tired of looking into the far distance. I
had to accept the reality. There was no one around me except my
suffering companions, SS-guards with machine-guns, the ever-
beating capos with their sticks, the high voltage fences, and the
crematoriums which had been executing millions of innocents.
Not finding any amusement for myself, I went back into the
stinking and crowded barrack. What else had we been waiting
here for? Food! We had been listening for the clinking sound of
the cooking pots. The same way as a hungry lion waits in its
cage, we had been waiting for that hodgepodge. We knew our
hunger would be gone only for a few short moments and only
for a few minutes would our suffering disappear.
The food was delivered in red, round pots and each of them was
to feed five persons. We had to share the hot soup evenly
amongst each of us. They did not provide spoons for us. Each
five person's eyes stared in one direction - to the pot - then a
loud fight would start about who should be the first one to drink
from it. As soon one started to drink, the next fight was about
how much the person had already drunk. To stop the drinker,

we started to push and pull, and so, the "valuable" soup spilled out. This gave a new reason for another argument. The soup was burning hot, but no one cared about that. All that was important was to have as much as possible into our stomach as quickly as possible.

In the yard of the Birkenau camp I had seen piles of regular pots and saucepans which had been taken away from the arriving human transports within half an hour of their arrival. We were not counted as humans who should be given one of these items which were now just rusting under the open sky.

As soon the lunch was finished we continued to argue with each other as we had nothing else to do. We reproached each other about how much each person had ended up drinking. The person in the centre of the argument was always the one who we thought had drank the most soup.

Amongst the five of us, there was only one other Hungarian. The rest were other nationalities therefore the arguments between us were even more heated and used lots more hand signals than the groups with same nationalities. It was chaos every time, but at the end of the day the result was the same - our stomach was empty and in pain - either in pain from the burning hot soup or from the pain of hunger.

The only person in the barracks who was always satiated was the capo, the head of this barracks, who ate in a small office divided from us by a wall. From the pot he could eat as much soup as he wanted but he rarely ate the lunch soup. His privileged position made it possible for him to fill his stomach with more substantial food. He walked amongst us quite well fed and treated us inhumanely. He had a position he wanted to keep for a long time. He wanted to gain merit and this was best achieved by convincing the SS-officers about his inhumanity. Our capo could have remained in command of the block until his retirement. He was perfectly capable of torturing, commanding, and beating. From his room, he watched us with a cynical smile as we competed with each other at lunch. He did not try to keep order amongst us. When he saw a speck of dust on the ground, he would make us lie down on the floor and beat our back and head with his stick. He was sensitive about cleanliness, but he did not care about five unwashed mouths eating from the same pot, or getting the pot out of each other's dirty hands.

When there was a big fight around a soup pot, he would make us empty its contents into the latrine[64]. He could do that as no one questioned him. On the contrary, he was recognized for this as a good barrack's commander. He had a full authority there. He could do with us whatever he wanted to do. We had to "live" with this sadist capo for 10 days.

Finally, the 11th day came. We lined up and were ready to go. I was still sceptical. I knew that what had happened outside the camp in the past 10 days would change everything inside, so with one eye I was still watching the chimneys. As we moved away from the shadows of the chimneys the hearts of the deported Auschwitz camp residents' started to become lighter. I was there only for a few weeks, but I saw thousands marching to their death. Day and night I saw the chimney of the terrible Death Factory, from which the dense dark grey smoke was rushing to the sky with incessant flames.

Our marching group arrived at the gate. The road on the left led to the Death Factory. I had seen many groups who never returned marching from that direction. The road on the right led to somewhere else. I arrived from Birkenau from that way. Whoever went that way had received a delay and was allowed to live for a little bit longer.
These were exciting moments. Our group stopped outside the gate, but we did not turn either to the right nor to the left. We had to wait for our escort for a very long time. Finally, when it arrived, our group was surrounded and the group was led towards the right. I breathed in relief. Now I did not doubt they were taking us to work. On our right, through the barbwire fence, we could see the streets of the lagers while we walked.

As we looked inside the streets we could see lots of movement and the working groups were leaving to the beat of music. Soon we walked by the Auschwitz train station. When we arrived there our train was facing towards Birkenau. We crossed the train tracks and passed by some operating factories.

---

[64] A latrine is a toilet or an even simpler facility which is used as a toilet within a sanitation system.

We came to a more aesthetically designed gate. This was the main site of the Auschwitz working camp. We saw many red-brick buildings. Numbered double story blocks were lined up side by side.

The main gate of the Auschwitz camp – Picture from:
https://parapsyc.files.wordpress.com/2011/06/auschwitz-camp.jpg

We were escorted to a small building next to building No 4. We received a cleaner version of the grey-blue stiped uniform. My number, A-17854, had to be sewn up on the left side of my coat and pants.

My work schedule there had been announced to me too. We had been split into a morning shift and a night shift. I was put into the morning group. We had to go to work the next morning.

I tried to get familiar with our new place. The big brick building had three storeys - basement, ground level and first level. All three levels were the same - long and skinny with supporting studs which housed bunk beds with flannel blankets.

I decided to take a top-level bunk bed, being far away from the crematoriums and more comfortable than the one I had at Birkenau. I felt quite relaxed and fell asleep. I was also happy to know I would be going to work the next day.

Picture from:
https://deanoworldtravels.files.wordpress.com/2014/12/birkenau-wooden-barracks-interior-100_1798-1024x768.jpg

The morning wake-up was very early. We had to start work at 6am and worked until 6pm. We had to line up in front of our barracks. We had our first "roll call" by calling everyone's number in German "Siebzehntausend-achthundert-vierundfünfzig" called out one SS, "Siebzehntausend-achthundert-vierundfünfzig" he called out again. No-one had put his hand up, so the capos and officers started going through the lines and looking for the number on the uniforms. The next minute one stopped in front of me and started hitting me hard. I fell onto the ground and he kept kicking me and yelling "Siebzehntausend-achthundert-vierundfünfzig". A few minutes later the beating stopped. "Welcome to my first working day," I said to myself. I could barely stand back up into the line. "Sándor, you must learn your new name," I said, starting a conversation with myself. "Yes, but they were speaking so fast and I didn't understand what they were saying. I do not speak German," I repeated to myself.

We left towards the gate and I could hear music. On the left side of the gate there was a classical music band with many instruments and they were playing well known songs. On the right side, in front of a two-level building there were some high ranked SS officers looking at us as walked out to work. We had to take our hats off and march with tall posture as we passed front of them.

The morning act was well organized. Anyone who has never been close to the crematoriums at Birkenau must have thought "The Lords of the Third Reich are greatly appreciating the foreign auxiliary workers. They are even providing music for them, and the workers are full of enthusiasm."

icture and more info from: http://www.whale.to/b/auschwitz_orchestra.html - Auschwitz orchestra

Picture and more info from:
https://i.pinimg.com/originals/f2/59/26/f25926e6190cc1dd4e583927fa1ff2a7.jpg - Auschwitz orchestra

Our way led towards the train station. We had walked for about 15 to 20 minutes when we arrived at our workstation, a large building – The Union factory. This factory produced a large amount of ammunition.

We stepped into a very big hall which contained many large and very loud machines. The glass windows on the roof had been painted with a dark colour which, from inside, looked like purple, so it could operate during the night as well. This way the spy planes of the allied forces could not see the lights coming out of the buildings, so it could not be a target during air strikes. Many young males and females worked there.

Along with pulling, stretching, and compressing machinery there were more machines which had been performing complex operations, all of which were operated by the prisoners. The work was directed by blue caped foremen, and along with them SS male and female officers who used their batons and whips very often. Talking between the prisoners was forbidden and was brutally punished.

I had experienced their brutality and on the second day I noticed that the female officers were even worse than the male officers. One of the Hungarian girls had breached the rules in some way and the female SS officer's whip started to beat her immediately on every possible part of her body, without any warning. It seemed to me the louder she screamed the harder the officer's whip came down on her.

One of the German technicians started to take a look at us, then he started to ask work-related questions. This was our second and final "interview". When it was my turn I said (with a translator) "I was working as a locksmith in a factory." I knew my lie would be discovered soon because I did not know anything about this profession at all.

We all had to follow the tall technician who knew the factory very well. As we walked he knew how many persons were needed in each working station. Those who knew each other tried to stay together, but I did not know anyone. I was alone. We arrived at the next station and only one man needed, so I stepped out. I analysed the station and the workman there. I was stationed next to a small and stocky Russian prisoner. He tried to communicate with me but I did not speak his language and I did not understand one word. I was a bit anxious in case he asked me technical questions, so I just shrugged my shoulders.

I was able to tell him my name and where I was from, as I believed this was important as we might be working next to each other for a long time.

As I looked around I was pleased to notice there was not any actual locksmith work to be done there. There were machines which we had to look after.

He put me next to a huge machine, not tall but rather long. From the base of the machine a steel bar, about one metre long, moved in and out of a long steel tube which stretched bullet cases to about 15cm. This bullet case was later filled with gunpowder.

I had to start the machine working. I placed the steel case into a socket then switched the machine on. I had to wait until the steel bar moved the socket and, in doing so, stretched the case. When the steel bar moved back, I had to stop the machine. I had to do this very fast to make sure the steel bar would not crush my hand into the socket as well.

Supervisors and SS-officers monitored if we were working fast enough. There was no rest. Beating sticks and whips "encouraged" us if we slowed down.

Other than this, I had to carry the boxes filled with the large bullet cases into the next room where more processes were waiting for them. I was happy that this workflow did not require any special professional knowledge, but suddenly the machine stopped. I was trying to figure out what had happened and what might have caused it to stop. I noticed that the driving belt had jumped off the driving wheel. My colleague pointed at the machine for me to put it back on. So I walked there like a professional but my knowledge did not extend any further. I touched and pulled it, but I could not place it back on. When I almost had it done on one side, the other side popped off. I was sweating very heavily and my colleague shook his head with anger. He realized the level on my skills. Even an apprentice could have placed the belt back on with ease. He had noticed I was ashamed and he quickly rushed over and placed the belt back in with a few clever moves.

Luckily there had been no guard, who would realize my clumsiness around us at that moment.

We were very hungry from the little food we had been provided with so it was difficult to stand and work for 12 hours. There were guards everywhere, so we could not even have a little rest, even in the toilets. The toilet was inside the big warehouse where during the day I had to go quite often. Already on the first day I had been taught to be quick. Just as I sat down, one guard kicked the door open and from a water hose started to spray ice cold water on me. I coughed and sneezed from the cold shower. The next time I had to go to the toilet and do my job, I was ready to jump any time.

As new workers we did not know about the rules of the place. The guards laughed together at our sufferings. They enjoyed watching us when we had to pull our wet clothes on quickly. From the earlier transports there were many Hungarians there already, especially women. Next to me on the hole punching machine was a woman from Szabolcs-county, who cried a lot. She was mourning the loss of her parents and younger siblings. I should have comforted this weak and fragile girl but I needed some consolation myself. Although physically I had not yet weakened, spiritually I needed some comforting. I was not strong enough to help others.

What could I have said to her? From their home, which had been robbed from them, they had taken away her parents and siblings who had perished into smoke through the crematoriums. She was now in a body and soul-destroying military factory, where every step and move was watched and punished by the SS-guards.

With thinned, narrowed and in-drooping chest she had placed the sleeves in to be machined. Only her eyes shone from her pale face and that was how she looked at me. We looked at each other a lot while we were working, because we were from the same country, so we felt a little closer to each other. I managed to sneak her something from my little lunch. She thanked me gratefully with a small facial gesture.

There were other female workers here from Hungary with whom I was trying to make contact, but these women where further away so it was more difficult.

This acquaintance made this unfriendly war factory a bit more friendly. I had to support and encourage, and be the guardian of, the weaker sex. In this environment, this responsibility had made me a bit more determined.

Every morning my eyes looked for the girl from Szabolcs-county; when I finally found her, I started the work calmly.

One or two weeks had gone by and one morning I could not find her at the start of the shift. The women working a bit further away from me had started their machines with cried-out eyes. My neighbour's machine looked lonely. It had no operator. I could not understand her absence.

I gestured vigorously to find out what had happened to her. It was lunch time when I finally received the sad news.

After work the night before the entire women's barrack had gone through a health check. The ones who had any skin or other kind of infection had been sent to the gas chambers.

It hurt me unspeakably when I found out what had really happened to her. I looked at the empty workstation for a few days. I did not have to encourage, support, or be her guardian any longer. The crematorium of Auschwitz had done its work. A Polish girl had been stationed there as a replacement.

My Soviet fellow prisoner started to be friendly with me. I was sorry for being unable to talk to him. He could have passed me a lot of great advice. When we started to get used to each other, one of the work foremen stationed me somewhere else.

I had to separate the good from the bad, the greasy and empty bullet cases. Gently hitting them on the concrete floor I could hear the different clanging between the shoddy and the intact cartridge cases. Almost every 10th cartridge was shoddy and was useless to the Nazi army. The free labour force managed to slow down the empire one way or another.

The intact cases were taken to another part of the factory where female Greek workers had been filling them up with gunpowder and before they were sent off to another room to place the bullet heads into them with a big machine. There were no "Work Health and Safety" regulations in place, nor any protective wear. Many work accidents which did not have to be reported to anyone had been happening there.

I also heard that many accidents had been happening in my workplace earlier. Unfortunately, I was eyewitness to one of those too.

One afternoon I heard a terrible scream. The injured person was from my 4th barracks, a Dutch worker. His hand was not quick enough, and the machine had cut off two of his fingers at the base. The medical treatment was very basic there. His hand had been bandaged up and he was been sent back to the barracks to rest. For a few days he got new bandaging in the evenings then the diagnosis was easy, "Unfit for work". Six days later the guards came for him and took him to Birkenau. After that I did not hear from him, but I knew what his ending might have been. Injured workers were useless to the factory. The soup made from some grass, the bread made of some sort of bran, and the jam made of beet, was worth giving only to the "healthy ones".

"This is not a health sanatorium!" was how the Nazis described this camp to each new arrival. The injured deportees were all sent to the gas chambers. It was an easy and quick administrative solution. Another number had to be crossed out.

A few weeks before, I had been praying to get further away from the shadow of the Birkenau crematoriums, but this place was not much safer either.

One morning the sirens warning of an air strike went off. We did not believe this could be real. We could not believe that there was someone who would like to drop bombs onto about 18,000 Jews, war captives, Nazi resistance fighters, etc. It would have been more believable if the strike had targeted the crematoriums. There were only a few hundred crematorium workers there and this group had been killed and replaced with new prisoners every three months from the start of its operations. This had helped with the number of liquidations also. The death factory was further away at the back of the lager, far away from the buildings where we worked and "lived".

If one bomb had fallen onto this munition-factory, the entire place would be blown up and would put the Nazi army into an ammunition deficit.

We did not know where to hide. One guard stood at the door with his machine gun to block the way out. All the other "hero soldiers" has gone into hiding.

We managed to find a small cavity inside the wall, and pulled a few concreate blocks on to us to block the entrance.

I heard the sound of the falling air-strike bombs and the walls of the building were shaking from the noise of the low- flying planes. Someone moved closer to me but in the darkness of the hole I did not know who it was. I pulled one concrete block aside to let some light in and in the semi-darkness I recognized one of the Greek female workers. I wondered if I could give her some reassurance in this situation. I immediately said a few calming words to her. Even though we did not speak each other's language, the calmness of my voice must have given her enough strength and courage.

None of the bombs landed on the factory building so the work had to be resumed as normal. First, we had to clean ourselves from the dust. I helped the Greek girl, for which she thanked me with a smile.

Only on the way back to the barracks, an upon our arrival, we managed to see how much damage the air-strike had made and how many people had passed away. There were some great bomb craters in the ground and sadly, a lot of the deportees had passed away - but unfortunately not enough of the SS.

Only these few SS guards received a very big funeral with a gun salute. The inmates, as usual, went to the crematorium.

During the ceremony I wrote a letter to the pilots in my head: "Dear Captain of the American and English Air Forces, may I ask who has given you the coordinates of your recent targets? Did you know who and what are the real points of attack? What instructions have you received from the higher ranks? Why do you have to drop bombs on 18,000 poor souls?"

One afternoon a few days later the sirens went off again, not just at our factory but in all of the ones surrounding us. However, we could not hear the rumbling of plane engines. Our SS-guards made all of us to line up and we had to march towards our lagers. We did not understand the situation as it was not yet the end of our shift, but we suspected something awful, as the guards had been using rougher voices than usual.

On the way back we saw other marching groups too. We were all escorted back into our barrack #4. The SS-guards stood at all doors and soon Gestapo-officers entered with the serious accusations. The workers of the Sondercommando had blown up one of the big crematoriums and escaped the camp. All of them had been captured and after the interrogation they were burnt alive.

"If anyone has any information then he should step forward now, otherwise we will start the interrogation one by one!"

As not one person stepped forward, the SS-guards selected ten people and escorted them out of the barracks. It took a few hours before seven beaten-up workers re-entered the building. Three had been kept in the Gestapo's jail and the returned ones had no information useful to the interrogators.

Then the next group was taken away. This time, all of them returned a bit faster than the first group, and these men were less beaten-up too. Maybe the beaters had become tired. There were lots of us in the building #4.

After the next group it would be my turn. However, I had nothing to do with this plot and I had no information either. These few hours were very stressful for many of us.

Nine men came back but the guards did not take any more group for interrogation.

"What has happened?" we all asked.

"One man from the last group could not handle the torture any longer and has confessed everything," said one from the last group.

"And what did really happen?" we asked him, as many of us had no idea about it at all.

"The women from the factory, who have been working in the gunpowder section, have been stealing the powder in small portions and taking it out of the factory. Their barracks were very close to the Birkenau-Death Factory and they managed to get it to the sonder-commando team. They made a bomb and - we know the rest. It was a well-organized collaboration," he said[65].

The people involved in this were heroes in our eyes, but of course they were rebels in the eyes of the Nazis. Their destiny was clear: EXECUTION!

What the American and English pilots had not managed to do had been done by a few brave women and men in the shadow of the death. It did not matter if they were from Poland, Hungary, Holland or Czech, they had worked for the same goal - stop, or slow down, the execution by gas and diminishing the activity of the crematorium for once and for all.

The big red brick building had collapsed. This warned our prison owners that "the unarmed silent army" would not surrender easily.

During the daily 12 hours of my job during these past few weeks, the little amount of food became even smaller. The number of calories in it had made my body very weak, my cheeks had fallen in along with my eyes and my skin looked pale. In one word I was almost like a living skeleton. It had become difficult to work and it made me even more tired.

One day my work-group leader decided to place me to another workstation. This machine was huge, but the work seemed easy. All I had to do was to slide the already stretched (about 15 centimetres long) cannon ammunition cases onto a base template and press a pedal with my feet. The machine would come down

[65] Oct 6 1944, Soviets march into Hungary & Czechoslovakia. Oct 7 1944, Uprising at Auschwitz-Birkenau concentration camp, Jews burn down crematoriums - https://www.onthisday.com/date/1944/october

very heavily with a big noise and punch four holes in the side of the case and one into the top. The supply of cases were provided by other workman and women. If there were too many cases waiting for me to do, my guard would encourage me to work faster with a few hits and punches. My hands and feet had to work fast and had to be coordinated too. It took all my effort to keep going. My whole body was in motion when I did this new work.

One morning I was in a hurry to process all the cases piled up next to me. I placed the case on quickly, pressed the pedal, pulled the item off, placed the next one on, pressed the pedal and so on. In my mind I had wandered off to my hometown and was eating some delicious food in my mind when I pressed the pedal a bit too soon. My left hand was still under the machine which slammed down onto my thumb. The pressure split my finger and the blood sprayed everywhere, on my clothes and on other items around me.

It felt that I was unconscious for a few seconds from the pain but I did not fall, and when I realized what had happened, I tried to stop the bleeding by squeezing my finger with my right hand. My fellow workman managed to get some paper from somewhere, but my thumb bled through it very quickly. I did not want to go to the medical station. I remembered my other colleague who had lost two fingers a few days earlier. I was already unable to continue this work because of the pain. Besides the SS soldiers and guards there had been non-German taskmasters overlooking our work. Not all of them were heartless. Luckily one of these kind men had noticed my bleeding. He knew I could be executed with this type of injury and he immediately redirected me back to my previous station. To select the cracked or perfect cannon ammunition cases could be done with one hand. To hit it to the concrete and listen to the chiming of it was an easy job, however my finger was terribly painful. This day felt longer than any other.

Finally, the shift was over and we marched back to our barrack. Someone suggested I should pay a visit to the "hospital", some said not to. I reminded them about the last accident and its outcome. This caused a change of mind of some, so we went to sleep. Of course I did not have any sleep. The pain was unbearable.

During the next few weeks I had to make sure my injury was not noticed by our guards at work or by anyone else who could send me off to the medics. I managed to collect some paper during work so I could change my bandaging from time to time. It was not very hygienic but I did not have much choice. Luckily, I did not get any blood infection and a few weeks later my finger started to heal. The zigzag scarring was a new addition to my left hand. Three times now I had survived the gas chambers.

The international football player

It was towards the end of the summer. I had already lost a tremendous amount of weight from the long working hours in the ammunition factory. One night as I returned from work into the barracks, two inmates were waiting for me. They had received a strange assignment from the capos. They must gather eleven great football players to represent the prisoners of Auschwitz for a match. They had appointed me to be part of this selected team as they had heard about my previous football career outside and inside the camp. One of the teams would be made of prisoners regardless of their religion or nationality, and the other would be made of the prominent distinguished arm-banded capos who were entrusted with the management of the work of the prisoners as barrack commanders. The names of the two teams could have been the Hungry and the Well Fed. With about 50 to 60 kilograms bodyweight (and constantly losing it) we got placed in the Hungry team, and the capos, with their rounded bodies and with great physical conditions into the Well Fed team. To meet the request, we undertook to be part of the international team with very little enthusiasm. In that environment I did not feel honoured to be part of the best 11 players of the Auschwitz team once more. I had become uncaring so I was not proud of my selection.
When I had arrived in Birkenau at the beginning of July, I was still in a relatively reasonable physical condition, so I took on the challenge with great courage, and I had hoped to receive more

lenient treatment from becoming a player. I was part of that team for four weeks and during this period of time I was less deprived than the others, but this was not the case now.

Soon I received the briefing that the game would be on the following Sunday. To have a training session was out of question - our handpicked team did not deserve that much, not even an extra portion of bread to have a bit more energy. We did not even have a reason to win, the game had no stake at all, and for a long time I could not bother to be proud and driven to win. For a piece of bread, I would happily have traded off my membership of this international football team. I regretted taking part in the game. I was neither psychologically not physically fit to play and the location did not provide an idyllic atmosphere for football.

The day of the game arrived - Sunday. The start time had been scheduled in the early afternoon and only then did I find out the location of the game. When I signed up for this, I had hoped for some exercise on some green grass outside of the camp with a change of scenery. However the location was far from my hopes. It was on an exceedingly small area, with rock-hard soil, between two barracks. Our spectators were the ones in the two barracks watching us from the windows. The two temporary goal-boxes had been marked at the two ends of the "field".

From somewhere, perfect football shoes and jerseys came out. We put these on in one of the barracks next to the field. I managed to find myself a pair of football shoes which fitted perfectly, but the purple chequered jersey was very baggy on my skinny body. As I looked at myself from every possible angle, I realized how much weight I had lost. I had barely any muscles left and those remaining had lost their elasticity.

I had always loved to chase the round ball and I always participated with great pleasure in every game. I believed in playing hard without any fouls or rudeness. I was never sent off the field with red card. Now, I waited for the match to start in an unstable mental state and with a deteriorating physical condition.

I did not know any of my team players, and I was the only Hungarian nationality on this team. The rest of the team was made of Italians, Czech, Polish and Greek. It was truly an International team. My companions beside me could not be proud of their muscular development either. We looked more like a collection of bones than a team.

Our fellow inmates had been eagerly waiting for us at the windows. They greeted us with a loud cheer when we entered the field but we waited for our opponents with heads down and without any enthusiasm.

The well fed, and some even overweight capos, arrived in blue-white jerseys. They looked fearful with beating sticks in their hands but now, having changed from their uniforms into the jerseys, they looked even more scary. There was about a 300kg (if not more) difference between the two teams in bodyweight. I had been placed to play as a right forward, and my opponent of the left defending position was an enormous man. During the game I was afraid even to go near him. On one occasion when I received the ball, he ran into me with such force I flew a few metres through the air and could hardly get off the ground. I tripped and fell a lot, and my teammates did the same.

At the beginning of the game we managed to stay on our feet, but later we lay on the ground more than we stood. Our spectators' interest and enthusiasm were very quickly lost. They watched the game with much sadness.

At the back of the capos goal-box stood the camp's main hangman. With his huge protruding teeth he looked like a serial killer. Whoever could do so, stepped out of his way. With one wave of his hand many had been sent into the gas chambers.

I was also afraid of this SS soldier and even when I could run up with the ball for an attack, I slowed down. Our team did not have much energy to prepare an attack or put pressure on the capo's team. However, for some reason, I did end up with the ball in front of the box. I may have been able to score too, but I was afraid to do so, because this SS had been snarling at me with his huge yellow teeth. Scoring one goal was not worth that much for me because I could be punished with a gas sentence. The goals ended up in our box only. The final score was 8-0 for the capos. Every time they scored, they hugged with great pleasure. They had managed to score against an international team whose members were hungry, tired and vulnerable.

For a good performance of a football player, beside the good physical condition, it also necessary to have a great mental state. An established crematorium a few kilometres away, which was working at full capacity, provided a reason for permanent mental depression. It had also contributed to the certain or uncertain fate of our family members. Overall, the circumstances were not suitable for playing a football match.

Nearby, thousands of people were destroyed every hour and by the end of the summer of 1944 the number had reached the millions. Football should not be played in a graveless cemetery. It was soulless to organize a match and we should not have taken part in the game. Our team could not score one goal. I did not really care about this lack of success. I had enough trouble with how I would recover after this game. Every part of my body hurt from fatigue and I could barely take my gear off myself. We could not even get any joy and respect for our prisoner spectators by scoring at least one goal. To compensate for the beating, one goal would have meant a bit of malicious joy for them.

We had not managed to please our spectators, but it was better this way, as after the game the distinctive sign of yellow armband of the capos was put back on their jackets, and maybe every goal would have drawn consequences for all 11 of us.

It was not the loss of the game that hurt us, it was than the physical fatigue.

When I laid down with sore muscles onto my wooden bed, I listened with sleeplessness to the victorious singing of the capos who celebrated their win over the international Auschwitz team with lots of alcohol.

The spectator

Over the main entrance of the Auschwitz camp there was an inscription made out of bronze letters "greeting" the visitors "ARBEIT MACHT FREI" – WORK MAKES YOU FREE.

Right next to it stood a two-storey building. On ground level SS-guards were stationed, and the upper level of the building had a hidden special and mysterious purpose. From whispers, I heard that the upper-level windows were hiding females. For the long period of months, I had not seen female inmates in the main lager. Only male workers were kept there and they were escorted to perform different work. Opposite the two-storey building was a rectangular area where a classical band, formed from prisoners, played rhythmical music for those going to work in the morning and for those arriving from work in the evening. Each morning all members of the SS camp leaders were present to watch the entry and exit of the working groups. They watched all prisoners, closely looking for the smallest irregularity for which they could pull the guilty ones out of the line and punish them. Taking off our caps we had to march in step with the beat of the music. It was expected from us, fatigued workers as we were, to face our prison-guards with an enthusiastic look after the 12 hours of hard work.

The function of the band was not only to uplift the workers leaving or arriving from their shift. Occasionally the camp leaders invited all camp inmates to "enjoy" the performance of the classical band. These live outdoor performances also had a soul-torturing reason. Beside the physical torturing, they provided us with mental torturing as well. They knew what desires the "Blue Danube" piece from Johann Strauss would arouse in the shadow of the crematoriums surrounded by electric barbwire. I was reluctant to participate in these outdoor concerts but I had no say in it. The capos escorted everyone out from the barracks.

On one late summer evening before the sunset we were put onto this square again to listen to another musical performance. The musicians were wearing white uniforms and there were about 80 of them. The best musicians had been selected from all over Europe. You did not have to be a music enthusiast to hear how perfectly the band delivered the best classical pieces one after the other.

Next, a composition from Verdi was played. The notes were flying beautifully up in the air from the instruments. A teardrop started to roll down on my cheek when I was listening to a piece from the Traviata there in "The Empire of Hell".

As I was mulling over the awkwardness of the situation, I involuntarily looked up the upper level. From behind one of the windows a young woman was looking right at me. She was one of my many companion inmates. Maybe because of the desolate and horrible place, I found her face over the glass window most beautiful. It was not out of sexual feeling or desire did I examine her face. Other feelings were swirling inside of me. I knew first hand that the most beautiful women had been set aside already at the time of arrival at the ramps of Birkenau. These women kept their long hair and were escorted into this building. There they were handed over for the pleasure of higher ranked SS-guards. These unfortunate girls would live only for a few weeks. When they were worn out by the brutal and violent soldiers, they ended up in the gas chambers. There was daily transport from every European country so there was an abundance of choice. The old ones were replaced by fresher younger ones. They could build their own harem from the most beautiful European women. They did not adhere to the Nuremberg Racial Aryan Law [66] any longer. This kind, humiliated, death-sentenced woman had been looking at me at this open-air concert on this late afternoon. Despite the distance, we had communicated between each other with our eyes. She was more severely humiliated than I was and my condolences were expressed deeply. We did not manage to find out more about each other - only that we both have fallen as victims to the arm of fascism. We had arrived in an identical fashion, locked down in animal wagons, and had been selected and dragged out from the loving arms of our family, and had become "nameless numbers" in the hands of these wild animals. We were waiting to be part of the millions gassed and burnt in the crematoriums.

We searched in vain for each other, but our eyes could not establish a closer contact. Where were we from, and what nationality were we? Where were our mothers and fathers? What sin had we committed that we must be punished so severely? The music continued to flow and I made sure I was looking towards her with the utmost care while not being seen by any guard. This would have been a "sinful act" and maybe both of us could have received a ruthless punishment. I took my eyes off her for a moment and when I looked back, I saw only the white curtain. I waited for a while but without any luck. Maybe her

---

[66] The Nuremberg Laws (German: Nürnberger Gesetze) were **antisemitic and racist laws in Nazi Germany**. They were enacted by the Reichstag on 15 September 1935, at a special meeting convened during the annual Nuremberg Rally of the Nazi Party (NSDAP).

guest, for whom she had the deepest hate, but nevertheless had to give herself to, had arrived.

The concert was over and I hoped she would still be watching me from the safety of the curtain. I wanted to salute her with a small bow so I had turned towards the building, which may have looked like I was saluting the musicians for the play. I had hoped she could still see me and understand my gesture. I never saw her again.

Meeting with Dr Mengele

I had reached my goal in the lager. I had moved away from Birkenau and now lived my days as a factory worker. The days were long and monotonous. The work was 12 hours a day. The food was meagre. The living conditions were poor.

In the few months there I lost about 15kg of my body weight. I was now around 65kg and skinny, just like everyone else around me. I was always tired and hungry.

We had no idea what was happening outside the camp. Sometimes we heard some news but it was never good enough to excite us. The best way we could know what was happening on the war front was the way our guards treated us. If they were brutal, we knew the Nazis had lost somewhere. If the hitting was gentler, we knew they had gained back or taken over some new territories.

We knew the Soviet army was closing fast but we did not know if it would be fast enough for us. Would we live that long - for that day of liberation of this camp?

The days became shorter and the nights colder. We did not see the beauty of the changing seasons as there was not one tree to be seen. We could not enjoy the trees turning from green to yellow, the falling of the leaves and the smell of the autumn. The view was always the same - high voltage electric fences, guard towers with soldiers in them with machine guns, capos, hitmen, and many skinny living skeletons in grey and black striped uniforms. The discipline was tight and the beatings were delivered in a most brutal way. There was no mercy there. When we marched to work I dreamed about the beautiful "Large Forest" in Debrecen and the smell of the fallen leaves under me when I lay down on the thick layer of them. From there I looked up to the sky through the maze of hooked and twisted branches. Sometimes I lay for so long and so still that even some deer had come very close to me.

This kind of thinking in this camp was almost a death sentence. There, we were not allowed to think, be sensitive, or sorry. Whoever still had the smallest sprinkling of human emotion would die very quickly or would suffer a lot. I had not spent long enough time there yet to lose these feelings like many others had. To become careless, emotionless, or even detached from my past I would have had to spend more time there.

As I was a great observer, I analysed some of my inmates who had spent years there already. These men and women did not know how to be sorry or to grieve for someone any longer. They could face everything now, the beatings, the tortures or even their own death. Therefore, you could not be resented by any of them. Most of them had lost all of their friends and relatives. Some of these had even been killed right in front of their eyes. These men and women no longer knew how to cry. We could not expect them to be compassionate towards us, the newcomers.

We had heard news that the war was coming to its end. I was hoping it would not last longer than a few more months. I knew this amount of time would not be enough to change me to becoming like one of those who had been there a long time. I could still cry. One day working in this big factory next to big noisy machinery I remembered one of our celebrations at home. I had been seated around the table with my siblings. We had drunk a little bit of wine which made all of us enjoy the day even more and we were all joking around. I could see my mum's skinny and lean face as she cried from happiness as we all ate, with great appetites, the food she has prepared. From this great memory my eyes became watery, but then I could not stop... I cried so much my whole body was shaking. Many workers around me noticed my weakness and regardless of nationality or gender some started to cry with me. They also could still cry. They were also relatively newcomers like me. I was ashamed being at being a weeping man in front of them. I promised to myself that I would change if I wanted to live. I would train myself to do that. I would train my brain and emotions so I could control them. This did not depend on being a highly-educated person. I had seen many intellectuals who had lost control of their emotions and become spiritually broken. From that stage there was no return. It was not long before they lost their physical abilities and their destruction occurred quickly.

My environment made it easier for me to endure the suffering that was waiting for me. I had to be realistic. There was no room any longer to be romantic, to be weak or to cry. I wanted to become a resilient person as I had a strong will to live. I could not become an emotionless person from one day to the next. I never did manage to get myself trained enough to succumb to the hardened ordeals of the lager.

Soon a new challenge arose. One Sunday morning our barracks commander entered the building.

"You all get a day off and do not have to go to work today!" This was the first time since I had been there that this had happened. We knew we were not getting a day off just as a kindness of our hosts. We suspected a catch in this "act of kindness".

Soon the new order was announced, "Everyone will be checked by the medical staff!"

Right away I remembered the day when all the females had been medically checked and for the smallest diagnosis of a skin problem or other medical reason these women had been sent immediately into the gas chambers.

I had made full use of the factory's or the camp's shower facilities and there was not one affected spot on my skin. Yes, I did lose some weight, but I did not classify myself as the skinniest there. The "older camp workers" did not even have their breakfast as they were very stressed, but they had not said a word to the "younger camp workers".

We had to line up front of the barracks and the strict headcount suggested that something big would happen soon.

We were all escorted to the big shower facility in tight lines. We all had to take our clothes off outside in the cold and keep our uniforms on our arms. The residents of other barracks had been lining up the same way. Everyone was standing there quietly. We all had been waiting for the final verdict. The sentence would be made without questioning, without listening to witnesses. There would be no mitigating or aggravating circumstances. There would be no introduction about how good or bad the person was, how he lived his life, what his profession was, where he worked or how many children he had. The verdict would be announced in a matter of moments and on the basis of only one circumstance - what kind of physical condition the person was in. The verdict would be simple - to die or to live. If you were selected to live, you would be allowed to work a few more weeks or a month until the next selection.

It was well choreographed. The selection of the nameless humans with only a number on their arm had been done by a doctor. Any of the SS guards would have been able to do the selection, but if a professional doctor made the selection it could not be overruled by anyone else. This person had the authority to send hundreds, thousands, one hundred thousand, no, no - millions and millions - into oblivion.

Soon our group was the next to be observed so we had to speed up our steps and soon I would find out the verdict from this professional doctor who vowed to save lives on the day he received his doctor's degree.
We had moved quickly inside the shower room and I was soon to be viewed. I did not know what verdict the people directly front of me had gotten because I was too busy with myself. I was also curious to see who the man selecting us was.
There he was, the man who did the selection on our day of arrival; the man who had an immaculate uniform; then and now as well, the head of the executioner squad, Dr Mengele. He was full of enthusiasm on that day. Maybe he had just arrived from the train station of Birkenau and had already sent thousands into gas chambers.
According to the medals on his coat he was a great war hero. He had become one by selecting children, women, the elderly, the

sick or the infirm, and sending them to death with one movement of his arm. He was also made a hero by conducting live human experiments in the name of medical research; by selecting the weak ones after months or years of 12 hours a day, seven days a week work, whom they had fed with soup made of some weed grass.

And now I was front of him. I was fully naked, and he was well dressed. On our first meeting back in July I had been like an athlete among the elderly and the females, and he looked fresher. That day he looked tired. He must have been busy selecting the few hundred usable humans from over half a million Hungarians in the past few months. He wanted to do his job with the perfect German precision. He wanted to be there when the trains arrived on days and nights. He wanted to "introduce" himself to everyone when to wagon doors slid open, even if it was only for a few hours for some to remember him.

I was next. I could feel my heart beating in my chest and I had a lump in my throat. I hid my left hand by my side, and walked past him on my right side. All I received from "the master of the selectors" was a one second look. That was enough for him to diagnose my health. I walked out on the other side of the bathroom and the fresh September wind felt great on my naked skin. He did not see my injured left fingers. One of my roommates grabbed me and started to hug and kiss me: "We are saved! We can stay! We will live!" He was almost crying these words into my face which he was holding in his hands. The area was full of happy faces and hugging people, but my heart was heavy. I knew not everyone had been let off. Many had been selected as "unfit for further work". These people were guarded by a big number of SS soldiers until late afternoon. We could not even get close to them. The truck had been loaded that afternoon with thousands of living skeletons who were not fit enough to work any longer. As Mengele solemnly stated, "I have reduced the Auschwitz camp's stock by a large number of unsuitable persons in the workforce". Thousands of food portions did not have to be distributed that night. The capos had a feast.

I knew we had been saved only until the next selection process which would come again, faster than we thought. From that day onwards I checked the condition of my body every day. I did not have a solution of how to slow down my physical deterioration. I had no answer. The living and working conditions had not changed, nor had the food portions become bigger. All I could do was to hope for the Soviet troops to reach us, but even that could have had a negative effect on the Germans. The selection process could become more frequent and the number of "unfits" could become larger at each selection. These thoughts made me depressed and I had no intention of making friends. I had become closed off from my surroundings and after work I just lay on my bed until the tiredness pushed me into sleep.

The scavenger

One day I was ordered to go outside of the factory and sweep the ground. As I was doing my job I noticed an SS couple sitting on a bench. They had not noticed my presence as they were all over each other. Soon the man pulled out something wrapped in paper from his bag. I became so curious I started to sweep closer and closer to them. It was a sandwich, white bread, salami, butter and green capsicum. I could smell the fresh capsicum from meters away. I was hoping they would have some left over and now the question was what would they do with it? Soon they stood up and walked towards the factory. The leftovers remained in the paper on the bench along with the bag. I was so hungry as I had been watching them eating and the beautiful smell made my stomach hurt even more. Millions had been killed in that place, people had been beaten to death or shot in the head without any reason. I knew if I stole this small amount of food the Nazis would have reason to do the same to me, but I was extremely hungry. I picked up the "rubbish", stuffed it inside my uniform and walked behind the factory building. There was only the crust of the bread and the base of the capsicum inside, but it was food for me. I stuffed these few bites down very quickly. However, this made me even hungrier and my stomach felt even emptier. I got back to work. Soon the lovebirds came back, and the man picked up his bag and they looked at me. From their look I understood "We know you have taken the rubbish, but we are not mad at you. We understand your situation."

Even in this deathcamp some had not lost their humanity. Being of German nationality did not necessarily make a person a thoughtless killing machine.

60 minutes of hope of freedom

Life was not boring in the camp. Shocking events made our life unsettled day by day. We all knew we would die there, and many just could not wait. Some tried to make their life easier but this caused conflicts.

One night as we arrived back to the barracks after work we went through the usual headcount. One person was missing. The guards went through the headcount a few more times but they were always one short.

This meant we had to wait to go to bed until everyone was present. The night shift was already working in the factory, but we had to stay outside the front of the barracks in the cold and dark until the number was right.

The irony was this: millions had been killed here and disappeared without a trace, but one missing person had raised the alarm. More and more SS soldiers appeared and looked for the one missing person everywhere. We did not know who the missing person was, but they probably found him as we were let to go to sleep.

Next morning in the factory I got the news who the missing person was and how he became missing.

Trains delivering materials for the factory had also transported the products out of it. One Czech worker hid himself under one of the train wagons. The train had to use the same trainlines out of Auschwitz as the incoming human transports. After the alarm was raised upon his disappearance, they searched every inch of the camp. They had found him under the train which was waiting to leave the camp. He had chosen the risk of a death sentence which was part of the escape.

On the way back from work we could see his sentence. He has been hanged and the wind was gently swinging his stiffened body. We had to march in front of his body and look at him. This was their way of intimidating all of us. He paid a terrible price for his 60 minutes of his hope of freedom.

Third meeting with Dr Mengele

The following weeks were even more difficult and October arrived bringing some cold weather. We did not receive any warm clothing and the thin uniforms let every slow cold wind through. I was not just hungry, I was also freezing. However we had received more and more good news about the approaching alliance troops. It could be months before they could free us, but I did not think I could last that long nor did I believe I would have enough luck to survive - and I was right. One evening, as we marched back from work, all barracks' residents were waiting outside the buildings in five lines. Usually, we could go to rest after work, but we had to stay outside. After everyone was there and lined up, the groups were escorted towards the big showering facility. The word got around - we would be going through another selection process. I was shocked.

Since the last selection a few weeks ago I had continued to lose weight. I was not sure how my third meeting with Dr Mengele would end. Would I be selected as fit or unfit for further work? As I looked around myself, everyone was checking himself out desperately, with very scared looks on their faces. I was just as scared too.

Many had gone already, taken a deep breath of cyan gas. They did not feel anything anymore. They were at peace and as the lines moved forward into the building I felt jealous of them. We were all naked again and all of us looked the same - skinny and broken-down living skeletons. More than 10,000 of us were waiting for a death or life sentence - but we were innocent. We had no guilt. We were not murderers or rapists, nor thieves. We were guilty of only one "crime" - we had been born to Jewish religious parents. The 'Superior' German race had categorized us as a lower race. That was the reason I was standing there and was waiting for the crucial decision with thousands more around me.

This October night was colder than during our previous selection. Standing there naked was very cold. Just like before, my uniform was folded on my arm. I was next. I decided I would pull myself up straight to look more muscular, but this made my legs look even skinnier and my stomach even more hollow. My body must have looked rather grotesque.

It was him again, Dr Mengele. This was our third face-to-face meeting. As I was about to slowly jog by him, he reached out to my hip and pushed me towards the clerks who were waiting for the death sentenced prisoners. Everything went black. I had been selected for death - which would be delivered by gas.

The Polish clerks wrote down my number from my arm and the number of my barracks. Interestingly enough, I was allowed to go back to my bed instead of waiting for the trucks to take us to the gas chambers like the selected group during the last process. When I walked inside, one of my Polish roommates was laying on the ground crying hysterically. His number also had been put onto the list. There were 60 people selected from our barrack Number 4, and I was part of this group. A few roommates were trying to tell us differently: "You will be going to inland Germany and you will be fed well until your condition is better," one said. Of course, I knew this was not the case.

I had no inclination to eat my dinner, but another sentenced older man spoke while he was eating his portion of dinner: "I have lost my entire family already. I am not sorry at all. At last, I will meet with them".

I could not fall asleep. All I could think of was how deeply I would breathe in the cyan gas so I could die faster. Many of my great memories came to my mind, but at the end I always saw the crematorium, the one I had been so close to so many times while I was playing football on the other side of the fence. I don't know for how long I was awake, but yelling awoke me: "17854 - Siebzehntausend-achthundert-vierundfünfzig – Seventeen-thousand eight-hundred fifty-four, Seventeen-thousand eight hundred fifty-four". I knew my number in German by now very well. I jumped to my feet and stood in the line which formed in the middle of the room. The rest of the roommates were saying goodbye to us.

As we stepped out from the barrack, the morning was still dark and the fresh cold air gave me the shivers. We had been escorted to the end of the barracks where there was an empty square. We had to wait until all of the selected skeletons from all of the other barracks had arrived too. There were about 800 of us there, waiting for the trucks to arrive. SS guards with bloodhounds surrounded us, "Soon you all will be transported into Birkenau!" stated one guard. Now even my smallest hope had been destroyed.

Meanwhile, the hospital was also liquidating its sickest patients. They had no clothes on except a long shirt. They had been dragged out from the building and been dropped onto the cold floor without any warm blankets. Their future was the same, death by gas.

The morning started to become lighter, the sun had come up, but it was still very cold. Outside of our cordon, many friends and relatives had arrived and started to say their final goodbyes to the selected ones. I was in my own world. I did not want to talk to anyone. I had already asked one of my Hungarian roommates to find my relatives in case he made it home and to tell them of my sorry, final ending.

Suddenly, I saw an SS officer approaching our group with fast steps and he had a quick conversation with our head guard, then he stated, "Whoever is a worker from the UNION factory must step forward and return to work immediately!"

These were the most beautiful words I had heard in a long time. I was able to leave this death sentenced group which was heavily surrounded by SS-guards and bloodhounds, high voltage fences, and guard towers surrounded by machine-gun armed soldiers. All I could think was that I had been saved once again. I did not know how but I was able to keep going and hope for the Allied forces to reach us in time. I did not realize how cold and grey this October morning was. All I had in mind was that I had escaped the gas-chamber. I would be continuing to work as a slave, being hungry and cold, getting punished for everything possible, but I was alive. All 60 of us from the 4th barrack left the death sentenced group. We were very sad for the others but we could do no more for them. When we arrived back in the factory everybody was surprised to see us. They all knew where we had come back from. The German group leaders told us "We need only 15 of you, the rest can go back". These were very stressful moments again.

I tried to wave to my work group, but they ignored me. With my injured finger, I was not a perfect candidate to be selected for further work. The unwanted 45 of us had to go back. One of my fellow inmates was trying to sneak into the 15 selected group but one of the guards noticed him. For his action he received a beating after which he was thrown back into our disembarking group.

SS-guards escorted us back into the lager. The realization that they identified us as slaves was hard to bear. When we arrived back the guards left us on the square and they moved into their office. No one really cared about us. After a few minutes waiting I came up with the idea of vanishing back into our barracks.

"This is madness! You know what happens with the ones who disobey the orders!" one inmate states.

"I know, but we are sentenced to death anyway. Nothing worse can happen to us," I argued.

"We should go back to the death-selected group and accept our destiny," said another and a few decided to go that way.

However, I did not agree with the "voluntary marching to death" and calmly I walked back into my barracks like I had just come back from work. My Polish barrack commander, Stasek, was surprised to see me, but he immediately realized what had happened. He grabbed my arm and escorted me to the kitchen. He did not say one word. He pushed me down into a group sitting on the ground peeling potatoes.

No one looked for me in the next few days. My death selected group had been transported into the Birkenau gas-chambers. This was the last group to be sentenced to death by gas. The reason for this was the fast-approaching Red army. The Nazis were able to hide the real fact of the reason for this and for other camps. The Alliance countries did not want to believe the news which had been delivered by a handful of deserters who had managed to escape from some camps. The Nazis were trying to hide its real purpose with success, for a while at least. The prisoners of Auschwitz were working on the dis-assembling of the crematoriums from thereafter with pleasure.

Crematorium in Auschwitz

On the bank of the Vistula, there is a factory,
Its red bricks have been mortared densely.
It is a special plant facility,
Burns people with its technology.
Burned four million Europeans,
With high-capacity furnaces,
In the feverish work of three shifts,
Generations have been destroyed to ashes.
The building, creative, working people.
Scorched into a handful of ashes,
The red blood turned into grey ashes,
Living as a black smoke through the chimneys.
It spreads high and blending in the sky,
To infinity the dark clouds grimly fly.
Plant, which was built for genocide,
Different nations on conveyor belt died.
The kilns were still waiting for many millians
Russian, Polish, French, Hungarian, Sicilians.
The best of Europe was destroyed for annihilation,
By the greedy madness of the Fascism,
But the bloody death factory trembled,
Against it, Nations assembled.
With tools they pounded the walls,
In the wake of the tanks, it is falling apart.
The "great work" has become a ruined piece,
The Four Million are guarding over its peace.

September 1966, Debrecen, Hungary

The kitchen worker

Thanks to Stasek I was now alive and had new work. I was peeling potatoes with other men. We were seated in two lines, facing each other on the concrete floor. In between our lines were big pots filled with water into which we had to drop the peeled vegetables.

Next to us was the cooking place so I could watch what had been put inside our daily soup which was cooked in large metal cauldrons. Now for weeks, this was our main food. Next to the cauldrons there were large vegetable grinders. The potato and some kind of large green leaves of a plant and beets were ground into the water with a bit of margarine and that was it. That was our soup. When the kitchen management staff did not steal the canned meats, we could also be lucky to find it in this hodgepodge. If it happened, the lucky one would happily break the news to his fellow inmates.

I was happy to do this job at first. It was easier and with less responsibility, so I thought. However, the looks on the workers faces spoke otherwise.

It was forbidden to talk to each other, to look up, sideways, or behind us. The capos here were German criminals, bank robbers and killers. Their crooked beating cudgel was a fast-moving tool in their hands. It was used without any reason and without any gentleness. The main target of course was anything on the upper body, head, back or shoulders. The head manager here was a well fed, fat SS-officer. He enjoyed seeing his men's brutality. He was infected with the same intentions and often helped in the beating.

When I received my first hit, as I pulled myself smaller, I looked back to see who hit me and why. Of course, he did not like that, and it was against the kitchen rules to look back. So this gave him the reason for more beating; "What is the matter? You are not happy?" he asked me. I was now an offending Jew prisoner in his eyes and now he could use all his power to hit me. These men were well fed prisoners here. On many occasions I saw them exiting the cooking area with bread, margarine and some sausage in their hands. They could steal as much food as they liked, and on the other hand, thousands were dying or had been eliminated because of being underfed.

The rather small and muddy pieces had to be finely and professional peeled. No waste was allowed. Soon I realized this work was the hardest of all. I had not been able to fill up my stomach since my football playing days in Auschwitz, which was many months ago. Looking at these little pieces of vegetables, the stomach pain got even worse with this job from day to day. I could not even think of stealing one piece or even take a bite as my second senses warned me against it.

Sometimes I was called into the cooking room to give a hand. Now I could see with my own eyes how much food was actually there. I would not have believed it if I had not seen it with my own eyes - bread, margarine, sausages and more. The treasury department was not keeping the gold bars as safe as the food was kept here. There was no way of sneaking any food out. This made me even more depressed.

Now that I was a kitchen worker I had to change my barrack. My new home was the barrack number 1 which was identical to the barrack number 4 - on three storeys with three-level bunk-beds, with about 800 to 900 of us living there under bare minimum conditions. We were a mixture of nationalities and professions. As there were more Hungarians here I was able to make some friends and have a bit more social life after work.

Here in this barrack there was a little stove. On the cold nights we could warm ourselves up a bit.

The pig food

One of our roommates was working on the pig farm. This was a fine selection of animals only for the higher ranked SS-officers. The left-over food from the SS canteen was delivered, mixed with bran, and was dampened into a thick paste before giving it to the animals.

I could call myself lucky as I had my own maroon coloured small pot, which I was able to tie to my hip. Having a huge gap where once my abdomen had been, I was able to hide it under my uniform. Not all of us were so lucky but this roommate of mine had his own pot as well.

From time to time he could steal a small amount of pigwash. As this was such thick paste, it did not spill out of the pot from under his uniform. One night he heated up his stolen portion and made the entire barrack smell rather good. He had to guard his pigwash very well from all the hungry looks.

I decided to follow his idea and being a good observer, I decided to steal some potatoes. I wanted to get some more energy, perhaps even put some weight on to stay healthy. I had a plan, I had the tools, and now I just had to deliver it.

I took notice of the habits of the supervisors, the routines of the body searches after work and everything that could possibly be important, to convert my plan into real action.

The vegetable thief

We had been ordered to pack the potatoes, which had been dumped on the court, into big bags. I managed to place some in my pocket and under my uniform at the level of my chest. No one was guarding the work nor the big gate, but I had to pay attention to the windows of the kitchen at the guard houses. I placed the potatoes outside of the main gate frame hoping they would still be there after work, and I was successful. I picked the potatoes up, stuffed them in my pockets and, on the way back to the barrack, hoped I would not cross any SS-guard or any capo. Another occasion I managed to find four flat potatoes. I pulled my shoes off carefully so the guards would not see it and placed two pieces in each shoe, under my feet. It would have been easy to see what I was up to and pay the price for it, but I was determined to stay alive. After work we had to line up for a body search and walk towards the guards. I must have been walking like Fred Astaire as the potatoes had really been pushing on the soles of my shoes but I could not give away my secret. This was my last attempt at stealing.

On that Sunday night I cooked my little potatoes and, with the little margarine from dinner, mashed it up. A teacher friend of mine called Haász from my hometown Debrecen had come to me in a very hungry state. It felt very good to share a few of my stolen vegetables, but he was not the only guest I could help out. It felt good to give even a little from what I had.

That night I had slightly less stomach pain from hunger, and I slept much better. I managed to avoid having nightmares too.

I could have lived on these stolen potatoes as long as I was there, but the Soviet army was closing very fast. This caused a lot of stress amongst our guards and we were the perfect punching bags for them to release some stress. We did not have to give any reason for them to punish us before, but now the number of hits per hour had been multiplied, and the swings has gotten stronger too.

Even the SS-commander of the kitchen had gotten worse, which we did not think could be possible. Later we found out he has lost his family during one air raid. Thereafter, the beating was so brutal we started losing some of our potato peeling colleagues to the hospital. I got many hits too but it did not put me into the hospital. I had many large bruises, especially on my back, and lots of bumps on my head. This was the only place I could be hit as we sat on the concrete ground.

Unfortunately, I was not this lucky every day. From the start of the morning, our guards had been walking up and down behind us. I knew it would be a difficult day as one of the most brutal guards was on "beating duty". I was peeling the potato in my best possible way, when I heard him stop behind me. Suddenly his beating stick landed on the back of my neck with full power. The sharp pain instantly ran down on my entire spine but I was finally able to breathe after the pain eased off. I had to stop halfway during my first breath as the excruciating sharp pain came back right away. I was trying to hold my breath to keep the air in but that was painful as well, so I had to breathe out. I tried again. I breathed in but the pain was there again, so immediately I exhaled. During this time, I had to keep working as well so as not to get another hit on my back. I was about to faint as I had little oxygen in me, but I had to stay conscious and to avoid getting removed from work and being placed into the hospital. During this time my German "executioner" just kept walking along looking very bored.

I do not know how, but I managed to finish my shift. That night, however, I was unable to sleep. My pain did not ease off all night. I had to come up with some solution as I knew I would not be able to go to work the next day, but I also wanted to stay alive. If I went back, I would have a chance of getting beaten up again and perhaps getting some more broken bones, which would be the passport to death. As I was a great observer, my brain worked very fast. There was no roll call at the kitchen. It was not a permanent working place like the factory was. Most of the workers were there only for days or a maximum of a month.

The man of hiding

Next morning my neck felt a bit better but I was very tired from little sleep and also from very little food. I did not go to the line-up and roll call. I was just lingering about. I found myself in front of my old barracks #4, and as I looked inside it was empty. The morning shift had left for work and the night shift had not arrived back yet from the munition factory. The calmness surrounding this huge building invited me to walk inside, I entered and made my way to the lower level. It was tempting to take one of empty beds and just rest and sleep. I knew this was not the best decision as the returning room commander could find me easily and of course I would be punished for it. So, right next to the door I squeezed myself under a bed and stretched myself out on the concrete floor so my head almost touched the base of the bed.

This building was the best place to hide and, as I used to live here, I knew the cleaning routine and I remembered that this room was cleaned very early in the morning. When the night shift was sleeping upstairs our morning shift used to sleep her. I did not have to worry about anyone looking for me here. Of course, I could have been unlucky and if the lager commander had ordered a full camp search, then I would have been caught as a rebel. I assessed the situation and I decided I would give it a go. "It cannot be difficult to lay down," I told myself. However, after the first few hours I realized the truth. The concrete floor was very cold and hard and I could not just get up and go to the toilet without risking running into someone. I had to stay totally silent - no coughing, no sneezing - and awake in case I talked in my sleep or maybe snored. There was not much room under the bad so turning around was not an option either.

My first day of hiding went alright. During lunchtime I climbed out, walked back to my barrack as if I just returned from the kitchen, ate my portion, then sneaked back to the 4th barrack and back under the bed for the rest of the day.

When the day shift arrived back, the shower facilities were opened up and I climbed out from under the bed and joined the workers for a shower to warm up my joints from the stiffness. Next day, I did the same. I walked out of my barrack like I was going to work in the kitchen to peel potatoes, but I had no intention to go back to be beaten up again for no reason. Maybe from the cold concrete, my back felt much better in the morning. However after hours of lying still it had become stiff.

This next day was a bit more eventful. The commander of the barrack had visitors - the other capos. All of them looked very well fed. Some were even overweight. As they sat down in their personalized uniforms they started to talk about the war, where the liberation troops were, politics, and other events that had happened in the camp. I did not understand all the words of their language but understood enough to know the topics. In the meantime, different professional workmen were arriving one after the other - the tailor, the shoemaker, and the barber to shave and to cut hair if needed. The payment for these professionals was bread, potato, salami, or cigarettes. If the commander liked a workman, he could manage to keep him and help them to avoid selection or transition to other camps. In other words, they could manage to keep them alive, just like our football team had been kept alive a few months back.

At lunchtime the commanders placed a few goodies out on a table. I could smell the beautiful foods but I had to be careful not to swallow or not to let my stomach rumble loudly.

One of the commanders had passed a small package around with some explanations about it, and when all had looked at it, he stood up and walked towards my direction to only a few beds away from me. He placed this package under a pillow. Of course, I had become extremely curious and I was hoping it had food inside. There was nothing I needed right now more than food. I decided I would try to get hold of this package and if there was not food in it, I was hoping it held some value for me. By now the hunger pain was more unbearable than any other physical pain. My brain was concentrating on one thing, to feed the body. I started to slide as silently as a snake. I had to be careful otherwise the commanders sitting there would make their death sentence in one second, based on three guilts - unlawful hiding, stealing and the biggest guilt of all which even my uniform stated, being a Jew, a yellow star. This would have been enough to beat me to death.

If they caught me I could not say, "Sorry, I did not read this rule," as there were unwritten rules here. Neither could I say, "Sorry, I was just a bit tired and needed some rest and I'm taking a few days off work." Knowing all this, I still decided to commit to break the rules. My hunger was stronger than my common sense.

The cleaners always did a spotless job. Every morning when they finished collecting the bigger rubbish they washed the concrete, even under the beds. I had hidden there after the cleaning in the mornings, so I did not have to worry about collecting any dust or dirt by crawling slowly.

The target bed was about 10 metres away from me and the barrack commanders were further 3-4 metres away from there. I had to go slowly and soundlessly, but I had a great advantage - the commanders had been drinking schnapps which made the group a bit loud and helped me to stay safe. I needed about one and a half hours to crawl the 10 metres from bed to bed on my back, but finally I was there.

I tried to peek out to see whether they were standing or sitting, and the location of the beds gave me enough cover. I reached up from underneath the bed and I slid my arm slowly under the pillow, millimetre by millimetre, keeping quiet and not making any sound or mistake.

Finally I reached the package under the pillow and my heart started to race from the excitement. EUREKA[67]!!!

I still did not know what was in the package, but I had decided if it was not food then I would try to trade it for food. As I started to pull the package from underneath the pillow it felt very light and I was hoping the contents would not disappoint me. I placed the package under my shirt and started to make my way back to my hiding place. I knew this would take me an hour again but I now had a bit more confidence. I made my way there without notice and now I also had my new treasure too.

I arrived back to the last bed close to the door, which was my former hiding place. I knew it was slightly hidden from the fireplace where the commanders had been sitting. I crawled backwards on my hands and knees like a crab so I could keep an eye on them, and I slowly pushed the door open with my back and sneaked out. As I held the door with my hands and closed it as slowly and as soundlessly as possible, my heart was in racing mode again. I was out safe and sound.

"Sandor, you are a genius. You are one ballsy, crazy man!" I said to myself. "Now let us see what is in the package".   I had to find a good hiding place. After a short browse I settled on the back of an empty barrack. I did not take the package out from under my shirt to open it. I was about to learn that I had become the new owner of 200 cigarettes. It was a whole carton of 10 packs of 20 cigarettes, and they were German made.

The trader

I knew the black-market value of the cigarettes. Every evening you could trade behind the barracks and the cigarettes had the

---

[67] Eureka effect: the sudden, unexpected realization of the solution to a problem

highest value of any tradable items. One box of cigarettes was worth as much as a whole loaf of bread, which meant I could have 10 loaves and finally get rid of the aching pain of hunger - at least for some time.

I went back to my barrack and I had to find a good hiding place for my new treasure. My bed was on the top level, which was very close to the ceiling. I could slide one piece of a tile to the side. After looking around to make sure no one could see what I was doing, I took one box and placed it under my shirt and hid the other nine boxes in the ceiling. I did not know why the barrack commander had placed this gift under someone's pillow. I did not know who the intended receiver was, so therefore I did not have any guilt taking this box. I knew I would be using it to trade for food and knew that perhaps, as I always shared my food, I would help some of my friends.

With this in mind, I took off to trade my first box of cigarettes. I knew I must avoid meeting with the commander who had placed this item under the pillow. It was easy to pick the right prisoners - the skinny ones who had been trying to trade their small piece of bread from dinner just to have one cigarette were not my type of people. I was looking for those looking well and healthy. I knew these people would be able to access the items I needed. I was whispering from ear to ear when finally, I found my man. He did not ask where I got my stuff, neither did I. I had to follow him into his barrack. When I received my bread, I had to pull my non-existing stomach in further to fit it under my shirt. I did not eat the entire loaf of bread. I broke off a small piece and it took me three or four days to finish off the rest. Of course this did not fill me up but it eased my terrible hunger-pain a bit.

I knew I could get almost everything from our "black market". The big "guns" managed to trade everything, even jewellery, and some were trading with the SS-officers too. There were a few civilians who had been working in the camp who had been trading with the prisoners. This, of course, was dangerous and those who got caught had paid a heavy price.

Now I started to imagine I was spreading butter on my bread with a knife. That was a satisfying feeling so I had to get a knife on 'the market' even though I knew it would mean one less loaf of bread to eat. Furthermore, I wanted to have some scissors and a handkerchief. I traded one box of cigarettes for these three items - but I was happiest about the pocketknife.

The delivery men

The next day I sneaked back into my hiding place. Having a bit more food and resting during the day helped me to keep my current physical condition and not to lose more weight and that was the most important for me at that moment.

During lunchtime I sneaked out again and as I was wandering back to my barrack, one commander has asked me to help out with a fellow prisoner. We had to pick up the big wooden barrel with two strong branches and take it to the kitchen. The barrel was then filled with the soup to be delivered for lunch. It was a very difficult task. The barrel was very heavy, and we had to march in synchronized steps so as not to spill the soup. We knew exactly how much treasure we were carrying.

When we arrived at the barracks we received the greeting of Hollywood superstars. Everyone was happy to see us - and the fresh hot soup.

The other good side of being a delivery guy was that we could have the leftovers. We pulled out our spoons and cleaned out the barrel so well we got even some splinters in our mouth from its internal wall as we managed to scrub the fat from the pot.

I liked this job, so next day I lingered around the barrack where the internal workers of the camp were stationed. They worked directly under the barrack commanders. Unfortunately, I was not always selected to be the delivery man. One day I just followed the great smell of the soup. I was trying to get some from the pot but the two delivery guys did not like this so they protested loudly. I pulled back to make sure I did not get punished if a capo heard us. I did, however, follow these guys at a distance. When they arrived at the concrete staircase of the building where they had been ordered to deliver the lunch I turned back with sadness. After a few steps I looked back and saw the younger one of carriers losing his balance at the top of the staircase. As this happened, one of the wooden branches slipped out of the barrel and the soup started to run down the staircase. Like a bullet shot out of a gun I ran towards the building. During the run I managed to untighten my small pot from my stomach area and I placed my dish where the soup was running the fastest. I did not care about the dirt or how many persons' shoes had been walking up and down there. All I cared about was filling up my little pot. The guys saved as much soup as possible and I also managed to fill up. I took a few steps away from the building and started to drink the still warm soup greedily. The fluid filled me up for a few hours and I was happy that with some luck I had managed to keep my weight on again this day.

The lounger[68]

This is how my days went by and I found it easy to find my way around the lager.
It was November now and it had started to get cold. The news from outside was still not what we wanted to hear. The Soviet army was closing in very slowly, too slowly for us.

One morning when I was going to my hiding place I ran into the night shift which was returning to rest. A friend from Debrecen, who happened to have the same first name as mine, spotted me. I jumped into his march and we had a quick chat about ourselves. He asked me to go with him as he was happy to share his bed with me. As the concrete was getting very cold and the position under the bed was very uncomfortable, I accepted his invitation.
His bed was wide enough for our two skeleton bodies, and it felt very comfortable. I was looking forward to a great sleep. He complained to me about his heavy workdays and the constant pain in his abdomen from hunger. I told him my story with

---

[68] a person spending their time lazily or in a relaxed way

which I put him to sleep. I stretched myself out long and felt happy to exchange the cold floor for a warm bed. With this in mind I fell asleep.

We were wakened by SS guards yelling in the barrack. We did not know why this had happened but we had good reason to panic.

The news went around very quickly. They were looking for loungers like myself. It was my unlucky day that I ended up there to escape the concrete floor. Whichever direction I looked there was no way out. Capos and SS-guards were standing in every possible exit. I had to escape from there in some way. The only possible option was the kitchen. With head down and eyes on the floor I just started to walk towards the kitchen while, in the meantime, I was waiting for the call to stop. I was already at the top of the stairs when I had enough guts to stop and look back. Not one guard was looking at me. I sneaked out through the door and again I could not believe my luck. I walked through the kitchen out to the big yard and joined the workers collecting the potatoes which would be cleaned for lunch that day. I promised myself I would be more cautious in the future.

A few days later I found out about the result of the random search. The SS-guards caught 11 men in hiding. We never heard what happened to them but not one of them was seen after that, so it was easy to guess.

To amuse myself after the long days of hiding and after my night shower, I used to walk towards the big gate entrance and watch the arriving day shift workers and the departing night shift workers. Ironically, the marching was accompanied by the music played by the camp orchestra. I studied the faces of the workers marching perfectly as they passed in front of the SS officers with their hats off to show them respect for this camp life. It was like a military parade but without the guns and the salute. I was walking towards the gate, not paying attention to anything or anyone around me as I was deeply in my thoughts. I failed to notice the SS sergeant who was walking in the opposite direction. The rule was to take your hat off if you saw one of the officers and to walk with a great marching posture as a way of respect. A fist-punch to my face awakened me from my deep thoughts - and then more followed. I lifted my arms up to protect myself, but this angered my punisher even more, so he took his machine gun from his shoulder and, with the bump stock of his gun, he started to beat me up. I got onto the ground, but this animal did not stop hitting me. My fellow Jew prisoners were just standing and watching this beating from the distance. A group of Russian war prisoners were the only ones who came to my rescue by yelling loudly at the officer. I think that was the only reason he stopped punishing me for my terrible crime - not paying respect to him by lifting off my hat.

When the beating stopped I could not get up right away. My abdomen was extremely sore. As I rolled over to my elbows and knees I started to cough up blood. When I managed to stop coughing I did a damage check. My lips were split, so was my eyebrow, and I was bleeding from my ears too. "What now?" I asked myself. If I go to the hospital we know how that will end. We did not have the gas chambers any longer but the Nazis had many more ideas of how to get rid of the unwanted specimens. Many had suffered from different illnesses or diseases although they were not visible. I looked awful. My face was swollen and I had bruises on it too. I managed to clean up the blood but now I had more reason not to go into public and to remain in hiding. The lower level where I was hiding was darker than the upper level, so I felt safer there. The way I looked I decided to skip lunch and not to show myself to anyone. I came out of hiding only at night. My wounds, the abdomen pain and the pain from hunger were unbearable, but I had no choice if I wanted to stay alive. I had to keep going hour by hour, day by day. I did not tell anyone about my problem and even in hiding I had to stay quiet. Many times I could have just growled and groaned but this could jeopardize my hiding. On top of all this, the weather turned even colder, the days shorter, and for days it was raining. This worsened my mental state.

Every night we had to line up under the open sky for our roll call. As the sun had already set, big reflectors provided the light for the line-up and the fine rain was very much visible - falling non-stop. No one was able to leave until everyone had been called and responded that they were present.

On one of these winter days we lined up for more than two hours. We did not know the reason for the hold up. Either the numbers did not match or our owners had decided to mentally torture us even more. My abdomen was still very sore from the beating weeks ago. The only way I could ease the pain was placing my hand on the affected area with slight pressure. From the warmness of my hand my abdomen felt a bit better. The officer who was leading the roll call did not care about us freezing in these conditions and as I was not standing in line the correct way, he called me out. As soon as I got to him he delivered a great fist punch onto my face without any warning. Immediately I fell onto my back into the wet mud. I was happy to notice that he moved along, and I did not receive any more of his punishment. "Looks like you are having a bad run, Sándor" I told myself as I got up and moved back into line. There was no way for anyone to forget where he was right now. These little incidents kept reminding us about the reality.

Many could not keep their strong mental state and decided to end their life one way or another. The easiest and most common suicide was to run towards the high voltage fence to deliver a quick and final shock to the system. For some reason I still had enough physical and mental strength to keep going. For how long? I did not know.

The loader

Most of us were working inside the camp in small groups. Some worked at the kitchen, some worked fixing the roads, the roofs, the piping in the showers etc. Some days I joined some of these groups to break up my daily hidings. We had been escorted into a big storage building. Here they were keeping IG Farben[69]

---

[69] **IG Farben**, in full **Interessengemeinschaft Farbenindustrie Aktiengesellschaft**, (German: "Syndicate of Dyestuff-Industry Corporations"), world's largest chemical concern, or cartel, from its founding in Germany in 1925 until its dissolution by the Allies after World War II. - https://www.britannica.com/topic/IG-Farben - In the middle of 1942 a new section of the concentration camp – Auschwitz – Monowitz was established, close to the site of the I.G. Farben works, to house the prisoners working there and thereby save the time-consuming daily march from and to the main camp – Auschwitz 1. - http://www.holocaustresearchproject.org/economics/igfarben.html

products. The different types of chemicals had been stored there in bags and in smaller or larger boxes. We had to move these items from upstairs or downstairs into the underground section. Despite my questioning I did not manage to find out what kind of chemicals were stored there.

It was difficult to carry these heavy items up or down. The guards, of course, did not care about our physical status and they made sure we were not just wandering along with the weight on our shoulders. They managed to speed up our walks with some well-placed hitting on our bodies.

One of my workmates ended up losing his balance and as he dropped the bag it ended up ripping from the fall. Its contents spilled out on the ground. I quickly came to his help and we were trying to scoop the colourless material back into the paper bag. One of the guards had seen what was going on and he came at a fast walk to start punishing us for the damage. I was not ready for another beating so I grabbed my paper bag and walked away as fast as I could. The guard realized that there was only one clumsy person and the other was just helping out to clean up. Unfortunately, sympathy and helpfulness were just as big of a crime then many others.

By now I had received so many beatings in a short time, I did not even notice the pain, only if it had landed on a soft and more sensitive spot.

The doctors in Auschwitz had been performing different types of experiments on the human body. The endless human transports had been able to provide enough guinea pigs for them. One of the experiments was how to reverse human evolution and turn us back to be a cave man. For this they locked people for months and months into the same sort of cage as you could see in the zoo. They lived there without shaving, without washing themselves, and the food and water had been given to them at specific times. During the night they were woken up by the prodding of an iron bar and they had to walk up and down in their cage.

Of course, a cave man thousands of years ago did not shave and ate raw food. However he did not live in a metal cage but in freedom, he drank fresh water from creeks and lakes and, in his cave, no one had been poking him with an iron bar.

Outside of these the small cages, thousands of us were living in a bigger cage. We had been closed away from the world with one of the greatest inventions of the 20th century, the electric barbwire fence. The Nazis had tried to turn everyone there to become wild humans, but the wild humans were the taskmasters - the capos and the various officials. They had been beating, hitting and torturing us inhumanly. Sadistic joy had been flickering in their eyes when they saw the suffering of the victims as they lay in pain on the ground before them. They also differed from the prehistoric man in that the cave man fought or killed only when it came to killing his prey to ease his hunger or to defend himself his family, his herd and his hunting ground. The wild people in this camp were the well-fed who were beating and killing for fun and to satisfy their souls.

Christmas in the camp

It was the end of 1944. The camp was getting ready for Christmas. One day a truck arrived with a large pine tree. It was erected as a Christmas tree opposite the main entrance to the lager.
As Christmas is the celebration of peace and love as well, I believed in it, and during the days, I often walked towards the tree. I thought it would give me and many others a bit of safety in the camp. I wanted to believe that on these few days, these beasts would suspend everything which was cruel and deadly. Something involuntarily pulled me towards the Christmas tree. I had not seen trees, bushes or flowers for months. I do not even know what attracted me to the green clothed tree. Was it its colour, or was I hoping to draw strength from it? I could not decide. On the other hand, I did not want to reject the influence of the Christmas tree. This symbol of peace did not fit well in place - on the main square of the concentration camp. Here, where so many people's lives had been destroyed and so many had been killed, the Christmas tree, which is known as a symbol of peace in family homes, looked odd and strange.

Our SS guards did not skimp on Christmas tree decorations. They even brought a long ladder to decorate the many-metre tall tree. I must admit it was well decorated with well-placed bright and shiny adornments. It even had colourful lights on it. During the night it looked so magnificent it could have been placed on any mayor city's main square.

It had been erected many days before Christmas while the tired and exhausted workers had been marching by to and from their 12-hour daily work shifts. This was probably done for psychological reason too. I believe they wanted to use this to further punish and weaken the mentally and physically broken prisoners. When something that was deliberately organized has unfortunate outcomes for people, it is fairly certain that there were some dark thoughts behind it.

On a quiet, sunny winter Sunday morning, the leadership of the camp invited the occupants of the entire camp to a musical outdoor performance. The large camp orchestra was dressed up in snow-white outfits and started to perform beautiful pieces often played at this time of year. When they started to play the Blue Danube Waltz my uniform started to feel very tight, so I had to undo the collar button of the shirt as I felt it was suffocating me. My entire skin felt painful and itchy in this uniform and more than ever I was longing for my freedom. I am sure I was not the only one.

Here, where millions of lives had been ended, the music composed by Johann Strauss did not match and was not appropriate to the location. This music was created by a fantastic creative mind for dance and joy, but now the dark mind of The Third Reich was using it for the further destruction of our souls. After this night we all started to talk about our home, our families, our past happy Christmases, the presents we had given or received, the happy faces of the young children and, of course, the great choice of food.

When the shifts were marching in and out of the camp, they had to walk past the tree. Many of the sad faces that looked stealthily at the decorated tree couldn't help but think of the warmth of their home, the pine tree they had decorated with great care year after year, the kids with sparkling eyes, the gifts placed under the tree, the warm soup, or the fragrant smell of the steak emanating from the kitchen.

I do not know whether it was because of the spirit of Christmas or for any other reason, but five prisoners attempted to break out of this prison. Unfortunately, this outbreak was unsuccessful, and all five prisoners were captured alive. This act was punishable by death. Although they belonged to a Christian nation, the Germans camp leaders simply disregarded the sanctity and peacefulness of Christmas.

They no longer cared about the peaceful atmosphere of Christmas and instead they appointed some prisoners to construct the gallows. The assigned workers from the camp had a great helper - one of the notorious SS officers whom I knew back from my football career, the one with large front teeth that protruded like a shovel. In addition to his 'signature' look he had an outstanding character. He was known to hit defenceless prisoners the hardest of all. There were SS officers who did not look brutal but this particular one had a look which could easily have imposed a 10-year imprisonment. The whole lager was afraid of him. When he got drunk, he even dragged sleeping prisoners out of bed and beat them into a bloodbath. When he got tired of beating he would look at his victim with joy and admiration of his own latest "artwork". Whenever I was able to do so, I stayed far away from him. This officer had put his comfortable life aside and was showing off his great carpentry skills by assisting to build the wooden structure of the gallows. The camp leaders had taken off their human-like face masks, and now the sight of the five hanging ropes overshadowed the beauty of the Christmas tree.
So, it was as it was supposed to be. We had not clothed ourselves in the Christmas illusion any longer. The tall pine tree could be splendid with all of its glitter, but the hate inside us was growing greater towards the person who had instructed the erection the Christmas tree and who had ordered the erection of the gallows.

We felt the camp leaders had been preparing for a big play. They were excellent organizers and directors. The big performance took place in the late afternoon of Christmas eve.
It was a cold, snowy and foggy evening when the day shift workers arrived back into the camp. The searchlights had been lit

up and even their strong lights were having difficulty cutting their way through the thick fog.

An announcement called for all prisoners to make their way to the main square. We all lined up in long queues opposite the gallows. Many thousands of prisoners had been waiting for this development silently and wordlessly.

Next to us the Christmas tree had been lit up in its colourful lights and one reflector had been directed to shine on the gallows to draw more attention on it. No one any longer paid attention to the red, green, yellow and many other colours that dressed the tree - we were all thinking about our five fellow inmates. When they were escorted out they took a short peek at the tree but their fearless look gazed directly at us. The five 'death-sentenced' carried their gaze all the way to the many thousands of their prison comrades. They wanted to help us in these moments as well. Their heads and eyes acknowledged us encouragingly. They could not make signs with their hands, as they were bound tightly behind their backs. The anxiety and the deflated feelings of the crowd of thousands was the opposite of the brave behaviour of the five prisoners who did not beg or look for mercy, but stood without batting an eye under the five hanging ropes. They did not break as the organizers had wanted. The performance would have gone perfectly if they had.

The five sentenced were put on five high boxes. The five nooses were placed around their necks at the same time. The SS hangman placed the ropes with the greatest care on their necks. A command was uttered, but before the boxes could be kicked out from under their feet, the five of them yelled out clearly and loudly together, like they had rehearsed it, "To the defeat of Fascism, death to Fascists!"

We could clearly hear their last wish. This was their last will. This was heard by all in the camp - prisoners and our arrogant guards alike. With the utterance of the last word, five of our companions going to death also pronounced the death sentence on the guards. They foretold that the end of the Nazi regime would come - only the date wasn't marked. We knew that the power of the fascists was weakening, that the time would come when these people would shiver from fear and hide and wait for judgement. They would certainly not be so brave. They would not dare face the executors of their judgement so heroically. They would crawl and slide on their bellies to avoid liability. In a short amount of time, we had got to know so much about them. We got to know their characters. We took our hats off during the execution act, which was over quickly. We took one goodbye look at the swinging lifeless corpses of our five fellow inmates. On this cold Christmas night, the 24th of December 1944, we sadly left their stiffened bodies and went past the Christmas tree with our heads down.

Next morning, we did not have to go out for a roll call and the ones who had been here for longer told us about the special Christmas lunch. We did not know the menu and not even the best informed were able to find out, but everyone was excited and full of hope. All necessary items had been cleaned and were ready to receive the Christmas special lunch.
One of our barrack inmates ran inside the building. He was sent out to keep eye on the "present". "They are coming, and they are bringing two different containers!" he yelled out with much excitement.
"What? Are we receiving a two-course lunch?" asked one inmate.
"Where are we going to put the second course?" asked another, "I have only one thin cup".
"I know," said another "Here" and he pulled his cap off his head, and everyone else followed.
"Problem solved," I said, and we all had a small smile which was very rare around there.
The menu was cooked potato with gravy. I pulled out my pocket knife which I had traded earlier for the cigarettes and sliced the potatoes into the gravy. I enjoyed the great smell of the food and began my slow lunch. I wanted to enjoy this meal as much as possible and for as long as possible. For a long time, I did not feel full after meals but this time it had some ingredients which finally did the job. Since I could not risk working and stealing from the kitchen, I had to be happy with the so-called soup. This was a great Christmas gift from the camp leaders.

Everybody's mood was much better. There was some joking around too. It was difficult to describe how much a good meal could lift the spirit for all of us. I lay down to have a good nap and I thought about the next year. I could not wait another 365 days to have a good meal. On the other hand, I knew I would not spend the next Christmas in Auschwitz. Maybe our camp leaders would be spending their next holiday season behind bars. At least I hoped so.

I did not know if I would live until the next Christmas because it was clear that Auschwitz and the other camps would be closed by then. The news from the fronts was clear - Germany would lose this war too.[70]

The second day of Christmas was not a day off anymore, so all working groups had to get back to their 12-hour shift work. And me? I went back to hide under the bed. The lunch from the day before was gone and my stomach was empty again. I had traded all my cigarettes so I could not even get some more bread.

A few days later we celebrated the New Year. We did not have anything to pour into our tin cups and "clink our glasses", but the camp leaders did. They had already started the celebration by midday. Maybe they knew it was their last New Year's celebration and they would no longer be able to do to other humans whatever they wanted. Later that afternoon they were very drunk and they lingered around the lager to look for some victims to satisfy their sadistic tendencies. I did not go to bed. I hid behind it. Luckily, they did not come into our barrack - only their loud voices. It was early morning when the lager finally became silent.

A new calendar appeared on to the wall. It had '1945' written on it; but we had to keep the days in our mind. We knew this year would be the decider of our fate. We would either be rescued or we would vanish with the other millions. Either way, it would bring us closure.

In the early days of January I received the tip of an upcoming thorough camp search. The guards knew there had been a lot of

---

[70] **1944, Dec 26** Budapest surrounded by Soviet army. 1944, Dec 31 World War II: Hungary declares war on Germany.

prisoners in hiding. This tip later became well known to all in the lager. Maybe the guards had started to become more conscious about their situation. By now everyone knew the Nazis would lose the war sooner or later. Maybe they hoped all those in hiding would come forward and present themselves for work to avoid any punishment.

I gave up with the illegal hiding and I presented myself to work. I joined a mixed group of men. I did not know who they were and what kind of work they were doing, I just moved into the back of a line. There were a few more who decided to do the same and we all looked very new to this bunch. We did not get too much questioning from the existing group at all. They just let us join in.

We exited the lager through the main gate and walked up to a pile of rocks. Everyone picked up a large piece and we walked out onto the road- which was not new to me. This road was the same as I had used to walk to the ammunition factory. We did not get that far. We ended up turning into a factory building which had the sign "DAV" on it. Large halls were located in different parts of the courtyard. We were escorted to a big pit where we dropped our rocks. The job was to fill up this pit. When we finished we waited patiently for our next task.

A grey-haired, broad-shouldered SS-officer arrived at our group and said: "If anyone has knowledge of furniture and joinery-making, step forward". I did not think for too long, I had been in this situation in the past. I had enough courage and bravery to try another profession, even if they found out about my pretended knowledge and I could potentially lose and get punished. I was probably more confident now that the crematorium had been demolished, or because we could feel the easing of the brutality in the camp. The German alliances had been losing ground day after day, and the Nazis had been losing their confidence too.

I stepped out of the line with a few others. Of course, none of us looked like professional furniture makers. By now all of us looked like living skeletons. Even a surgeon would not look like a medical professional, so this officer took us to an underground fabricating place in a large hall. This was a well-equipped place where you could find all necessary tools and machinery like a circular saw, planer, and many hand tools as well. All workers there were inmates and prisoners as well. The other thing I realized as we stepped inside from the winter cold was that this place was heated. Right away I felt the need to become part of this workplace which felt quite different from the death camp. The smell of the wood and the glue was making this place feel more homely than all the other factories I had been to so far. While awaiting further instructions we looked around trying to find out as much information as possible about the workers there. Of course, this was not easy. They all looked like everyone else, except the hair. They had a 5 to 6 centimetre shave at the top of the head. They all worked like professionals, so I assumed they had been working there for a while now.

Our officer came back to us and asked: "Do any of you know anything about locksmith or metalwork?"

I was the only one who stepped forward and I was relieved that I knew more about this profession than cabinetmaking.

He started to ask me questions in German, but I could only mumble for a while - then I changed over to Hungarian. To my biggest surprise he started to talk to me in Hungarian, fluently. Seeing my surprised face, he said "I'm originally from Kolozsvár[71]. Now answer my questions. Where are you from, and where have you worked?"

He was probably pleased with my responses and asked me to follow him. We went through an open area into another factory. He talked to one of the work foremen and left. I never saw him again. The foremen asked me a bunch of questions, but he soon realized I did not speak German very well. He made a wave with his hand to shut me down, then he asked me to follow him. We came to a very tall and strong looking inmate - then he left us as well. My new boss was a Russian prisoner, again. He showed me the way to my new workstation. I had to drill three symmetrical holes into door hinges. He pointed at a large pile of hinges in a box and luckily the drilling machine did not need too much knowledge to be operated. I was happy with this new job. The

---

[71] Cluj-Napoca (Romanian) is a former city of the Hungarian Kingdom known as Kolozsvár is the fourth most populous city in Romania. On 11 October 1944 the city was captured by Romanian and Soviet troops. It was formally restored to the Kingdom of Romania by the Treaty of Paris in 1947. The earliest Hungarian artifacts found in the region are dated to the first half of the 10th century.

Russian showed me how to do it then he went back to his job. I pulled the first hinge out of the box, started the machine, and I drilled the first hole, but I was unable to stop the driller. I probably did not pay enough attention to my master. I was trying to twist and turn every button, handle or lever I could find on the machine, but nothing happened. Now I probably looked worse than an apprentice. I started to sweat heavily and looked left and right seeking some assistance. The man at the next station came to my rescue. Now I knew how to start and stop this drilling machine. However, I did not manage to drill the three holes symmetrically on the hinge. The more I tried, the worse it got. My Russian boss came to see my work a few times and he'd probably had enough of my bad performance, as it spoiled his perfect performance, and that of his team. He grabbed my hand and showed me to follow him. He took me to the front of this large hall where a bunch of workers were cleaning large 60 to 70 centimetre metal boxes for bullets. The boxes were rusty and with the given sandpaper we had to make them clean, then cover them with beige textile. The number of ammunition boxes which had been piled there was endless. During this very physical and boring work I managed to familiarize myself with this very large, cold hall. On one end the prisoners were working with different large metal fabricator machines and at our end we were performing restoration work on the ammunition boxes.

This workplace also had fewer SS-guards and capos, but the food was the same - un-filling soup. The IG-Farben [72] and the Krupp[73] company owners and shareholders probably made a lot of money from the cheap workforce who were fed with soup and had been constantly replaced after being found unfit for work. With the 12 hours of constant work and close to no food we lost our weight rapidly and with it, our good immune system. We

---

[72] I.G. Farben was a German Limited Company that was a conglomerate of eight leading German chemical manufacturers. In its heyday, IG Farben was the largest company in Europe and the largest chemical and pharmaceutical company in the world.

[73] The **Krupp** family, a prominent 400-year-old German dynasty from Essen, have become famous for their production of steel, artillery, ammunition, and other armaments. The family business, known as Friedrich **Krupp** AG, was the largest company in Europe at the beginning of the 20th century. It was important to weapons development and production in both world wars.

needed only a few months to look the way we all did, but some of us managed to keep surviving for a longer period.

The Water of Auschwitz

From a swamp, like a rotten taste when you drink,
Can't use it even to wash, should go down the sink.
The dweller of the camp is given this dirt,
A few drops given to the throat between hurt.
Bacillus adheres to the unwashed skin and dirt,
Purulent wounds, lice and flees under the shirt.
Typhus and tuberculosis have its breathing ground,
Fresh water would clean the flesh wound.
We are hungry but only about water we can think,
Our dry throat doesn't want to eat, want water to drink.
Many are dying but they don't get either,
Their cracked lips don't make the SS nicer.
We are thirsty, we want only aqua,
Nearby rumbling the full bed of Vistula.
The river roars, its noise can be heard here,
But only the cows and the SS can it commandeer.
Water surrounds the numerous swimmers,
We envy them during the weak dinners.
Millions are on the beach, enough water for everything,
So many superfluous it is a torment just to think.
Birkenau, Auschwitz, waterless days,
Dreamless nights, suffering ways.
To stop at a well, pull up water constantly,
To drink from the cold water endlessly,
I would not exchange for treasure, I would give everything,
In exchange for water, water to drink and worshiping.

Three pieces of pork crackling [74]

A well-fed SS-officer with a monocle [75] stepped inside the hall. Behind him followed his best friend - a large dog, unleashed. The officer had been watching everyone and everything from right to left with eagle eyes. The workers were looking towards him from the corners of their eyes with hate, but not one would disobey the rules - work, work, and more work. He did not seem to find any abnormalities, so he continued to walk through the hall. He was near my station when he stopped. He reached into his pocket and pulled out a piece of paper. He opened it up and took three pieces of crackling out of it, then he threw it front of his dog. Living on the weak soup for months I had not seen any solid food since the Christmas potato presents and I became extremely excited to see the pork skin pieces. The dog looked down on the ground, poked his nose at them and with a small movement of his big nose took a few sniffs at them. He must not have been hungry at all as he left his master's gift on the concrete floor and walked after him. When they had walked a safe distance from me, I launched myself at the leftover food and shoved one of the bits of crackling into the safety of my mouth. I had no time to do the same with the other two pieces as my inmates jumped at me and twisted them out of my hands. I was very unhappy to lose such a great gift from this four-legged animal that had showed more mercy and humanity than the two-legged guards. I made sure not to grind it quickly, I sucked on it for hours to enjoy its taste. I felt fuller than I had been in the last few months just from the constant taste of that piece of skin and believed I had become stronger too. The restoration work felt easy after this little dessert. Unfortunately, I did not meet this gentleman dog again.

Soon we received a small break and we had our lunch. I decided to explore the factory and also to look for some familiar faces. I knew there was an elderly joiner named Lusztig from my hometown who used to work here. Unfortunately, Mengele had pulled him out of the line on that October selection day and he

---

[74] Roosted pork skin

[75] A monocle is a type of corrective lens used to correct or enhance the visual perception in only one eye.

was sent to be gassed. I did not find anyone I knew from the few Hungarians, but I started to talk to a younger man from Győr[76] and we kept finding each other's company during further breaks. We mostly talked about food and the hope of the Soviet army's fast arrival and the possibility of freedom. However, we did not talk about our families. We were quite sure that we had lost them already and did not hold much hope about their survival.

As we waited for the liberation army we were afraid of the final days and the evacuation of the camp. We knew how much the Nazis had been keeping us under their surveillance and how much they did not want any of us in the hands of the Allies. More survival meant more evidence against themselves.

The Soviet offensive had started and it caused different levels of excitement amongst everyone. The guards feared being held accountable for the atrocities they had committed against many prisoners, and for us the hope of salvation kept the prisoners excited.

With a young fellow we met, we planned an escape and considered the possibility of hiding during the last hours of the camp. We found and designated a few different hiding places here in the hall and outside of it as well. The question we considered was for how many days would we have to hide after the evacuation, and if we would be able to survive many days without food. We also speculated how the evacuation would be done, with or without resistance, and whether we would be kept alive or maybe all of us would be killed. Until that day I had to keep rubbing the metal boxes with sandpaper.

This also made me realize how technologically different the work was organized here. We were using physical work with the sandpaper, but at the next station the boxes had been painted with proper spray guns.

The good thing was that in the new workstation we could talk to each other during work if we had the breath to do so, and I believed the reason why this was so was because we did not have any female workers, hence no female guards. They had

---

[76] Halfway between two of Europe's most elegant capitals (Budapest and Vienna) lies **Győr**, a charming Hungarian **city**. The **city** once served as a fortress to defend Vienna from Ottoman invasions.

been more brutal than the male guards. The bad thing here was that it was extremely cold and it was difficult to rub the boxes. Boxes not perfectly cleaned were returned to us. I even received a few back with some aggressive words from a co-worker. Luckily I did not understand any of what he said, nor did he understand my response. I never agreed with the treatment we have received from our guards but I have put it down to them being our enemies. However, I never understood why inmates would be aggressive or brutal to each other and display no solidarity at all. Without a fellow inmate's humanity, suffering was even more painful. The Nazis always kept their eye out for some "carrier hungry" individuals. This kind of "volunteer policeman" made their life enjoyable and easier. They did not have the sufficient number to overlook the whole camp and they enjoyed watching the prisoners beat each other up.

I saw with my own eyes a capo beat up another weakened inmate in front of an SS-guard. The guard did nothing, just stood there with pleasure on his face, knowing his work was being done internally by someone else. Of course, this behaviour has backfired. When we all had to leave the camp to move west, they did not receive any special treatment. These capos became unfit, soft and mentally weak when the tough times arrived. I did not want to be gloating towards them because their fate was sealed more certainly. For helping to make everyone else's life even more painful they hoped to get some special treatment, but at the end we all walked together into the march of death.

The detective

It was mid-January 1945 [77] when there was more and more excitement amongst the prisoners. We even heard that some SS-

---

[77] Jan 2 1945 Allied air raid on Nuremberg, Jan 4 Germans execute resistance fighters in Amsterdam, Jan 12 German forces in Belgium retreat in Battle of Bulge, Jan 12 The Soviets begin a large offensive against the Nazis in Eastern Europe, Jan 16 **Adolf Hitler** moves into the

guards were already packing their bags. On this Sunday I found out for sure about the liquidation of the camp. The work had finished in the early afternoon and we had returned to the camp. I was walking around in the camp with open eyes as I knew fateful days were approaching. I took my route towards the showers. I saw a few guards carrying heavy bags towards the water boiler room and emptying them inside it. When they have gone to get some more, I became interested about their load. I pushed down the door handles and when I stepped inside the semi-dark room all I could see on the ground were thousands of pink cardboard filing papers. I looked around and as I had not seen anyone, I picked up a bunch of them and slid them inside my striped uniform. I sneaked out and looked for a safe place to see what these were, and why they wanted to burn them. These were evidence of crime, which they had to destroy. On the filing cartons there where the numbers which had been tattooed on the arms of each prisoner who had survived the first selection on the ramp upon arrival and into the camp and had been selected for work. Furthermore, the information showed where the person had been rostered for work, age, nationality and finally the medical diagnosis for each person who had passed away. They all died from **Tuberculosis**[78], according to these papers. This is how they tried to cover up the millions of murders. The pink filing cartons contained a registration of all those who lost their strength during the 12-hour shifts and were selected to be gassed by the lager's main doctor, Mengele. This is how he diagnosed and treated those who were sick.

All these documents had been perfectly recorded using typewriters and kept on file. I had experienced incredible luck not to be registered on one of these pink documents too. It was dangerous to keep these documents with me, so I decided to take them back. I managed to place many of my nameless inmate's death certificates back onto the floor of the water boiler room. Not long after that the smoke of the boiling room was visible. This time they did not burn human bodies but instead the

---

Fuhrerbunker, his underground bunker in Berlin, 15 Jan 1945 Red Army frees Crakow-Plaszow concentration camp; **17 Jan 1945 SS-units begin the final evacuation of prisoners from Auschwitz concentration camp, marching them on foot towards the interior of German Reich.**
[78] **Tuberculosis** (TB) is a disease caused by bacteria called **Mycobacterium tuberculosis**. The bacteria usually attack the lungs, but they can also damage other parts of the body.

documents of human lives - the final records of their evil work. From the smoke of the chimney, there was no longer any doubt that the Germans had to flee from Auschwitz.
A few more hours or a few more days and the crucial time would follow.

The Concentration camp

Our body is eaten by lice, scabies, has infected scars,
From the SS whips our skin has deep, long marks.
Skinny, weak, lethargic, hardly existing,
Body feels heavy but still is (continue to) persisting.
To be alive ourselves we course,
Suffering, torment cannot be worse.
Death sentenced, but first they kill our soul,
Terrible feeling to be in this dark hole.
Gas-chambers, ovens will be our final destiny,
Flesh will melt of the bone before exiting, heavenly.
Till skeleton we can have amnesty,
Convicted by Hitler, this is the reality.
Heated furnaces of the Death Factory,
Millions disappeared without registry.
The Globe did not raise this many executioners before,
To hand out death, the Fascism was their mentor.
Mercy and grace are lacking in their hearts,
Medal of Honour for whom kills most, becomes art.
The letters of their Psalm teach them destruction,
Their Bible embraces to kill as misconstruction.
Scull and crossbones on their flag, their land is soaked with blood,
Their stone heart rejoices at death, their hand is clean, not even mud.
They become babies born of a mother,
Raised and trained SS-soldier and brother.
They wanted to become the Lord of the entire World,
To create concentration camps as their Underworld.

But the truth-seeking Heroes smashed it to grounds,
Their home, fences, playground became battleground.
Memorial columns warning at the camp site,
No more Fascism, No mor war, No more fight!

The march of death

The 18th day of January 1945 was a very cold morning. I was
ready to get dressed to go to work when the commander of the
lager walked into the barrack and stood in the middle of it. This
always meant he was ready to announce something important.
"Today we will be evacuating the lager," he started his
announcement. "Everyone must leave. Only the sick can stay
behind. The camp management will ensure the safety of
everyone. No one will be hurt," he stated. We knew the Red
Army was closing in, and we also knew how many lies the
Germans would tell to avoid panic.
Soon this place would be in the hands of the liberating army and
the whole world would find out about the secret of this horrible
place.
The SS leaders and the officers of the camp started to flee in
panic. Amongst them was Dr Mengele. He had to remove his
arrogant and confident mask. He was shaken. He denied his
rank and was running away from prosecution. Of course, he
carried with him his files of the medical research which he had
been conducting on live humans. He sought the help an
assistance of the Third Reich believers to be hide him and get
him out of the country.

Dr Mengele

Slender figure, pedantic elegance
With spread legs on the Auschwitz ramps,
Millions floating in his way
Left or Right - Mengele sway.
His well-groomed hand swings to kill
His heart does not tremble at the sight of a few mill.
His smile reassures with confidence
The uninformed crowd gently listens.
Stroking children's heads with kind encouragements,
Soon baby, mother will follow you in the chambers.
He turned his medical oath into lies,
For healing he recommended gas.
Wagons are arriving, opening the barrier,
On the ramp stands by the executioner.
He stands there in shiny boots, very tall,

Smokes his cigarette waiting for arrival.
He deals death in three shifts with his hands,
Four million got into gas with his judgements.
But Soviet tanks have arrived at the ramp,
He lowered his arm and the coward has fled.
He has run, he hides, trembling in Patagonia,
He found shelter in South America.
He lives there, hiding from four million Jews,
The executioner is terrified by the death curse.
Who handed out the approval of slaughters,
He covers his face even amongst monsters.
Let the thickness of the Jungle be his grave,
Only to be given death by a tiger's claws crave,
May the viper's venom speed through his bloodstream,
His bone and flesh devoured by a vulture team.

23rd April 1970, Debrecen, Hungary

In the last few days the camp leaders destroyed as much
evidence as they could but with little success. There was way too
many evidence and not enough time to complete the job. This
few hundred square-metre camp, where more than 2.5 million
people lost their lives, remains indestructible evidence forever.
We could not pull off the planned hiding as we were not
escorted to work into the DAV-factory. No one could leave the
camp, and this was not the right place to try to hide. The only
possibility was to hide amongst the sick and terminally ill and
wait for the liberating army to arrive in a matter of days. Of
course, this had its own risk. I could not assume that the SS-
leaders of the camp would leave all the sick alive to be found by
the Soviet army. We were sure every one of them would be
killed.
A few months after my liberation I found out that the sick left
behind in Auschwitz were kept alive and the liberating Soviet
army found all the celebrated living skeletons. The few hundred
mortified prisoners were left behind without any harm.
I never found out for what tactics or reason these beasts choose
to act with humanity. Their motto was to destroy everyone and
everything who knew their secrets, sins, evil deeds and

malfeasance. The sick and chronically ill were in such a bad state that their captors may have thought they would not survive, or maybe they suffered from bad time management and, in the hurry, they had no time left to kill all of them. The SS rank was more concerned about their safety and to flee themselves was more important.

I could not rely on my sixth sense working well, but in this case, I would have saved myself months of inhumane suffering. I did not know this, so I also had to stand in the line of thousands marching out of the camp. Before the marching, our leaders managed to organize a huge number of guards who would be looking after our "safe" retreat.

The inside of the lager looked like a beehive with people coming, going and packing. We spent a day in groups. Our secret hopes might not come true. We had been waiting for the liberating army and for the local partisans about whom we had been hearing for so long, to arrive. We hoped for a quick attack which would make the retreat impossible. These hopes had been lost by the late afternoon when dark started to settle in and we all had to get in line. There was no longer any organization about where to stand in the line like there was for barrack or work groups. We could stand wherever we wanted. I did not know too many around me but there were many Hungarians. As I looked forward and behind me, all I could see was a long line of living skeletons waiting to be marched out of the camp into the unknown. It was a very cold night and we all stood there with arms around our chest, in our uniforms and our shoes with wooden soles. We had no jackets or anything else to keep us warm. I was dancing from one leg to the other. The cold was biting the skin on my face and on my hands, but it had also sneaked under my clothes. I wished to be back in the barrack right now and being under the blanket, but on the other hand I wanted to leave this place as fast as possible. I had to force myself to give up my principles when the minus 18 to 20 Celsius cold started to bite my skin.

Among the many torments this camp had provided, I could no longer determine what was easier or harder to endure. I believed this was the idea behind all the mental and physical beating and suffering that the Third Reich had managed to put everybody through in this place. Just think of the Sonder-commando workers, who had been loading dead bodies into the crematorium's burning fire for three months. Many recognised their father or mother, siblings, or any other relatives or close friends as they carried out this task. They also knew their three months "contract" with the Nazi regime would be soon over and they would be loaded into the fire the same way.

Picture from:

It had become dark by the time the line started to move along. I wanted to stretch my steps to get some blood flowing into my limbs as I hardly could feel them by now. Each line was formed by five prisoners and I was on the right outside. When we arrived at the main gate there was one thought in my mind: "Sandor, you are a lucky man. Millions came in through this gate but not one person has ever has walked out of it." I managed to stay alive and left this place behind on this very cold January night.

Around me, everyone was in the same stripy uniform, everyone's lips were purple from the cold and everyone, representing many European nations - Polish, Greek, Italian, Hungarian, Russian and more - was as skinny as a skeleton. We did not expect much good from the night or the days ahead. Under my feet, the shiny road, which had become flat and slippery from the hundreds marching before me, crackled. I had to be careful how I placed the wooden soled shoes on it so as not to slip and fall. We had already left the gate, but we were still on camp land when we had to stop. I smelled freshly baked bread in the air. The bakery of the lager must have been working overtime to provide food for the hundreds of guards for the long march ahead. I was dreaming about some nice warm fresh bread when tremendous noise distracted me. As I looked around everyone had left their lines and suddenly chaos had broken out on everyone. The lager's bakers were throwing freshly baked bread towards us. The bread was for us, but it was hard to get. People were fighting for a piece and the strongest and fastest had an advantage. I managed to catch one flying slab of fresh bread and immediately hid it under my uniform. The fresh warm bread warmed my skin, at least on a small area. The flour was no use for us on a long walk and would have been difficult to carry anyway, so this was our goodbye dinner thrown at us to fight for.

Some could hardly get up after the fist fight for the bread. This provided one more last "enjoyable performance" for our guards. The bread could have been given to us in the usual and more organized and civilized way, but that would have meant no joy for our guards. At least I had forgotten the cold during this improvised entertainment, but as soon things started to calm down, I started to feel the extreme cold again. The warm bread under my shirt made me feel happy. I decided I would apportion my bread sparingly during the walk. I would not be acting like some of the others who did not apportion their acquired piece but ate all of it at once without thinking about tomorrow.

They started to re-organize our lines. The brutal beating started again, beating sticks flying and landing on many, mixed with loud yelling. There were only SS-guards, no capos or any other prominent members were helping them out. I quickly took my place in the line but this time, although I had different people around me, we still all looked alike, skinny living skeletons in striped uniforms. The fight was still going on about the bread in some places. In line with me, three rows ahead, one prisoner on the side of the line was still not in-line and he was still arguing. One of the SS-guards reached into his gun pocket, pulled out his revolver and shot the man in the abdomen. He hunched over, yelled for a few seconds then his blood painted the white snow red as he fell on his knees first then on his side. We all watched his last few shakes in shock before he passed away. This happened very close to me, but I could do nothing for him - just to look at his killer with bitterness.

We had not even walked out of the shadow of the lager and the killing had started. Of course, the promise to keep all of us in safety was another lie just to get everyone quietly into line and to avoid panic. What would happen during the rest of the marching I asked myself?

On both sides of the lines we had numerous SS-guards practicing their target shooting as they walked along. A Polish location was our destination. We reached it with a march of two days and two nights. We had lost many inmates along the way. Our walk was marked with dead bodies from start to finish, on both sides of the road.

On the first night we did not hear too many gunshots. As our muscles were capable of functioning, we could combat the cold by the walking. However, on the second day the weaker ones started to lose their strength and they started to slow down and fall behind. Everyone knew what would happen to them. Everyone was trying to stay with the group but not all could do so. Even the weak ones did not give up easily. They started to grab onto stronger ones who helped them for a while, but even they had to let them go if they did not want to fall behind as well. This happened all around me. The weak ones were praying and asking for help desperately. The fear of death had set on their faces, but more and more of them ended up on the side of the road. After our passing, the residents of the Polish village collected our lost colleagues.

I had been nibbling a small amount of bread from time to time. This did not cure the pain of my hunger but it did help to ease it a bit. I endured the first night's marching well, but I was freezing. I was trying to stay in line during this very boring and monotonous walk. I did not want to multiply my suffering by thinking of warm rooms or food. I was dedicating my entire mind to fighting against the cold and to overcome my tiredness and survive this march.

This could be achieved only with great self-discipline. During the march I was able to move my entire body as I had practised it on the football field, and now I was able to use it to my advantage. The long training runs now helped me out so many years later. My muscles were able to adapt very well.

The winter night slowly broke to dawn with lots of effort from the morning sun. I was waiting for the daylight as the march did not feel so scary then. The guards were more cautious with their killing as well, especially around the villages, because they liked to kill without witnesses. However the evidence was left behind on the side of the road. During the second day they did not care about witnesses any more. There was too many fatigued prisoners and we heard and witnessed more and more gunshots. My legs and lungs had been working perfectly, however something had happened to my neck. Maybe the injury I received from the guard in the kitchen when he has punished me for nothing had returned, and now I was sure he broke my neck. Every now and then I felt I could not hold my head up any longer. I had to walk with my head down. This made my walking more difficult. The long stretches of the road between the curves looked very long and endless. We did not stop for one second. They did not let us to sit down at all. We were forced to walk non-stop. We were in a hurry. It was not clear why we had to be on this "rescue mission". We did not have to escape or hide, only our guards had to do so. Perhaps the great big Germany needed these living skeletons for something else. It looked like we had not been used enough yet.

By the afternoon of the second day more and more had fallen behind the marching line. Our guards did not miss any of them. The targets were close and still, only a few centimetres away. It was impossible to miss the shot.

The lines started to become thinner and a very skinny young boy became my new walking partner. I did see him in the morning, but back then he was still walking with his father in arm, supporting each other. I did speak a few words to them. They had been deported from Békés-county.[79] His father had owned a tailor workshop back at home. The fast-paced walk had really tested the strength of this thinly-built tailor. He already had started to lose his strength in the morning of the second day and his son was trying to drag him along. He also begged him not to give in and keep walking. With his son on one side and me on the other, we grabbed his arms to help him to continue. Unfortunately, it showed in his father's eyes that he knew he could not continue for too much longer. My neck vertebrae were giving me more and more grief and pain and the son could not drag his father along any longer too, and had to let him go after a few kilometres. The same thing happened to this thin tailor as it did to the others. He was shot in the head right front of his son's eyes. His mother and his younger sister had been selected by Mengele to be gassed on the day of their arrival.

I do not know what happened to the young fellow as he had lost a lot of strength as well. He was just as thin build as his father and he probably followed the rest of his family a few hours later. No one knew how much longer we would be marching, but if it was for another day than I would be lying down as well. I had not much energy left. It was nightfall and we had arrived at a forest through which the road was cutting. As soon as we got a bit deeper inside it the SS-guards started to shoot into no particular direction. We did not see anyone at all. "Was someone trying to run away?" I asked the man next to me.

"No, the Germans are afraid of any partisan who may be hiding between the trees, but I cannot see anyone," he replied. "Looks like they are not afraid to empty their magazines to hide their fear," I replied.

Unfortunately, our hope to see some help never arrived.

Our marching line stretched over a kilometre long and about 300 armed guards were keeping us going or letting us stop forever. Complete darkness had taken over and we could not see even the side of the road any longer.

"Anhalten! Ausruhen! (Stop! Resting!)" The order was passed along the long line from guard to guard, and we had to stay at our spot. I immediately lay down with my back on the cold

---

[79] Békés County lies on the Pannonian Plain (Great Plain) in Hungary. Békés county arose as one of the first comitatus of the Kingdom of Hungary, in the 11th century.

snow. My neck was very, very sore but lying down on the snow eased the pain a little bit. "Do not fall asleep!" I ordered myself. "If you fall asleep you will never wake up again. You either freeze to death or you will be executed if you fail to stand up in time."

I kept talking to myself. I rubbed the cold show on my face to keep me awake.

The rest felt very good. I did not have any more bread left so I didn't have to worry about spending time eating. I rubbed my neck a little bit more as it made walking extremely difficult.

The rest lasted no longer than 15 minutes and then we had to keep walking towards the unknown destination.

Suddenly we could see some bright lights in the distance and deep loud explosions could be heard. It could have been 15 to 20 kilometres away from us. I had never seen such a bright light during the night. The hope was there. The Russian army had lit up the night sky with flares which were dropping down, and then it all became dark again. They used this technique to make sure their bombs were doing the most possible damage.

I just kept walking like a robot, placing my legs one in front of the other. I could no longer see anyone around me. I no longer registered the few blinks of revolver lights ending life after life or the sound of falling dead bodies that followed. Everything had become one bleary memory. I did not consciously direct my movements any longer. It was only my instinct and my strong will to live and tell the tales that kept me moving and going.

Angry loud voices awoke me from my bleariness and then I saw the reason for it. I noticed a large lighted building in the distance. I picked up my pace as we walked towards this building. It could only be a crematorium as the Germans had been keeping all important targets in the dark. Only the crematoriums had been lit up at night as they did not care about these buildings being destroyed. We were all in a physical state to be destroyed as well. This group of almost dead prisoners were no good for anything else. I looked around to see if there was any chance of escaping. This was the first time during this death march that I actually thought of escaping. Unfortunately, the closest forest was accessible only through an open area and I was sure my guards would shoot me dead before I could make it to the trees. I thought about this option for so long that we arrived at the building. I was happy to see it was not a crematorium, - it was a train station. If I correctly remember the name, it was Leslau.[80] We were directed into the railway-car-garage building next to the train station building.

One side of the building was open for the locomotives to drive in and out for service. Between the railways lines was a huge lower-level garage to repair the engines from underneath. "We are resting here!" This was the only command we received. We did not get any food at all.

I walked inside the office section where it was a bit warm but there was no space at all. People were lying down directly next to each other, some in seated positions along the walls, so I walked back to the cold mechanical

repair hall where the ground was wet. The snow which had been blown inside the building's open section was mixed with the black dirt from the locomotives and the dust. As I did not find one small dry area here, I climbed down into the lower-level pit where I managed to find a small dry spot. However, this January night was very cold and I could not get warm enough to fall into a deep sleep.

No train had come in for service and the SS-guards had probably managed to find the warm spots as I had not seen any of them.

The relocated

Loud yelling was our wake-up call in the morning. My uniform was black from the dirt and so were my hands, and I believe my face looked a bit like that too. As I looked around, everyone who stayed in this half open area was just as dirty. It was hard to stand up as the soles of my feet hurt from the wooden soles of the shoes after close to 48 hours of constant marching.

I tried to wash the dirt off myself in the snow but it was too greasy, so I did not have much luck cleaning myself up. In addition, my hands were already ice cold from the night. We had

---

[80] Włocławek is a city located in central Poland. Under the Nazi occupation Włocławek was again renamed Leslau. Włocławek was liberated on 20 January 1945 by Soviet troops

been waiting around in groups to hear some new commands or instructions.

The railwayman arrived with the good news. We were waiting for a train to take us further towards our final destination. "This is a miracle. We don't have to walk any further," said someone next to me with some happiness in his voice.

The sun's rays started to warm us up a little bit but it was still freezing cold in our one-layer uniforms. We were all waiting along the railway platform. As I looked along it seemed to me we had lost about half of our marching group since we left on the first night. The cold weather, no food, no water, 48 hours of marching and the SS-guards had done a good job. Of course, we had all left in a bad physical condition to start with. These guards may walk free after the war and not one of them would stand trial. To tell the truth I would not remember anyone's face to identify the culprits anyway.

During the last two days I had seen many dead bodies in many different positions, however I managed to find one similarity amongst them. All of theirs faces and open eyes showed the same expression - they radiated the same terror, reproach and threat. These faces will haunt all of the killers till the end of their lives and this will be the unintended sentence for their actions.

The time was crawling by slowly but there was no train coming. The railwayman had gone so there was no one to ask about the time of the arrival of our train. There was no one here except us. The Polish community was also hiding from us and from the SS soldiers. During our crossing we did not see any civilians through some of the villages but I saw a few corners of curtains being pulled aside. Our death march had been watched.

During our waiting time there were no trains passing by but finally we could see a train approaching in the distance - its smoke making it even more visible to us. The arrival of a train had always made my heart race since I can remember, and once again, the approaching train's rumbling, its noise and its whistling, made me feel excited.

This was a very long train comprised of open cattle wagons. When the train pulled into the station our SS-guards arrived. They must have had a good night's sleep and some food as well

as they started to yell at us with renewed energy. "Ausziehen!"
(Get on!) sounded the command.

We all climbed into the wagons and I looked for the most
suitable place. We had plenty of space and I even managed to lie
down. Of course this was not because of the organizing SS officer
had ordered the right number of carriages. It was because we
had lost so many during the march.

Around noon the sun managed to warm me up and I fell asleep,
but I do not know for how long. My fellow inmates woke me up
when we arrived at a station. I did not know where we were or
in what land. When I climbed out of the wagon I read the name
of the station, Gross-Rosen[81].

As I looked around I could see mountains and quarries. The
town was almost empty and whoever we saw wondered who we
were and where we had come from.

As we stepped through the gates of the camp, a new chapter of
our chaos started. Our SS-guards escorted us into a large
building and we did not get to see anything else of this camp.
We were so crowded there that we were standing on each other's
feet. This, of course, started a bit of an argument amongst us.
Soon, large pots were carried to our building with some hot
hodgepodge in it. We had not eaten for days so I did not mind
what it was as long it was warm and filling. I had started to
forget the taste of foods and all I wanted was to silence an ever-
demanding stomach.

Model of the Gross-Rosen main camp, picture from the Rogoźnica Museum website

Gross_Rosen, Nazi concentration camp, entrance gate with the phrase "Arbeit Macht Frei"[82] – Picture from: https://www.museumoffamilyhistory.com/ce/cc/nf-camps-gross-rosen-01.htm

The food was portioned out at a very slow pace. Our impatience was not comprehended by the distributors and it felt like they were almost enjoying stretching the time. They did not have enough plates either. As soon one person finished another was trying to pull the plate out of his hands for their turn. Some even tried to get a second portion.

All those in line recognized this practice and it caused more yelling, pushing and shoving of each other. "We will stop the apportioning until there is order!" said the person in charge of distribution. Those waiting with their pot got in line to be served. After a torturous wait I finally received a ladle of the soup. The extent of the pushing and shoving had tired me out. The food was cold by then and it did not fill me up at all.

---

[82] More info: http://www.holocaustresearchproject.org/othercamps/grossrosen.html

I went outside the barrack to get some fresh air. I could see the quarry and some of the machinery from where I was. I could not talk to any of the Gross-Rosen prisoners because we could not leave our area, and they could not come to us either. We, the prisoners of Auschwitz, had been receiving special attention and treatment.

I went in and out of the building until dark. There was no air inside from the crowding, and it was too cold to stay outside for too long. When it became dark we had to get ready for bed, but this caused even more of an issue than receiving our lunch.

The room had no beds so we could only use the floor. However the building was way too small for all of us. We could hardly stand next to each other. Some decided to lie down anyway, but that was not a good idea. People started to fall over them as all of us were trying to get some more space and in some sections two and three people ended up on top of each other. This caused another sequence of shoving, pushing and yelling to win a bit of ground to lie down and sleep.

The loud noise was heard outside of the building and soon a group of capos with beating sticks also made their way inside the building. They hit whoever they could reach and soon order had been established. The order was to sit down in each other's lap. I sat on an unknown person's lap and another sat in my lap - three stacked on each other. The entire room looked grotesque by the end. People sat in three-level lines. I could not lean back, I could not stand up, and soon my neck started to hurt again from this stiff unnatural position. I had no blood in my legs and I could not feel them any longer. As soon I tried to correct my position to make it just a bit comfortable, people around us started to growl. There was no question about it, no matter how tired I was (or the entire group), not one of us slept. The noise did not get better all night, it just got less loud as we were all afraid of the return of the capos.

It was about midnight when I could not hold on any longer and I made the decision to go outside to pee. I did not want to urinate between two humans even if I did not know any of them. I had taken my wooden shoes off as there was no ground to step on anywhere. Everywhere I tried to step there was some part of a human body. Even with my best effort, I stepped on someone's leg, arm, or even hair. This caused further argument and I received kicks and hits below the belt all the way out. I managed to get out into the open but the painful punishment was my reward. The fresh air felt good after the airless building, but the icy rain did not make it too welcoming there either. When I finished and turned around, I had to face the dark truth at the door. They would not let me back in and I received punches and kicks right at the doorway. The icy rain bit all the way into my bones and all I was thinking about was the warmth inside, so despite physical punishment I decided to try to walk through the human pile which felt like climbing a mountain made out of human limbs. I had been forced to stay outside, but I was not the only one. A few more inmates had the same experience. They could not go back so they also had to spend the night outside. I moved right next to the building's wall to try stay out of the rain. However it had no eaves to keep the rain off.

The people sitting at the door clearly could see that some of us were stuck outside, but not only did they fail to call us back, they even prevented us from getting back inside.

By morning, more prisoners had come out to satisfy their needs and I had taken the opportunity to push myself back inside. It took me several hours to warm up after being outside for almost the entire night in the cold rain.

I certainly had managed to catch a cold during the night. I started to cough and my throat started to hurt as well. I did not know how I had managed to have so much energy to survive all these tortures so far. Only the strongest immune system was capable of surviving against these elements. Pathogenic elements had been attacking not just my body but my soul too, trying to weaken me from day to day. I probably looked awful by now. I was dirty. I had no bath for a long time, did not shave for weeks, and every bone of mine was visible under my skin. I was quite happy that I could not find a mirror to look into. The Nazis' experiment did work at some level. The 20th century culture had been washed off us. They had managed to re-convert us into some ancient century's slaves. Perhaps even the galley slaves had a better life than us. I think they were provided with more food than we were. People were dying in many ways and the underfeeding and the hunger managed to take lives day after day.

This day passed by without any more to complain about but the night was just as bad again. I believe the capos had been given definite commands to make our life as miserable as possible. They entered the building looking like jungle explorers who were trying to cut their way through the bush using a long machete, except they used their beating stick and hit anyone they managed to find. Maybe they even had a competition to see who could hit the most prisoners and who could get through to the other side the fastest.

During the forenoon we were ordered to line up outside the barrack: "You will be fed first before your further transfer inside Germany" advised one officer. I was happy to hear this as I did not think I could survive another night compressed inside this building. This lager had caused a lot of grief for me in this short period of time.
The food containers had been set up to apportion out the food. Interestingly enough, all of us received a plate this time. We did not have to wait for someone to finish and then fight for a plate like the day before. We got some cooked carrots and a small piece of bread. The carrot was almost raw. They had not been cooked for long at all and we were forced to eat in a hurry. I almost swallowed the carrot pieces without chewing them. I decided to put the bread away for the unknown trip ahead. I did not have to bother to collect my belongings as I did not have any. Even my little red pot was no longer around my hip. During the march I had thrown it away to offload any unnecessary weight to carry.

Passenger of the "Death Train"

We arrived at the train station, but we did not even guess what we would have to go through during the following few days. Auschwitz was called "The Death Factory". The train on which we embarked could have been called" The Death Train" by the end of our trip.

The train on the Gross-Rosen train station was assembled from mixed wagons - some were open, some were closed. I chose a covered wagon to climb into. I was hoping the roof would save me from the cold and the changes in the weather. I stayed beside the door while more and more climbed up onto the wagon. An SS-officer was organizing how many persons could be shoved into one wagon. The wagon looked full but still many were standing next to the train waiting to enter. Soon enough, an SS-officer jumped up and started to point and wave his machine gun towards everyone. Of course, we all started to back up and he looked happy to be able to create more space for those in waiting.

I was there only for a few minutes when I already started to feel how little air the wagon had, and still people were being pushed up into the car. I realized this would not work. I would not be able to cope with these conditions for too long. I made the decision to escape from this wagon before we left. I managed to slide myself down between the side of the door where I had embarked and down onto the snow. I then climbed up to the next wagon which was and open car.

About 120 persons had been shoved into each wagon, ours included. It was impossible to move but I knew the advantage of this open car. I had experienced the insufficient amount of oxygen in the closed car for a few minutes, but here I could breathe it in without restraint.

None of us knew where we are going or how long our trip would be. We thought it could not be too long in these conditions but these warped people were capable of anything. A loud-voiced Czech started trying to make some order. It was in everyone's interest to try to make the trip as comfortable as possible towards the unknown destination.

We all stood into a line as we realized this was the only way for so many people to travel in this wagon. The lines which took a lot of effort to form did not last too long. No one was able to keep to the organized lines.

Between the two cars was a small guard cabin where an SS-officer was sitting guard in his warm furry jacket. He placed his elbow onto the little window and watched us with a smile as we pushed and shoved each other to make some more room for ourselves.

We did not leave the train station until late afternoon. When the train started moving it was even harder to stand still. The fight for some extra centimetres escalated. Some nationals managed to find and help one another. We Hungarians did not manage to do that even in this situation. We could not form a team to defend our countrymen. The weaker ones were pushed away and many lost their strength to stand.

We had been traveling for four days when I too lost my balance in the ever-fighting crowd and fell on the floor. Many fell onto me as well. Bodies were on my head and my chest. I was suffocating and was yelling for help as much as I could, but nobody cared about it. Dead bodies were everywhere on the floor. I did not want to be one of them so I kept yelling but the ones standing on me did not move. I could not be this way any longer. I used all my strength which was increased by the fear of dying and I used my nails to scratch and my hands to twist arms and drag on them. With unheard-of strength and will, I managed to stand up and stick my head up for some air like someone who had just emerged from under the water. It took me a long time to catch my breath.

The trip lasted for five days and five nights. I had about a 20-gram small piece of bread which I had saved back in Gross-Rosen. We did not receive food or water for the entire trip. We were not let out at any train station. The fight for survival was not just about a place in the small area - it was also about for food and water.

Someone said he could see some mountains. In was his belief we were in Bavaria[83]. We could see a line of mountains in the distance. The snow had started to fall and I was trying to eat every snowflake possible. The ones that landed on the shoulders of the men around me ended up in my mouth. I picked up every one of them to get some fluid into me. I looked with sadness after the ones which were blown away by the wind at the last moment, before I could eat them.

---

[83] Bavaria (German: Bayern) [1] is the largest federal state ("Bundesland" or shortened to Land) of Germany, situated in the south-east of the country, and extends from the North German Plain up to the Alps in the south.

In these conditions, many people lost their mind. Many poor inmates, who tragically lost their lives in these conditions, were lying everywhere on the floor of the wagon.

A small-built, very skinny man had been driving himself through the crowd. Even though he was Hungarian he was yelling out in German: "Hilfe, Hilfe!". No one helped him out in this life and death situation. He walked around for hours and he passed me a few times. The last few sparks of life were driving him on. The awareness was already missing from his gaze and what he was doing was almost an involuntary act. His face was beaten up badly, the blood had run all over his face, but he did not care, and he did not wipe it off. As soon as he pushed himself into any national group he was immediately rejected. My heart went out for him, but I was too weak to help him out. I was close to dying too. I was still suffering grief myself and the only way I could keep calm was to remember how weak and vulnerable I was. I could not fight an entire team for him alone.

We started to have more and more room as many of the dead were lying on the floor. These human piles gave us more seating ground. We did not believe we had violated their grace by sitting on the dead bodies, the victims of the last five days. They did not feel our weight any longer, but it did help us a bit by easing our tiredness. I did not look around to see who was sitting near me as I was falling into just a light sleep. The danger of falling into a deep sleep was still present. I would drift off and be pushed under the crowd. I was sitting like this when, from the human pile, I could hear a weak voice. I immediately looked towards the voice which had come from the human pile I was sitting on, and only then, did I realize I was sitting one someone who was not dead yet. He was speaking in Hungarian and he was just begging for mercy. He was asking the ones sitting on him not to crush him and not to take away the air from him. "I did not hurt anyone, please do not hurt me!" he pleaded. Of course, I stood up as quickly as I could, and I was waiting for the others to do the same. To be fair I was sitting right on his neckline. As soon I stood up, I could see the happiness and relief on his face. He had a small locksmith workshop in New-Pest suburb. I was looking into his eyes when he said, "I have always lived and worked fairly." These few words just came out of his mouth like a sigh. The others sitting on him did not notice what I did. They were not Hungarians so they did not understand him. However, even without knowing the language, you could have understood the situation. The locksmith did not have enough energy anymore to push the sitting inmates off himself. As he knew his prayers did not find listening ears, he cursed the ones still sitting on him, then his head fell back onto the others on whom he was lying. Even having close to no energy, I started to beg the three others still sitting on him to stand up. My facial expression and my trying to pull them up worked. They unhappily stood up and moved over to another pile of dead humans to sit on. The tormented smith reached out for my hand and have gave me a weak squeeze as a thank you.

Our Death Train was still driving into the days and nights. The fight was still going on but with less energy now. This was another well executed plan from the SS-Waffen leaders. The wagon guards could report to their SS leaders, "Most of the prisoners died by fighting against each other. We could not do anything to stop them!" This way there was no blood on their hands.
One of our inmates had been shot dead by the SS-guard from the braking room. He was a Hungarian teacher. He also talked into the air with blurry vision. He behaved very quietly but sometimes he looked at me with deep grief on his face. His deranged look sometimes disappeared and then he talked about his hometown Sátoraljaújhely[84]: "I was a primary school teacher there. I was deported with my fiancé to Birkenau. I do not know what happened to her. I have been teaching a lot of young girls to write, read and how to speak correctly in Hungarian."
He talked about the many indignities he lived through in Birkenau and this was the time when he turned very sad. He did not complain that he had been marked as an unwanted man in his own country and that he had become homeless, or the fact that Hungary did not stand up for its own citizens but had provided a clear pathway and full assistance for the Nazis to deport all its unwanted citizens from the country. During our journey I had not listened to anyone this much. I did not have

---

[84] Sátoraljaújhely is a town located in Borsod-Abaúj-Zemplén county in northern Hungary along the Slovak border. It is 82 kilometres east from the county capital Miskolc.

much strength to reply to him. We spilt apart and I was leaning against the side of the wagon when I saw him climbing up on the wall to escape. I tried to reach him to pull him back, but our SS-guard was quicker. He shot him in the head from close range. The teacher's body was already so high up that the gravity pulled him out of the wagon instead of back onto the floor. He had managed to escape but he had paid for this freedom with his life. I did not see the expression on anyone else's face in the wagon, but his tragedy definitely shocked me. It happened quickly and I could not do anything to help him. His body remained along the railway line and no one would carve on his tombstone: "Here rests a young teacher who was a victim of Fascism and a long-suffered martyr of Sátoraljaújhely".

Previously I did not think I could survive without food or water for days in a very cold climate, but now I knew I was capable of doing so, and longer than many others. Before the war, in one of the hotels in our town, a Hindu fakir [85] had been lying down for days without food or water. However, this was his "performance" and people had to buy tickets to see him. Of course, many wanted to see him, and everyone talked about his unearthly ability. We did not need any unearthly talent and, arguably in more severe conditions than the Hindu fakir, we had survived for five days without food or drink. The fakir had been lying down comfortably and he did not have to face the cold weather in a single layer of clothing. He was not squeezed in with 120 other humans, and he did not have to avoid being stepped on every second. Our stunt was even more impressive. However, we did not volunteer for this and no one had to buy a ticket to see us.

One inmates realized how to help himself against the cold weather and his idea become popular with many others.

They began to take off the clothes from the dead and put them on, trying to protect themselves with a double layer against the cold. Whoever did not manage to get clothes from the dead were watching the ones dying in anticipation of the opportunity to pull them off from the still warm bodies.

---

[85] fakir - a Muslim or Hindu mendicant monk who is regarded as a holy man fakeer, faqir, faquir Moslem, Muslim - a believer in or follower of Islam dervish - an ascetic Muslim monk; a member of an order noted for devotional exercises involving bodily movements

In normal times their actions would have been a serious violation of respect and an insult, however no such judgement was recorded here. We had become outlaws, first in our country and then as soon as we stepped inside the gate of Auschwitz. There had been some record of us but the files had been burned and, at this stage, we were not documented anywhere.

The human face changes at the time of death. Some will have little change and they will look like a quiet sleeper. The eternal sleepers of our wagon had gone through a lot before passing away and their faces changed a lot. Our dead fellow inmates were lying around us everywhere and their faces were even more noticeably different when their naked bodies lay on the floor. They looked more awkwardly unfriendly than they were when wore the striped camp suit.

I did not touch anyone's clothes, not just because of mercy but because I could not bring myself to put on a dead man's clothes. The double layer of jacket or pants would have helped me against the cold but I just could not do it. I did not have any shoes as they had been trampled off me a long time ago. I was standing in only a thin pair of socks. My clothes were very ragged and I lost most of the buttons from my shirt pushing in the big crowd. Luckily, I had some string and I could join my shirt up to avoid the wind to blowing under it.

I did not watch the landscapes passing by. I was not interested about it at all. Even if I wanted to see anything, I had to try to stretch myself as tall as possible to look over the walls of the wagon.

We had been slowing down as we were passing a city so I had become interested. When I looked out I could see a city which was built on the side of the hills. Even in these conditions I gazed at this magnificent place. Someone close to me said this was Meissen, the world-renowned original porcelain factory. It looked like a treasure chest as it sparkled in the January sunshine. This beautiful place had shaken me out of my lethargy. What I was thinking about was how many beautiful places could be found in Germany, and how Fascism could do so much evil against Europe. I was not far from the place where the world-renowned porcelain, whose brand was known to millions of people outside of Germany, was getting made and hand painted. I was an admirer of Meissen porcelain and now I saw the city where many artists were learning and being educated.

As I stretched my neck to look over the side of the wagon I could see this beautiful historic city. As soon I pulled my head back, right away a different view was front of my eyes. Naked, dead bodies were lying everywhere. I am sure there were some dead here whose homes had some Meissen porcelain displayed in their living room in the glass cabinet. But these collectors were lying down naked and dead on the floor of the wagon gazing at the sky with opened, unseeing eyes.

By the time I finished my thought, the train had passed through the city. I drifted back into my lethargy listening to the monotone clicking of the wheels of the train. I could see how the number of living had decreased and the number of dead had increased. I could not see myself, but I assumed I looked just like the others. The living did not look any more alive than the dead. We only differed from them in that we moved and breathed.

Some people again started to stretch their necks. They could see something. I looked out also and I could see a big city. I saw a lot of factories and warehouses on the outskirt of it. I could see a mountain on the other side of the city and from the moving train it looked like all streets were running into the mountain in straight lines.

We had arrived at a large train station. I could now see the name of the city. We had arrived at Dresden[86]. We stopped in front of a large and clean train station. There were many standing on the platform, probably waiting for their train. We stared at each other. Their gaze revealed nothing - no regret nor hatred. They probably had learned well that the manifestation of their eyes was also a danger to them. However, I had not had such an experience before.

Back home the Hungarians blamed us for the war and threatened us many times. The Poles and other nations questioned our friendship. However, here they have just stood quietly. They did not threaten. They did not withdraw. They just

[86] Dresden is the capital city of the German state of Saxony and its second most populous city, following only Leipzig. It is the 12th most populous city of Germany, the fourth largest by area (following only Berlin, Hamburg and Cologne), and the third most populous city in the area of former East Germany, following only (East) Berlin and Leipzig.

watched us passionlessly. They did not even react when we started to beg for water or food. They still gave no signs of passion. The "Dresdenians" were particularly silent spectators to the passengers of the train. The train pulled out from this train station and I still could not understand their behaviour. However, I could still count the days and this made absolutely no sense. We have been on the run for five days now and I felt I would reach the end of my strength soon.

We arrived at another city. We had run along many railways. This place was called München-Allach[87]. We stood there for a long time then we reversed. We thought we had arrived. We saw blue-grey stipe marching prisoners in the distance and because of the long waiting time, we strongly believed we had finally reached our destination, but soon the train started to run again. It did not matter that we had started to guess where we were going as none of us had any idea. We had been riding for a few more hours before we stopped again at an unusual place without a train station. We waited for something in an area with lots of trees. Soon many vehicles were closing towards us - trucks, horse-drawn carriages, handcarts.

Our doors were opened and we had to get off. However this was not so easy to execute. I approached the door from the side, stepping over dead bodies. I could feel the blood in my hole-filled socks. My feet were slipping on the bodies covered in it. Half of the passengers in our wagon was unable to disembark. They were lying on the floor still.

The five-day long train ride had ended but now it was difficult to get off. I did not manage to climb off. I just fell. My muscles had become very stiff and to use them first I had to stretch them out. As I landed on the ground I fell on the snow. With two hands I stuffed it into my mouth. I did not care that it was very cold. I had to satisfy my burning inside. I ate a lot of snow and stopped only when I had satisfied my thirst.

The dead bodies were thrown onto the vehicles. From the covered wagon next to us came a very unpleasant smell. Of the

---

[87] Allach, the largest sub-camp of Dachau concentration camp, opened on March 19, 1943 because of a workforce shortage in the armament and building industry of Nazi Germany. The camp was also the manufacturing site of Allach porcelain and German Dress uniform Swords and daggers. Allach remained open from March 1943 through its liberation on April 22, 1945, by the US Army.

120 prisoners, only a few appeared to be alive. The rest had not withstood the airlessness and the deprivation. From the side of the track hundreds of the dead bodies were collected and transported directly into the crematoriums. They were my fellow passengers with whom I have been traveling for five days and had been lying next to me. I had to say a final goodbye to them because they have not been able to survive the cruel vicissitudes of the transportation. We had arrived at the Bayern Dachau - another concentration camp, another scene of horrors.

Prisoner of Dachau[88]

I could barely move after the five days journey of fasting and thirst. My feet had become frozen on the snowy road in my perforated socks. I had no strength. I did not walk, I just swayed. Next to me similar bodies were crawling towards the lager. Many could not stand any longer, but they avoided climbing up onto the trucks as they were afraid they would be taken along with the dead bodies into the crematoriums. This was how we were trying to get through the main gate.

The delegates of the Dachau lager were SS-soldiers and undertakers, hardened people who saw a lot, but even they stared at our group. It looked like they had never seen such tortured people. We differed from the dead only by being able to move, but otherwise there appeared no other differences between us. Our skin colour and our skinniness were similar to that of not living persons.

Thousands, maybe even tens of thousands of us, left from Auschwitz and now I could see only a few hundreds of us crawling and walking like zombies towards the lager. It is possible that during the train trip some part of the transport had been disconnected and others had been transported towards

---

[88] Dachau concentration camp was the first of the Nazi concentration camps opened in 1933, which was initially intended to hold political prisoners. It is located on the grounds of an abandoned munitions factory northeast of the medieval town of Dachau, about 16 km (10 mi) northwest of Munich in the state of Bavaria, in southern Germany.

another camp, but I was not sure about that. I was the witness to thousands of my fellow inmates' death during the one week of retreat inside of Germany.

There was no headcount during the travel. The departing and arriving camps counted the prisoners, but no one had to account for the gap between the two numbers.

Finally, I could ease my thirst. Luckily they could not make the snow disappear from in front of me. Due to this gift of nature, I could access slush. It was a pity it was not good enough medicine against hunger, tiredness and physical fatigue. I do not know how far we had to walk. Maybe it was not much in metres but it felt a long way. I stopped very often, and I was breathing heavily like an elderly man. Would I ever be able to get stronger again?

I would have to find myself in particularly favourable circumstances if I was to build my health up again. Could I dare to think that the SS would provide an opportunity for me to strengthen my condition. If they sent me to work in this state I would perish in a few days, I thought to myself.

I could see the entrance of the camp. This camp was one of the bigger ones, probably the second biggest after Auschwitz.

We had been escorted onto a big field. In good times, perhaps they played football on this field, as I remember seeing two goal boxes at each end of the area. It looked like there had been plenty of sport enthusiasts in every camp. Football was the favourite sport of the SS. Not only the sport's noble side of the competition took place in these camps, but the sadistic satisfaction was also sought.

A few years ago I was chasing the ball on the soft grass from love, passion and happiness. I loved the morning dew on the grass in the Sunday morning games. Yes, this had been my biggest passion. I was standing on a football field once again, but this time reduced to bones with no muscle tone. I would not have energy to run even a few metres. This was how an ex-football enthusiast was standing here now - hungry, freezing and dizzy in this ragged and striped uniform.

We had to line up and were taken for registration, and it took a very long time until we were organized into one group. We had to stand up and it proved to be a difficult challenge for the capos.

With great effort they managed to do the headcount, then we were escorted to the front of a single level building. I recognized it right away, this was a bath house. I knew the order - shower then disinfection. On occasions like this, all our items, even the trashiest ones, were taken away. I had a knife, a ragged handkerchief, a few nails, a few green soap cubes, and a spoon hanging around my neck on a string inside a small linen bag. I was trying to save these items which were important to me. The line of prisoners was going in on one side of the building and exiting on the other side. Next to the entrance there was an old table which was covered with snow. I chose this table to become the hiding place for my items. It was not allowed to step out of the line, so I had to come up with a plan how to get my items there. All these items were in the bag already so I wrapped the string around it to keep it as tight as possible for the easier execution of my plan which must be unnoticed by anyone else. There was only a limited number of people who could be inside at once. The beginning of the line entered the showers and until we had been inside, we had to wait outside in the cold - fully naked. I had to use this time to carry out my plan. I looked around and none of the prisoners around me cared. They all just wanted to enter the shower. I targeted the table carefully so as not to throw too short or too far, and without being noticed. I saw, happily, that my plan worked. The small bag landed right under the table and sank under the snow. Step one had worked. Now I just had to cross my fingers that it had not been noticed, so that I could somehow pick it up on the way out, despite the fact that we had to exit the shower at the other end of the building.

We had to leave all our clothes outside as they were infection hazards. The Germans were anxious not to catch any infectious illnesses. They had clearly been given vaccinations to look after us. They were looking after those people whom they had tortured and turned into living skeletons. A special strange procedure which characterized our prison guards at other times as well.

Steam clouds exited the shower as I stepped inside. From the freezing cold, suddenly, I was in hot steam. This felt exceptionally good but suddenly I was about to faint. This soon progressed into feeling unwell. I did not want to pull myself away from the warm water. I had collected a lot of dirt during the last week and I intended to wash as much off as possible. I continued to shower with a great level of self-control although my heart was beating very fast and I was on the edge of losing consciousness. About 15 minutes later when I reached for the towel, I felt cleaner but more unwell.

I rubbed my disturbingly thin body dry. My chest had collapsed, my arms and legs were as skinny as a pipe, the back of my hands were frozen into blue and green and the skin had cracked from the cold wind. Thank God that Mengele was not there otherwise I would have been escorted right away into the crematorium. I was hoping I would not see him there and that I would be spared from the gas chambers.

I received a civilian suit, a pair of wooden shoes and a very odd-looking hat. There were so many types of hats and we each had a different type. No one wanted to laugh at this strange looking group. We looked like we had just stepped out of a costume rental shop. Except for my tall hat, the used suit was at least clean, but the shoes were about three sizes larger than my feet. It was not permitted to exchange between ourselves and we could not raise this issue with the stockkeeper either. We had to slip or squeeze our feet into whatever size of footwear we received.

I was trying to peek towards the table outside to see if my little bag was still there or not. I was happy to see that no one had picked it up. On the way out with the group I stopped and pretended I to be tying my shoelaces and I picked it up and placed it in my pocket. I was happy to own my little bag with its items in it. It was probably worth nothing to anyone else, but for me it was a treasure.

After our group had gone through the disinfection it was already dark when we arrived at an entrance of a barrack led by a capo. From the foyer we stepped inside a large hall which was full of wooden bunk beds. The beds were more like platforms covered with dry straw. The dinner was only some weak black coffee.

I was looking for a place to lie down. One prisoner pointed out a top bed where I could climb up and find some space. I squeezed next to some Polish prisoners who were not at all happy that they had to share their sleeping space with a foreigner and not a fellow countryman. I could lie down only on my side, otherwise there was not enough space for all of us to fit there. I was trying to get some sleep after the many sleepless nights. I was hoping to get to sleep very quickly.

The Polish prisoners could not come to terms with their new sleeping inmate and they constantly pushed and shoved me. They demanded that I get off the bed to bring them some more coffee. I was not happy about this request, but they were so demanding that I had to climb down and walk across the entire building to get some more to drink for these guys. Of course, my request was denied, as extra portions were not allowed there either. I had to walk back with empty cups and before climbing back up I showed them that there was no more coffee. When I wanted to climb up and grab hold onto the top bed rail, they pushed my hands off. I was of course not happy for their behaviour and a loud argument started to take place. This triggered the appearance of the barrack capo, a limping prisoner. I started my explanation to him, but of course he did not understand my language. He was not Hungarian. However he understood the complaints of the Polish prisoners and he immediately reacted. I do not know what complaints they used against me, but they managed to give enough negative description for him to lunge at me and beat me from every angle. It was difficult for me to get up after he has finished his punishment. I stood helplessly alone in the middle of this giant hall. I looked around in the semi-darkness but I could not see one free space. At the end of a line of beds some inmates squeezed into a small place for me to lie down too. The ones who helped me out were Hungarians. This surprised me very much.

As soon I laid down I immediately fell asleep. The entire place was full of noise from snoring and snuffling but I was so tired that even this noise did not keep me from sleeping. All the tired and worn-out men around me also fell into deep sleep too. Unfortunately, my sleep did not last long as I became very itchy. This woke me up and I started to scratch myself. I scratched my itching hands and legs and then I tried to get some more sleep, but I received another sting. More and more places on my body became itchy. In the darkness I could not manage to see what was causing it; I could only guess that it was fleas.

I either had a very tasty blood or I had still had more than the others. When I went to sleep, I was happy to have some break

from the SS-guards and their collaborating capos but now I had
to face other bloodsucking creatures. We were lying on very old
straw, on which who knows how many men had been sleeping
beforehand. These evil bugs had nestled themselves in this warm
place and they ruined my night. I scratched myself until the
morning. My anger was only heightened by my inability to
destroy any of the attackers. These fleas were experienced and
well trained. Immediately after their attacks they retreated and
by the time I managed to slap their place of attack, they were
long gone.

I was in this barrack for almost three weeks, but I could not get
used to the biting of these fleas. They did not leave me alone
during the days nor during the night. No one around me had the
same issue and they did not understand my struggling.

One night they attacked me so badly I had to leave the
comfortable hay and lie down on the wooden floor behind the
bed. I was hoping they would not leave their hiding place. I was
wrong. They did not spare their energy and they followed me
even on to the ground. I had to realize that I would not win this
battle, so I went back onto the bed and I gave myself up to my
destiny.

Three weeks had been gone by without doing anything. We did
not leave, not even to do any work. Despite not performing any
physical work, I still went to sleep every night very tired and
also woke up tired. As the fleas do not carry any diseases they
had not been exterminated. They were assisting our SS guards to
make our lives even more miserable.

Infectious disease is spread by white lice[89] and that was the only
insect which was feared by the capos of every barrack. I could
avoid these until now, but I had to be careful to stay clear of
them. The prisoners of the neighbouring barracks had been
suffering from typhoid fever[90] and their windows overlooked
our building. The stronger ones had been able to pull themselves
up and stand in the windows to talk to our groups. Our block

---

[89] Lice are obligate parasites, living externally on warm-blooded hosts which include every
species of bird and mammal, except for monotremes, pangolins, and bats. Lice are vectors of
diseases such as typhus.
[90] Typhoid fever is an acute illness associated with fever caused by the *Salmonella enterica serotype
Typhi* bacteria. It can also be caused by *Salmonella paratyphi*, a related bacterium that usually causes
a less severe illness.

commander had forbidden our inmates to get close to the neighbours and to make any contact with them. One day he saw one of our people under the neighbour's window as he was talking to one of the infected prisoners. Like a wild animal he ran at him and he beat him to a bloodbath with his stick.

The capos organized a lice check every three days in our building. Three persons have been nominated to do the full body and uniform check. We all had to line up without any clothes. One person checked each individual, especially in the body joints like the arm pit, as these creatures liked to nest in these areas - and one checked the clothes in the same regions. During the first check-up the barrack was clear. However, during the second search they found four prisoners with lice. This caused panic. In these crowded buildings it was easy for these bugs to spread and this could have serious consequences. In the case of the appearance of any diseases, the barracks were fully locked down and food was only given through the small windows. This was the barrack officials' answer for treatment - total isolation. It did not matter if not everyone in the building was ill. Few incidents could be kept quiet from the officials. This was in everyone's interest, especially the capos, as the closing of the barrack would have happened with them inside as well. Accordingly, they ordered a thorough cleaning of these people with brushes, in the bathroom. After that they had to stay in the bathroom for the rest of the day and overnight as well. During the day, the bathroom had enough space but during the night some additional roommates were received. The ones who died during the night were placed in there and it was not a very nice sight – indeed it was rather frightening.

The death of a high school teacher

I already knew this Latin and history teacher from Debrecen called Imre Haász who was teaching the younger generation. During my imprisonment I had met him twice.

Firstly, in the autumn of 1944 I found him, very skinny and pale, next to me in a barrack in Auschwitz. I almost walked past him as he was hardly recognizable in his striped uniform. His face had lengthened, his eyes had become baggy, and he pulled the coat tight on himself to beat the cold. A small smile ran across his suffering face when I recognized him. He was the weaker and more broken one of the two of us. He was not just suffering physically but also mentally, from the hardships and the humiliation of the past few months. Clearly, he did not cope with all of this as well as I did.

The tears weakened his voice while he explained that he was a member of a road repair command where, besides the hard physical work, the supervisors were constantly beating them. He pulled up his shirt to show me the bruises and the red scars on his body. The soup made from green grass had not provided enough energy for the 12 hours a day heavy physical work.

In front of me stood this high school teacher who, back home, was teaching Hungarian history, thousands of years of history with its most outstanding events - the influence of kings, commanders, individuals, and the history of the world. However, the fascist executioners gathered everyone indiscriminately. The Auschwitz crematorium accommodated the most exceptional brains without exception. They had no regard for scientists or talented individuals and so in vain, he had not been pardoned either.

Imre did not ask for anything from me but I asked him: "Is there anything I can help you with? Is there any way I can assist you?" He looked at me in a funny way, a wrecked Auschwitz prisoner offering help to another miserable inmate. Even I did not know how this offer slipped out of my mouth. What could I, a prisoner who suffered from hunger and was also as miserable as he was, offer him? At the end I did manage to help him. I had three shirts on me which I had managed to get from somewhere. I offered one to him as I saw how much he was freezing in this cold. He did not reject my shirt, but neither did he demand it. "Thank you very much Sándor. This is most kind of you," he said quietly to me with his head down. He had tears in his eyes because he could appreciate the smallest gesture in these inhuman conditions. My tears rolled down my face because I could help someone who was weaker than me and who had nothing at all.

This was our first meeting - but our second one was a bit more tragic.

During the night after the body search for lice in the barracks I had to go to the toilet. I just sat down when one inmate literally smashed to door open on me. "Gunya, quickly, get up as I can't hold it any longer!" I did not know who called me by my nickname which had been used during the football games back home. It was my friend Imre Haász.
It is difficult to describe what he looked like. The lack of food and water during the long excruciating journey had so worn him out so that his face was already showing signs of confusion.
He spoke to me in a state of semi-delirium. He was thinned to the bone and hardly had any human figure. I was wondering how he had managed to survive the past 10 days. He had lasted, but only the smallest spark of an instinct for life was keeping this high school teacher going.
I gave him my seat. When I looked back, he was curled into a ball. He was seating on the toilet like a dead body. Maybe these were his last minutes.
The next time I saw him, he was amongst the dead bodies who passed away during the night and been collected and carried out to the front of our building the next morning. The flat top cart, which collected all of the corpses every morning from each barrack, arrived. The cart was already half full with bodies which were lying like wooden logs as they had become frozen from the cold winter night. Peacefully, free from further misery, they had been piling up on top of each other. Engineers, doctors, craftsman, painter, movie directors, carpenters and amongst them Imre Haász, high school teacher. They were carried into the crematoriums. I was already very busy with my own misery, but not too busy to say goodbye to my friend from Debrecen.

Last few days in Dachau

I was slowly running out of friends. They were dying from day to day. Only one other who was living with us in that barrack full of fleas still remained. He was a son of a bank manager who was able to keep going. His name was András Markovics, but I just called him Bandi[91].

One day I was very close to saying goodbye to him as well. We had to line up to receive our small portion of the weak lunch, the green grass soup. The limping barrack commander was always watching the apportioning very closely. He wanted to make sure not one person would try to get another extra portion of this swill. I did not try to do so as I already knew since my first day in the camp how hard his fist was and how wild he could get. All I could think of was that he would have never made it through if he had been arrived at Auschwitz. Dr Mengele would have sent him to death because of his limping leg. He was lucky to be in Dachau.

Bandi did try to get another portion. When he finished his first course, he got in line to get his second course of the lunch. The capo somehow managed to realize Bandi's intention and he cancelled the lunch for all of us to show that to punish such a 'terrible' act was more important than anything else.

He ordered a chair be placed in front of our building and Bandi got tied to this chair in the minus 15 to 20 Celsius for the rest of the day. A sign was made which stated, "I wanted to steal from the others", and this was hooked onto his neck. I was investigating any possible opportunity to help him out somehow, but the commander kept him under constant surveillance. At night when he was finally able to come inside the building, he had a few frozen bites on his body. He never again tried to mislead the lunch delivery guys to obtain an extra portion.

The idea behind the punishment of this limping capo was extraordinary and clever in its own way. It delivered the message: "I'm looking after the hungry inmates!" However, he did manage to take four and sometimes five portions of the lunch for himself. He had also beaten me on the night of our arrival when I was innocent. He had raised his hand to me to give preference to others. He protected three or four people who

---

[91] Bandi is a well-known nickname for András.

261

were in better physical condition than me, the weak one. He falsely believed his idea of justice gave him the right to make sure his rules were followed.

During my life in camps I met lots of capo and barrack commanders. Except for a few, they were all fighters with a warped soul. I could not decide if the Germans just had good luck appointing these persons for these positions, or the environment and the surrounding situation formed them into villains and torturers. It felt like they all went to the same school to learn these skills.

I did not see much about the life of this camp. We did not leave the section which was surrounded with fences. Therefore we did not receive any news from the outside world. Nothing which could have given us the smallest hope. Wherever I had been previously, I had to face different types of physical and mental miseries. This encouraged me to try to get out or move away from these places. The suffering was always coupled with something new. In Auschwitz, in addition to fighting hunger, there was the horror of the gas chambers. In Gross-Rosen there were the beatings. In Dachau, the constant biting of the fleas presented the extra tortures.

Our block commander must have been very afraid of the possible diseases caused by the lice. He managed to organize a bath for the entire barrack. We were escorted deep into the lager towards a different shower block than the one we had used on the day of our arrival. The requirement was to strip naked before getting into the building. We also had to throw our clothes into one pile and wait for a long time in the cold before finally entering the shower. Of course, it was not just cold - we had icy rain as well. The ice drops hitting my skinny naked body felt like someone was poking me with fine needles. When we received new clothes, our old ones went through disinfection to kill the possible pests. The warm shower heated up my muscles and they became loose again after the freezing cold. I was trying to delay the end of the shower so I could enjoy this short time a bit longer. I even drank the hot water. I was trying to fill my stomach up with something. It had no taste, but it did feel better afterwards.

As I knew we are going to the showers, I did not take my small bag of items with me this time. I hid it deep inside the straw bed, especially my little pocketknife because it had its great value. If we received a small piece of bread, I used the knife to cut it, and many jealous eyes watched my joy of slicing.

I had put up with this place of many fleas for about three weeks when one morning the commander brought us some news: "Next morning you have to be ready to go. You will be taken to work".

The news brought me mixed feelings. I was happy to leave the place, full of fleas and lice, behind - along with the limping and always brutal building commander. On the other hand I had not been required to do any work for the entire three weeks.

I could not get to sleep that night, not just because of the many flea bites, but also, I was anxious about the trip ahead. Where were we going and in what direction? Were we really going to be taken to work? We definitely did not look ready for any type of work, not physically, and for some of us not mentally either.

This February night went very slowly. I knew the many tricks of the Germans. I also thought the worst and questioned the truth behind this announcement. We looked more like we are ready to be executed by gas than to do any kind of work. I had seen many times that a group, which had been selected for work, had been marched into the gas chambers instead.

Next morning we all got ready, lined up front of the barrack, and soon we marched out of this camp. This was the fourth lager we had left behind.

Lager No 5

Walking towards the train station I was eager to know where we were heading. I knew my body would not be able to cope with more days of marching, nor with strenuous work.

The inmates in the camps sometimes came up with stories. Many times they just wanted to amuse themselves and their fabrications did not have any real background.

When we arrived at the station there were a lot of passengers who were waiting for the train to Münich[92].

Many looked strangely at us. I was jealous of them as I could see their warm clothes and I knew they would be travelling in a heated car.

I saw one man with a briefcase with some pity in his eyes. He reached inside his case but the SS guards spotted him the same way as I did. Unfortunately we were pushed back from the civilian travellers and I lost him in the crowd. I was hoping that after looking at each other's eyes he would throw a piece of food towards me. This hope was lost and I knew the next trip would be done in the same hungry way as all the previous ones - no food, no water.

All wagons were covered, so I had no choice; I had to climb into one of them. Some prisoners were so weak they had to be helped up to enter the carriage. I was shocked because, after 40 persons, the guards stopped more from entering. This was the first time I had noticed such care in the past six and a half months. I had hoped to receive some humanity towards the end of the war, even from the Germans. I was lying down on the floor and I was trying to come up with the reason behind this decision.

When we disembarked from the train in the dark night, it was snowing so strongly it was not possible to see more than a few meters ahead. These conditions brought me back to reality. The small station was called Ampfing[93]. Leaving the train station behind us, we went past a few houses then we turned into a forest road. This road led through a very dense pine tree forest. We had to march in the fresh thick snow which was putting a strain on our weak bodies. The small groups were secured by SS-guards with dogs. To avoid the falling snow we all marched with head down. Our clothing did not protect us from the cold either. I did not see any of the branches hanging over our route and I was constantly getting deep scratches on my hands and my face from them. I was losing the small amount of blood I had on to the white snow. Beside all of this I had to face another challenge.

---

[92] München (Munich) is the capital of Bavaria land (state). The largest city in southern Germany and the third largest city in Germany.

[93] Prisoners in the "forest camps V and VI" (Waldlager V and VI), located near the town of Ampfing, were housed in earthen huts, barracks partially submerged in the ground with soil-covered roofs designed to camouflage the structures from Allied aerial reconnaissance. Prisoners frequently worked 10- to 12-hour days hauling heavy bags of cement and carrying out other arduous construction tasks. In late April, as the U.S. Army approached the camps, the SS guards evacuated some 3,600 prisoners from the camp on death marches.

The fresh snow had stuck onto the wooden soles of my shoes, and this made my ankle twist in different directions. I tried to scoop the snow off my soles but with the next few steps it was there again. In some places the snow was so deep it swallowed my entire feet and besides, my hands were purple from the cold and the snow. To slow down was equivalent to death. The ones who could not march fast enough were shot into the head from close range just like before. The guards did not think twice about it.

I put my freezing hands inside my uniform, but I had to keep scooping the snow off my feet too. My ankle was hurting so much I was crying from the pain, but if I wanted to live I had to keep going. My weird looking march caught the attention of one guard. He saw the reason for my movements but still he decided to punish me. He started to beat me with his gloved fist wherever he could. I had to be strong to stay on my feet as I would not have had the strength to get up again. One of his punches landed on my nose which immediately started to bleed. The snow was once again painted red with my blood. The guard finally decided to stop his punishment. Now, not just did my sore feet make the march difficult, my whole body was in pain. I wanted to lie down on the soft snow and fall to sleep in peace. I was not afraid of a 'frost-death'. It would not involve great suffering. During the march from the Auschwitz camp I had seen many frozen bodies and none of their faces looked like they went through a painful death. I was after this kind of peaceful death but I was more afraid of the beating of the SS-guards gunstocks, and the biting of their huge dogs. I was more afraid of that kind of death.

I did not know where we were. I did not see anything except the straight high trees and the thick falling snow. I did not have much more strength left in me. I could last only a few more kilometres - that was all.

I was looking to both left and right where I was hoping to see some lights where we could finally rest. Soon, on my left side, I could see the line of a wire fence. Now I knew I must endure whatever pain I had. "It must be a big camp," I said to myself, as the fence stretched a very long way. The camp was in such darkness I would have walked past it by myself.

When we arrived at the main gate I did not see any lights there either. We had arrived at another concentration camp. This was Mühldorf[94].

As we continued our walk in the snow, now inside of the camp, I could recognize some chimneys. We stopped close at one of the chimneys. There was a door which had stairs that led us down into one of the bunkers.

The wooden beds were only one level high. There were many empty beds there.

I lay down on one of the wide wooden beds in the underground bunker. I did not mind the cold just as long as my tired body could rest.

The Hungarian translator came to give us some instructions: "You will not receive any dry or fresh clothes, nor any blankets, nor any food until tomorrow. There is a fireplace at the end of this tunnel. Making fire is not forbidden, however you have to supply your own wood from the forest," he stated. He then left us in the freezing cold in our wet uniforms. He did not provide any information about our possible work either. After a bit of rest, I had to stand up and move my body, otherwise I felt I would have frozen. Sometimes lying on my back, sometimes in a standing position, I had to move my arms to stay warm. I could not wait for the morning to come.

Hungrily

The SS guards of the camp selectively choose,
What would be the best way to torture?
Scolding, beating us, giving us little to eat,
The flesh withers to the bone and
The back curves, the eyes fallen in the scalp,
Which has no life - just defeat.

---

[94] Mühldorf was a satellite system of the Dachau concentration camp located near Mühldorf in Bavaria, established in mid-1944 and run by the *Schutzstaffel* (SS). The camps were established to provide labor for an underground installation for the production of the Messerschmitt 262 (Me-262), a jet fighter designed to challenge Allied air superiority over Germany.

We stagger with every step, the muscle has no tone,
The guards don't give any permission,
The hunger hurts more than the constant beating.
Neither awake nor asleep,
The is no other thought
Just constantly to eat.
The death is salvation
For which there is no admission,
The electric fence is the solution.

There is no weight on us, we look like a creep,
Would be good to die when we fall asleep.
Grass soup is given only those who works the best,
There is nothing more you get to digest.
We play cooking when our eyes are shut,
We dream about food and filling up the gut.
The guards do not know about our dream-eating,
It would be a sin therefore we would get beating.

Our stomach is a dent, our pot is empty,
Do you hear it? What is rattling gently?
The music of the bones is so haunting,
The words are exhausting, the lips are bounding.
Gas chambers, pneumonia, starvation,
The sick were cured by cremation.
The SS has a license to kill,
He can kick and torture at will.

Eats the bacon in front of us, chewing loudly,
Showing his appetite braggingly, boastfully.
The prisoner's mouth clings together from dryness,
In his throat there is nothing but air and emptiness.
In the morning, at noon, in the evening waiting in wain,
Going to bed with hunger, tiredness and shame.
And once we live well and they become hungry,
Do not hurt them, stay humbled not angry.

August 1966, Debrecen, Hungary

My new "home"

The next morning I walked up the stairs to look around. All I could see in the exterminated forest were many more underground bunkers. The SS guards were staying in buildings which were above the ground. The news about a new "human transport" spread around the lager very quickly. It brought some change into the monotonous days.

Everyone wanted to hear about their relatives. The other question was whether I knew about any camp which did not exterminate their prisoners. Everyone wanted to have some hope about their loved ones.

I knew about only one man back in Auschwitz who had arrived to us from Theresienstadt[95]. He told me about this camp where families could live together, and the elderly received proper medical care. Once a week there was also movie night for the camp. His news was unheard-of and unbelievable to us. Only if there was one more person who could tell us the same story would I believe it. Without this, I could not believe him, not in the middle of Auschwitz where I had seen the true reason for these camps. Only after my return home did I hear about such a place which had existed, but of course, it was just another part of the Nazi propaganda, and a big lie. This lager accommodated many thousands of inmates. When different nations and the Red Cross questioned the truth about the Nazi brutality, the Germans used this lager as an alibi against such accusations.

People were coming out of the ground and moving towards me. Their strange walk and posture caught my eyes. I had some knowledge about the inmates in different camps, but nowhere had I met such odd-looking people before. As they got closer, I started to understand that our weakened bodies, of course with a

---

[95] **Theresienstadt** was a hybrid concentration camp and ghetto established by the SS during World War II in the German-occupied region of Czechoslovakia. Theresienstadt served two main purposes: it was simultaneously a waystation to the extermination camps, and a "retirement settlement" for elderly and prominent Jews to mislead their communities about the Final Solution. Its conditions were deliberately engineered to hasten the death of its prisoners, and the ghetto also served a propaganda role. Unlike other ghettos, the exploitation of forced labor was not economically significant.

bit of exaggeration, looked strong and muscular compared with them.

An 18-year-old young man looked more like a weakened, broken, and elderly human. With their physical and mental deformities, they walked around mechanically, slept, and ate as if they had never received any food. They did not have anything about them which showed they possessed any willpower to live. There was only one kind of recognisable expression in these blank and pallid eyes, to leave this oppressive life as soon as possible. I looked at this sad group of figures in shock. Their spooky look was strengthened by the white powder which covered their clothes, face and their entire head. They were part of a group which had been building an underground aircraft factory. During their 16 hours-a-day work they had to offload cement bags as heavy as 50 kilograms from the trains and carry them to the building site.

New and newer human transports had arrived to replace the fatigued workers. They told me that the ones who lost their strength had been beaten to death and their heads had been kicked to pieces. At the end of the day the surviving exhausted workers had to carry the bodies back to the roll calls inside the camp.

After one surprise came another - someone called me by name. A few persons gathered around me. The strange twist of fate is that I found so many familiar faces and friends here in this place behind God's back. I met a few from my hometown, Debrecen. Something must have still remained of my old appearance because they recognised me. I only got to know who I was talking to when they introduced themselves: Béla Singer the barber, the Glattstein brothers, Miklos Grosmann, Eisenberg from Hajdúböszörmény[96] and a few more.

I had met these young men during a forced labour work about two years before in Szolnok, where we built and fixed the railways together in Szajol. The number of our 'Century' work group had been 106/6 and the name of our commander was Friczi from Szolnok. When I managed to get out from the forced labour work with medical reasons, this work group had been

---

[96] Hajdúböszörmény is a town in Hajdú-Bihar County in Hungary 19 km from Debercen. The town has got 32.200 inhabitants (1990 census) nearly all of them are Hungarians.

working on the Széna tér (Straw square) in Debrecen. One night the commander of the Straw square working group set hundreds of straw rolls on fire. He pointed the finger at the forced labour workers. After the investigation, the whole work group was sent to the Russian war zone as punishment. This was all I knew about this hundred-man work group, nothing more.

I was now able to reconstruct their suffering from that time onwards. After many terrible experiences they were taken to the German front line. As the Soviet Union pushed the Germans back, they had also moved back - and they, the criminal-squad, were closely watched. The Germans made sure this squad would always be kept under close watch and that they would never be captured. They had arrived at this camp directly from the warfront. That was all they told me about themselves and I was able to fill in the rest of the story. They were more interested to hear about their families and friends from back home, so I had to tell them.

I had not seen these men for about two years but we could not give each other any gifts, not even the best gift of all, a small piece of bread. We had nothing to share. All I could do was to tell what I knew, which was not pretty at all. I had no time nor interest to make it sound nice. I told them the brutal truth. Their faces could not have gotten any whiter under the cement dust - so I could not see the pallor of their reaction.

A loud bell disturbed our meeting and storytelling. This was the call for the inmates to line up and get ready to go to work. Our group had to stand separately from the others. The SS medical person looked at us, said something, and walked away. This time we did not receive any disinfection or shower and clean clothes. This camp was not equipped with such a thing. They did not tell us what our job would be, or where our area of work was. All they told us was we would not go to work that day, we could rest, but from the next day we would be starting work. Later we received a bit of soup without any bread. This covered last night's dinner and today's breakfast.

With hungry stomachs we decided to go for a tour inside the camp. This was a side camp. We could recognize this by the small portions of the food as well. I followed my great sense of smell to find the kitchen the fastest way. I was hoping someone would be able to see my need for food and help me out. Of course, they were used to such a beggar as myself, so they did not care about me at all and just kept walking and working normally.

As I was standing there I saw one of the kitchen workers exit the building with a bucket of potato peel. Right away I followed him and I begged him to hand me some peel. He was a Greek so he did not understand what I was saying but from my hand-gesture he realized what I was after. He signalled NO! with his head.

I did not give up and continued to follow him, hoping he would feel sorry for me. Soon we arrived at an area which was a morass. The Greek emptied his bucket full of peel there, then he turned around and walked back towards the kitchen building.

I expressed my feelings about him but, being so heartless towards me, he did not understand nor care about what I was saying.

The much-wanted potato peel was swimming in front of me on top of the morass. I was unable to reach it, so I had to fetch a branch from the nearby forest and then I started to fish the pieces out one by one. I was able to drag some pieces out of the smelly wet area. Some of them where frozen pieces and some were even rotten as well, but I was just as happy as a fisherman catching big fish. When I had enough 'catches', I moved on to find a way of cooking it - to make some food. I went into many bunker to see if I could find some of the few Hungarians I meat earlier, so I was full of hope of finding a helping hand.

I managed to find a boy from Szolnok who had such a low rank in the camp, he did not even go out for work. He was happy to help and he managed to find me some 50 to 60 centimetre-long rusty pieces of wire. We bent one end of the wire and started to put the potato pieces and peel onto it. The boy looked around and led me towards a smoking chimney at the back of the lager. It was easy to reach as it was erected from the ground. He bent the other end of the wire and hooked it inside the chimney for me, than he wished me good day and walked back to his bunker.

I love potato in any way it has been prepared but here in the Waldlager (forest camp) [97] was the first time I had experienced the smoked version of it. Shame it was not a whole potato.

---

[97] Mühldorf Camp Overview. More information from: https://www.holocaustmatters.org/muhldorf-camp-overview/

The potato peel, which for me felt more like a three-course dinner at the time, was slowly getting smoked. I had to wait until it became soft. It was a shame that it became black from the smoke, but its smell was more like a baked potato. I moved closer to the forest to eat my cooking. I pulled each piece off one by one. Some of it was still raw and needed a bit longer time to smoke, but I could not wait until then. I was super hungry, and the great smell of the potato made it even more urgent to eat. This type of smoked-potato-peel-skewer was a well-used special here in the lager. During dinner time the chimneys were utilized this way. One day I did suffer a bit of a loss. When I went back to pull my rod out it was not there. Some hungry man had taken it out of the chimney from inside the bunker. I lost an entire stack of the gourmet snacks.

The wizened peel did not ease my hunger and I was unable to find any other food source. Besides that, my stomach started hurting again. Probably my previous stomach intestine infection from Auschwitz had recurred. Neither standing up or lying down eased my pain at all. I suffered from a lot of pain during the second night and the following morning I had to present myself at the work roll call with a terrible pain. It felt like I was getting stabbed with hundreds of knifes. I did not care where I was going to be taken or what kind of work I would do, I could not even think from the pain.

I was placed into a small group and we were escorted to the nearby forest to gather firewood for the SS guards and for the kitchen. We did not receive any great tools for this work. We were given a basic wood saw and axe but neither of them were in any way sharp.

I collected small branches until it was my turn to use the handsaw. I was on one side of the saw and another person was on the other side. As soon we started to push and pull the saw, I started to lose my breath and my abdominal pain got even worse. I asked for some rest time but my partner would not let me take any. I tried to explain my issue to him with my hands and gestures as we did not speak the same language. However he did not want me to stop and urged me for an even faster tempo.

This first day went rather slowly and when the little wheelbarrow arrived to take the firewood, the guards were not impressed with the amount of it. They raised their voices but that was all, and luckily, we did not receive any physical punishment. My other inmates arrived back at the camp at the end of the day and all looked alike from the white cement dust. Listening to their daily coverage I realized how lucky I was once again that I was given the easier job.

Next morning the wake-up call sounded even earlier than before. It was still dark outside. My pain did not ease at all and I did not think I could survive another day of work. I just wanted to lie down on the snow and wait for the final call. I could not put up with the terrible pain and the suffering any longer.

I saw some green tents at the back of the lager which were covering big stacks of hay. I did not see any animals in the camp so I was not sure what the purpose of these stacks was. I dug myself deep into the hay and covered myself well to ease the cold. However, the frozen hay made me feel even colder than being outside. I was in a half sitting - half lying down position to ease the abdominal pain. We had received only some black coffee like drink in the morning and some soup and a small piece of bread at night, so I did not have to be afraid of losing my portion of the lunch.

This day was just as long as the others, but I did manage to sleep most of it. When I woke up, I felt even colder but I was enjoying the rest and the smell of the hay.

No one had asked me where I had been, and I was not in the mood for chatting anyway. I felt very cold so I went to bed right away with the ongoing pain in my abdomen.

On the third day I woke up feeling very weak and as a result I just managed to carry myself about. I left to find a doctor, for many here were from Hungary[98]. I wanted to tell my problem to a professional. I did not have too much hope as most occupants of the lager could have been sent for medical treatment immediately. The doctors did not have much power and had no medical equipment or medications. However I did manage to find one and after he listened to my problems he reminded me of

---

[98] Most of the prisoners in the Mühldorf concentration camp complex were Hungarian Jews, but there were also Jews from Greece, France, Italy as well as political prisoners from Russia, Poland and Serbia.

all of the other prisoners who had also applied for dismissal from work.

I wanted to go back and hide inside the haystack but something inside of me told me not to do so. I listened to my instincts and joined the firewood collection squad once again. Soon I found out how good my instinct was. The SS-guards had gathered around the tents covering the haystacks and found eight prisoners hiding inside them. All were taken away and we never saw them again. My instinct and my luck had helped me once again to avoid the deadly danger. I had previously wondered about the purpose of the hay at a place where there were no animals. I came to the conclusion that it was made for the camp prisoners as a modern human trap.

The daily task was to cut out much bigger trees. This exceeded my physical strength and I struggled a lot. I started to feel worse as the day went by. Around noon I struggled with nausea and got into a serious condition. My sweat was pouring out of me and my weakness increased further. I vomited black, clotted blood and I immediately recognized that I had stomach infection and bleeding. I could barely keep myself together. This meant my end was approaching, and I was aware of it.

Even with careful medical care this condition could be deadly, but I had no chance of survival here in the forest far away from civilization without medicine and medical care. My end had come, and the realization was not easy. Against this condition even my once trained body could not win. A desperate feeling took hold of me. The power of helplessness took hold of me and my thoughts were of death. New and newer misfortunes had always fallen on my shoulders. I had not even got out of one, before the next was already upon me.

Maybe I should have given myself up in the past to some cruel, whimsical twist of fate. Then I would have been past everything a long time ago. I blamed myself for fighting on so much.

I did not say anything to anyone. I left the group of lumberjacks and I went to find the doctor. I did not care about the outcome of my actions or what the punishment would be because this had all become irrelevant to me.

I found a Hungarian doctor and I complained to him in despair about my condition. I begged him to allow me to lie down somewhere. "I will not take up the bed for too long as I will bleed to death in a few days' time," I said to him.

"I cannot fulfill your request," he replied. "They will hold me accountable if you do not tell me the truth and you are not actually ill - just simulating it. On top of all this, there are more serious patients than you here in the camp," he said.

"Come with me to the forest and I will show you my bloody vomit to prove you that I am truly ill," I said to him.

"I do not have any more time for you," he said, and left me in my deadly condition - hopeless and beyond care.

I went back to the group of lumberjacks and I lay down on my back on the snow. I did not care about the threats of the others. As I looked up, I was amazed how beautiful the pine trees were as they were holding the snow on their branches. I said to myself "If I ever make it home alive, one day I will go to the Big Forest park in Debrecen and I will lie down under the big trees to enjoy the beauty of the snow and the snowy trees. I will enjoy the beauty of the falling snowflakes and I will listen carefully to the crackling sound of the snow under my feet as I walk home on the lit-up streets".

The truth hurt my soul very much. My strong instinctive power left me. I surrendered myself to final and total destruction. All I wanted to know now was how long this would take, how much would it hurt, and how would I be able to tolerate it with dignity. I did not want to look like a coward in front of the other inmates and the guards.

Another bleeding attack began - now mixed with carbon black faeces from below. My small supply of blood continued to run out. The loss of blood made me so weak that it took few attempts before I could stand up. I could not see the colour of my face, but my frozen hands turned from blueish purple to yellow, the characteristic colour of those who die.

I decided I would make another attempt to ease my misery. I picked up a branch and I poked it into a piece of my faeces and went to find the doctor again, this time I had the diagnosis with me.

The doctor changed his attitude towards me this time around. He looked at me for a while, examined me and finally he felt pity for me and asked me to follow him. We walked for a while on a small forest lane, then we crossed through a gate to a separately fenced section of the camp. He escorted me into the hospital of the lager. I had never been there, and I did not even know about the place. There were three circular green tents next to each other and another one opposite these. This was the so-called hospital. Two of the three tents contained those with typhus[99] and the third one had all the patients with other diseases or illnesses. The one which was standing by itself was to collect the dead bodies. Following the doctor, we stepped inside the tent in the middle of the three situated together. I was shocked. The doctor must be mistaken. This was not a hospital. This was a crypt. The round tent had wooden bunkbeds, and, on each bed, there were two naked skeleton bodies squeezed together. From the skull of each skeleton, two big eyes were gazing at us. The remainder of the bodies were full of scabs - some were healed, some were full of pus and the wetness of it was clearly visible. I stared at these "corpses" in silence. The tent had a nauseating stench from which I could not escape or get used to while I was there. One of the reasons for this smell were the purulent wounds. The other was the metal container in the middle of the tent which was used by everyone as a temporary toilet.

The doctor called for the leader of the tent. He had been deported here from Tarcsa[100], and he was just called W (Arthur Weberman). The skinny old man, about 40 years old, did not let me say one word. "Undress!" he ordered, "This will be your bed," and he pointed to the top level of the bunkbed next to the entrance.

"Can I please lay down on the lower level as my constant bloody diarrhea will make the climbing up and down very difficult?" I asked him.

"No, this will be your bed," and he pointed at the top level again. I had no choice but to climb up next to a young skinny boy from Nyiregyháza[101], who was slowly fading away. His body was full

---

[99] The diseases are caused by specific types of bacterial infection. Epidemic typhus is due to Rickettsia prowazekii spread by body lice. Scrub typhus is due to Orientia tsutsugamushi spread by chiggers, and murine typhus is due to Rickettsia typhi spread by fleas.

[100] Mr Schwarz refers to Tarcsa only. There are Kis- (little), Nagy- (big) and Kerepestarcsa which are in the same area near Budapest, a village in Pest county, Budapest metropolitan area, Hungary.

[101] Nyíregyháza is a city in northeastern Hungary and the county capital of Szabolcs-Szatmár-Bereg. With a population of 118,000, it is the seventh-largest city in Hungary and is one of the leading cities of Northern Hungary and of the northern part of the Great Hungarian Plain.

of purulent wounds, scabs, and lice. I tried to lie down next to him as gently as I possibly could. I was trying to pull away from the poor dying body in disgust - but in vain. In the first hours I found it very difficult to bear the stench of purulence. It took me days to get used to this heavy intolerable smell. The tent was full. Due to space constraints, I could not lie on my back. I had to stay on my side. My back pressed against my inmate and I felt his feverish, throbbing body. I could not talk to him, not even one word because he was unconscious. He talked aloud all night with a quite murmur. He mentioned his mother and a girl named Ilka, and then he woke up shouting: "Do not hurt me!" On the next day he passed away. He was only 18 years old, anonymous, and he got to learn the most horrible part of his life - his faith as a Jew.

We said goodbye to him, and also to all of the daily four or five dead. Fifty-two deadly ill people laid on the wooden bunkbeds inside this tent. The dead were replaced by new living skeletons. This tent was furnished with bodies dying in just a few days. This was the budget. We did not receive any medical treatment nor medication. The food was the same, and I did not believe it was possible to receive it in an even smaller portion. But at least we could fade away here in piety, in a gentler way.

The fat, yellow-bodied lice managed to find me rather quickly. Now I was scratching myself from them instead of flea bites. Their bites were not as painful but they carried disease, and being next to a tent with patients dying from typhus it could be quickly carried over to us. The only defence was to strip us naked. They did not care about us catching cold.

One of the inmates was asking 'W' to make it possible for him to join me. He was from one of the townships of Debrecen. He justified his request by offering his help in any way he could. He did not look any better than me. He was also full of bedsores and wounds from scratching himself. Furthermore he also had itch-mite[102].

He was a son of a very wealthy family. He was running the family business back home. "I'll make you my business partner after our liberation and I'll give you 40 per cent of it," he said.

---

[102] The human itch mite, or scabies mite, burrows into the top layer of the skin. They cause intense itching when the skin reacts to the mite bites.

"Our deadly struggle and our freedom equals all of the wealth," I replied. This spiked a bit of argument between us, but it did not last long of course.

I did not become mad at my new neighbour for sharing his bugs with me. At least it gave me a kind of entertainment to catch them, and for their disturbance, I repaid them by pressing them against the side of the wooden bed with my fingernail until they exploded.

I was lying here for the second day now and I did not feel any worse. My nausea began to pass with the lying down. I was hoping that by some miracle I would be healed without a doctor or medication. As my bed was next to the door, I could enjoy the advantage of the fresh air. However, the downside was that I felt the cold air much more than those further inside the tent.

During the days the door was open. This allowed me to keep eye on the tent across from us and what was happening there. As this tent was the collection point for all the dead bodies from the three hospital tents, I could study the process. Each corpse went through one last body search before being laid down in a mass grave. They kept records of those who had golden teeth. They were pulled out by the dentist who was accompanied by an SS-guard. There was only one who did not care what happened to the tooth afterwards. The teeth had to be sent to Dachau, into the main camp, yet there were still abuses and manipulations.

One afternoon a particularly large number of dead were laid in front of the fourth tent. The Müldorf station was bombed and one bomb fell amongst the prisoners working there. It wreaked havoc amongst them.

However it was particularly devastating when the naked bodies of our roommates were taken out to the tent and being placed down on the ground. Every day we had to say goodbye to some of our companions. Some passed away from total weakening, some from the diarrhea. As soon as diarrhea made its way into someone's body, that person was gone in just a few days.

A few charcoal tablets [103] would have been worth a lot here. It would have saved millions. Here someone was trying to make it from an old beef bone by burning into ashes it in the fire. The experiment failed. The diarrhea continued to take its toll.

---

[103] Charcoal is used to treat stomach pain caused by excess gas, diarrhea, or indigestion.

'W' said goodbye to everyone who passed away. He was a religious man who knew the farewell prayer of the dead which he always said at such times. Every prisoner had a registration number which was kept on record at Dachau. He wrote this number onto every dead body's chest. Tears rolled down W's face as he and one helper were taking out our comrade who not long ago had been lying with us.

Most of the residents of the tent were Hungarians, with only a few Polish amongst us. Therefore, you could hear only Hungarian words. Soon we had more familiar faces joining us. One of the Gladstein brothers from Debrecen, Eisenberg from Hajdúböszörmény, and many others we knew - all of them in critical and very weak physical conditions.

I was the first there from Auschwitz transport. I was asked to talk about my experiences from Auschwitz. This was a difficult and cruel task for me and for every listener. I could not make it beautiful what had happened there. I do not know why these physically and mentally broken and weakened inmates wanted to hear something more about tortures. I did not know and did not understand what made them want to be tortured even more. They listened quietly as I told the cruel fate of the daily transports arriving, the selection process of the elderly, the mothers, the children and the fathers, and their final walk towards the gas chambers and the operation of the gas chambers. My listeners already had weak heartbeats and I talked to them about horrors. Their own suffering already pressed on their shoulders with unbearable weight and the knowledge that their own family members also had become the victims of the SS evildoer, further escalated their pain and misery. One of my companions could not even listen to me anymore. He started to yell at me with craziness and asked me to stop the telling of the happenings. "You are a liar! This is not true! You are a villain and a murderer!" he continued, Some others joined in, slandering me, raining scorn on me. It was only with great difficulty and a long time before they became completely silent. In the deep silence I felt ashamed of myself. These people were looking for some encouraging words and some hope but instead of that I told them the brutal and unbearable truth. I had dying people around me and I had broken the most basic rule against them that they should be treated with kindness. This was not the right place to break this basic rule. For this, anger flowed towards me from their eyes, for taking away their last hopes and their illusions about their living and maybe surviving relatives. We received our small portion of bread for dinner and I managed to keep most of it, unlike the others. When the bread was a bit moist, I managed to cut it into a few millimetres thin, 7 to 8 cm long and 3 to 4 cm wide pieces. From the 15 to 20-gram piece of bread I managed to cut about 20-25 slices. I placed them carefully into the cotton bag around my neck. I touched it a few times a day and I knew I would be needing them to build some strength. On the days when the bombing was on, we did not get any food at all. One day I pulled out a dry piece of bread from the bag and I was crunching it rather loudly with my teeth. I felt a bit uncomfortable when all eyes were looking at me for this, but I did not think of sharing my valuable possession with anyone.

Soon another piece of beef bone made its way into our tent. The bone was given around the tent from mouth to mouth to be licked and chewed on. I did not join into this pleasure. I did not want to put this bone, which had been previously been licked by many with purulence and by prisoners with diseased mouths, in my own mouth. You always knew where the bone was because the enjoyment of the chewing was quite loud.

Our tent leader W managed to get his hands on some bread, margarine and a few small pieces of potatoes every day. He toasted the bread in the sizzling margarine and cooked the potato on a handmade fireplace. The little brick cooktop had a small metal plate on which he prepared his dinner day after day. Many hungry eyes watched this daily procedure. This was the time for me too to suck on a small piece of my dry bread.

Every night, at exactly the same time, a sharp pain came inside my thighs. I did not know what this was but it kept me awake all night. I did not have this problem before its onset at night but as soon the morning came, the pain went away with the darkness. As I was not able to sleep, I could watch what was happening in the tent during the night. In the middle of one night two prisoners arrived from the camp to visit one of the dying men on one of the lower-level beds. First, they started to whisper to him, then it got louder. One of the men ran out and returned with a tool and then it turned into argument. They knew that this dying man had two golden teeth, so they had come to get them. They offered him food in return, but the owner of the golden teeth did not accept the deal. The owner was in a very weak condition and so they took the teeth anyway. He was left there tortured. A few days after this man passed away and when the dentist came, he did not find the registered items. The SS-guards ordered an investigation into the whereabouts and mysterious disappearance of the gold pieces. They questioned W and everyone in the tent. No one could take his own golden tooth over to the other side. The Nazis considered themselves the only rightful owner and inheritor of the gold. Soon the new unlawful owners were found and it was made certain that they did not use any more of the forest air of Mühldorf.

The days just went by and I realized that I did not have any more abdominal bleeding. I considered this a miracle, especially without medical treatment and seeing the daily failing of my fellow inmates.

Three Hungarian doctors arrived in our tent. They were just as tired and worn out as us. They had some tablets and some cream with them, but they were willing to hand these over only for some bread in return.

One of them started to have a conversation with W and placed a small jar of cream for treating itch-mite bites on the table. I was full of scabs from scratching myself and I desperately wanted to have some of that cream. I got off my bed and started to close in on the open tub of cream. They were in a deep conversation so I sped up my steps and made it look like I was crossing the room to visit someone on the other side of the tent. In the meantime, I stuck my finger in the jar of cream and scooped out some of the ointment. I could not even wait to make it back to my bed to use this medicine. I rubbed the cream onto the most burning spots on my body. I could feel its cooling effect instantly.

I was in the belief that my mission was unseen, but one of the prisoners had caught my every move. He must have been jealous of my success and reported it to W. W ran to my bed, and right away he forgot his strong religious beliefs as he started to pour all his swearing words at me, and started to beat me. Because of his untrue character and his selfish behaviour, W deserved all our hatred.

In the tent we had all different kinds of professions and different levels of education. There was a lawyer from Budapest who had the most amazing memory and style of storytelling. I became tired just from talking but this man was able to remember parts of famous writers' books like the Hungarian born Jókai [104] and Mikszáth[105] and the internationally recognized Jules Verne[106]. He could recite for hours from these books. To retain the interest of the hungry inmates for weeks, everyone was happy to listen to the famous stories and divert attention from the present. He could remember the poems from Ady[107], Petőfi[108], and Arany[109] too.

He had enough strength to entertain the tent. We were grateful for it from the bottom of our hearts. He did not ask for anything in return, not like many others who did.

One night, a priest who was working in a small village before his deportation, preached for us. He spoke about the need for faith, about the heavenly happiness and how the wicked would receive their worthy punishment. He mentioned suffering, which he said was a human test and preached that at the end, righteous

---

[104] Móric Jókay de Ásva , outside Hungary also known as Maurus Jokai or Mauritius Jókai, was a Hungarian novelist, dramatist and revolutionary. He was active participant and a leading personality in the outbreak of Hungarian Liberal Revolution of 1848 in Pest. Jókai's romantic novels became very popular among the elite of Victorian era England; he was often compared to Dickens in the 19th century British press. One of his most famous fans and admirers was Queen Victoria herself.

[105] Kálmán Mikszáth, novelist, regarded by contemporaries and succeeding generations alike as the outstanding Hungarian writer at the turn of the century. He studied law but soon took up journalism. In 1887, already famous, he was elected to the National Assembly. January 16, 1847-May 28, 1910

[106] Jules Gabriel Verne - 8 February 1828 – 24 March 1905) was a French novelist, poet, and playwright.

[107] Endre Ady (Hungarian: diósadi Ady András Endre, archaic English: Andrew Ady, 22 November 1877 – 27 January 1919) was a turn-of-the-century Hungarian poet and journalist. Regarded by many as the greatest Hungarian poet of the 20th century, he was noted for his steadfast belief in social progress and development and for his poetry's exploration of fundamental questions of the modern European experience: love, temporality, faith, individuality, and patriotism.

[108] Sándor Petőfi was a Hungarian poet and liberal revolutionary. He is considered Hungary's national poet and was one of the key figures of the Hungarian Revolution of 1848. He is the author of the Nemzeti dal (National song), which is said to have inspired the revolution in the Kingdom of Hungary that grew into a war for independence from the Austrian Empire.

[109] János Arany was a Hungarian poet, writer, translator and journalist. He is often said to be the "Shakespeare of ballads" – he wrote more than 102 ballads that have been translated into over 50 languages, as well as the Toldi trilogy, to mention his most famous works.

people would become the honoured inhabitants of the heavenly kingdom.

The words left his lips with total belief but we did not feel uplifted, nor did it not make our souls any stronger. After this he announced his real need for a little food. I had to be part of the givers and I shared two small pieces of my 1-millimetre thin dry bread.

After this we had to lay down the rules of any more professional speakers. We allowed them to perform only if they did not request any payment in return of their performance.

The cold winter passed, and the spring took over. We could see the rays of the sun a bit more often as it shone through the branches of the pine trees, and the forest started to come alive. On the warmer days we moved out of the tent and lay our skinny naked bodies down on the freshly grown soft green grass. Our ears started to enjoy the singing of the birds. Their tweeting concerts carried some sort of hope, and their presence made this death camp a bit more friendly.

Around middays, the quietness was disturbed by the rumbling noise of the American warplanes. They flew very close to the ground and released their bombs from their bellies. Furthermore, they used their machine guns to attack the nearby airport. After the liberation I had a chance to visit this airport and see the destruction they caused. There were a lot of planes everywhere on the big green field but they could not take off due to gasoline shortage.

The rays of the sun had regained their power by now and we laid down on our backs and watched the circling of the American planes. They were passing over our heads and we saw many bombs getting dropped at once. It happened at a great altitude but we did not have any strength to jump up and run. I just closed my eyes not to see the destruction of the incoming and exploding bombs.

I was waiting for the terrible noise, but nothing - nothing happened. I opened my eyes slowly and I looked over in the direction where my fellow inmates were pointing. There were four empty patrol tanks about 50 m away from us. I accused the Americans for choosing this section of their flight to get rid of some unwanted weight and to scare us to death. Soon I was also thanking them for bombing the nearby section of the enemy's ground.

Unfortunately, the forest could not provide us with any food. However it could please the passionate smokers. They managed to roll some kind of cigarette from the bark of certain trees. I happily sniffed the wonderful smell of it in the air. Listening to their conversations, I managed to catch some great information. The tent which held the patients with typhus contained a renowned gynaecologist named Jakab from Debrecen. He had been known as an outstanding doctor in many cities. His entire family lost their lives in Auschwitz, so he could not enjoy his freedom after our liberation.

Next to one tree I recognized a man named Farkas who was the chief editor of the Independent Newspaper, also from Debrecen. This highly intelligent man shared a lot of interesting stories with us.

The time flew by a bit faster by taking some sun and talking to each other. During the night I could not sleep much because of a lot of joint pain. From the warmth of the sun, it felt a bit better, so I had most of my sleep during the day in the tent under my blanket or outside. Most of the time I was dreaming about the different types of food and this helped me to fall asleep. Our personal storyteller from Budapest helped me to fall asleep too, but also woke me up if he got too carried away with his dramatic performance.

Besides him, we also had an explorer in our tent. He was a well-travelled man. One day he was telling us all about an English passenger ship he once travelled on. He had a great memory so he could describe the smallest details of it. We all listened to him with great interest.

I lived amongst these kinds of people for weeks. Unfortunately, the illnesses continued to take their toll. We said goodbye to a few men day after day. Besides the total weakening, the typhus, and the internal abdominal bleeding, some had to face other problems. During the winter many developed gangrene[110] or frostbite[111] on different parts of their bodies. The hands or feet of

---

[110] Death and decay of body tissue, often occurring in a limb, caused by insufficient blood supply and usually following injury or disease.

[111] Frostbite occurs when the skin – and sometimes the tissue beneath the skin – **freezes due to**

some reached a stage where amputation was required. The visiting doctors did not use any painkillers, local anaesthetics nor sterilizers when they cut off these body parts, which were made visible by sticking out from under the blanket. I witnessed a lot of this kind of surgery myself, inside our tent. Of course, these patients did not live more than a few days after the amputation. After W's farewell prayer, they all ended up on the daily carriage pulled by two well-fed oxen.

The two large animals always made my stomach rumble. All I could think of every time I saw them was the great taste and smell of the roasted meat on a campfire. Unfortunately, we never had the privilege of eating from the well-fed animals.

It was the beginning of April when two SS-doctors stepped inside the tent with a clerk. The doctors lifted up the blanket on the skinny bodies and dictated the numbers of some prisoners. This was our selection time in the tent. Probably it was too expensive to feed us with the green grass soup and they thought we had had enough of our inactive life. They wanted to reduce our numbers by an accelerating procedure.

As I was right at the door, I was the first one to be assessed. By lifting up the blanket they could see a living skeleton with about 35 kilograms bodyweight. My skin looked very dirty, as the dust settled into my pores. Amongst the dirt, the bites from the parasites were clearly visible. We did not have enough water to drink so bathing was out. I could not have provided an uplifting sight like this, uncovered.

The two doctors looked at each other and they signed for the clerk to write up my number. Almost everyone's number in our tent was written down. I unconcernedly noted the outcome of the medical visit. However, my closest neighbour became hysterical and his behaviour was followed by many. They had been here longer, and they knew the situation. The headquarters in Dachau had ordered a selection and this had caused the tension - the nervous vibes.

The methods were the same as in Auschwitz. The prisoners who were useless and unable to work were examined and liquidated. Apparently, this kind of liquidation happened a few months

---

prolonged exposure to cold temperatures. Depending on how long and how frozen the tissue, frostbite can result in severe, sometimes permanent, damage.

previously when a truck arrived at night and the very ill personnel were literally thrown up on the tray and taken away. The ones who had already seen this happen were afraid on this day also, and their fear struck me too. After this experience we all got scared from every noise which came from the forest. A tense anticipation appeared on every face and we glanced at the forest for any sign of the truck headlights. 'W' waited up all night with us, dressed, but as far away from us as possible. He was afraid of getting amongst us and accidently being taken away too.

A few nights went by and the truck had not come. We were unsure if maybe they had forgotten about us, or if the war situation has changed drastically.

The news arrived that the allied forces had been moving forward with great speed.

An elderly, short-built, well-spoken Hungarian prisoner stepped inside our tent. He probably fulfilled an important position in the lager and he also knew the latest situation on the warfront. He came with an important announcement.

"Before the allied forces reach the camp, the SS camp leaders would like to execute everyone in this camp and in the main camp in Dachau. The transportation to Dachau is being delayed as the Germans would like to kill everyone here in this camp. We, the healthy inmates, are doing our best to preserve everyone including all of you here in this isolated section, but we all must prepare for the worse. In the meantime, we are negotiating everyone's situation and a possible amnesty with some of the camp leaders. I speak the English language very well and I am also prepared for the arrival and greeting of the Allied forces. If this happens, I will make sure to notify them about the importance of your prompt need for medical care."

Finally, we now knew our situation. Our long-lasting suffering would end soon. Either we would be liberated or we would be killed. Until then we had to keep going, somehow.

As the ring of the allied forces was tightening around us and the transportation routes were bombed daily, the camp leaders had more important tasks than to feed us, so the portions either became smaller or we did not even receive any meals.

During these days we continued to say goodbye to more inmates. After W's farewell prayer they were all carried out from our tent and laid down on the ground in front of the tent opposite. My friend Eisenberg from Hajdúböszörmény fell into eternal sleep. One morning no one could wake him up. He died from total weakening.

The previous night we had a small chat as his bed was on the lower level of mine. "I miss my brother," he said. "If you do make it home please try to find him. He has a barber shop on Hatvan street," he told me.

"On Hatvan street?" I asked in surprise, "I used to live on that street and I was stationed in the ghetto there. "I know the location of that barber shop very well".

During our chat he never mentioned or complained about being unwell. He only mentioned his weakness. He passed away the same way as he lived, quietly. He did not disturb anyone with loud yelling, groaning or moaning. His bed-neighbour only noticed his stiff dead body in the morning. His farewell prayer lasted only a few minutes then W laid his body on the ground with his registration number written on his bare chest.

The land of Bavaria gave his much-suffered body an eternal resting place.

The Langer brothers from Kaposvár [112] had been stationed on the other side of the door. The younger one was called István[113] and the older was Károly[114]. They shared the bed with each other. Karcsi was a baker and he promised me, once we were free, he would bake me a big loaf of crispy bread and send it to me. I just shut him off with a wave of my hand for two reasons. One, he made me very hungry just to even talk about the bread. And two, I did not believe his promise. We talked a lot and as they were so close to me, I noticed how well they looked after each other and how much love they showed towards each other. Unfortunately, Pista was already very ill when they were placed into our tents and soon after he also suffered from the abdominal bleeding with diarrhea. We knew he would not be living long.

---

[112] Kaposvár is a city in the southwestern part of Hungary, south from the Lake Balaton. It is one of the leading cities of Transdanubia and it is the capital of Somogy County as well as the seat of Kaposvár District and of the Roman Catholic Diocese of Kaposvár.

[113] István -in English Steve, Steven (Nickname Pista)

[114] Károly – in English Charles (Nickname -Karcsi)

Karcsi was trying to warm Pista up with his own body by hugging him, wiping the cold sweat off his forehead and even more, he gave all his food to him to try to make him stronger. He did not care about his own hunger and health. He showed unconditional love towards his younger brother. Karcsi tried his best in vain as the younger brother became weaker and weaker day by day. Unfortunately, his care was not enough. One morning he did not wake up. During the night he went into eternal sleep like so many others. Karcsi pulled the blanket over his brother's face and came over to me to whisper the bad news to me. I did not understand his reason and why he was not telling W about the passing of his sibling until lunch time. Lunchtime arrived and the green grass soup, which was already cold, was delivered by a strongly built Ábris, a Jew from Poland. You could not see the hardship and the life in poverty in him. He was our usual delivery man and he made sure everyone received his small portion. The pot had been placed down by the two men who carried it to the front of the tent and Ábris stepped in through the door with the big ladle in his hand and looked around to see all of us, "the bone-collection". We had to place our small metal cup out for him to fill it up. Karcsi reached out with both of the cups. Ábris looked at him and found it odd that Pista had been covered up with the blanket. He pulled the cover off him with a quick motion to see the stiffened body of Pista. Ábris did not look surprised but he became very angry and, using the big ladle in his hand, started to beat Karcsi. He was not happy that Karcsi wanted to take an extra portion of the soup which legally was not his portion. In the meantime he was swearing at him and calling him names.

Karcsi was well beaten up. Ábris did a great job. Karcsi's face was bleeding and very swollen. In this state Karcsi could only crawl up onto his wooden bed and lie down next to his dead brother, turning his back towards the rest of the tent and the cruel world he was living in. He rested his hand on his brother's corpse until it was taken away later that day. Pista's number was crossed out and now we had one less person in this "hospital tent". Karcsi did not eat that day, not because he had given all his food to his brother to make him stronger, but because he did not receive his portion as punishment. His portion now was making its way into the stomach of Ábris. This was how he managed to keep his strength, eating the portions of the sick who had passed away. The next day, one less portion was allocated for us and a few days later I also experienced the viciousness of Ábris.

We had not received any bread for days now and my dry pieces of reserve had gone. The starvation caused everyone increasing physical suffering. I could barely walk now from weakness. In the soft April sunshine, half walking, half crawling, I made my way through the forest towards the kitchen. When the Greek cooks saw my naked body, which was just like a skeleton, but also covered with scabs and purulent germination, they could not have looked more surprised. When they looked at each other I could read deep sympathy in their eyes. This time I did not have to follow them to fish out any half rotten potatoes or peels from the mud. After a short period of my begging, they handed over a few potatoes into my bowl. My tears rolled down my cheeks acknowledging their kindness.

Crawling back towards the tent in the forest was difficult as one of my hands was looking after my newly received gift. About halfway I had to stop on a soft grassy area for some rest. Suddenly someone's shadow blocked the warm sun away from me. As I opened my eyes, I could see the enormous body of Ábris. His angry look did not suggest much good was to come. He asked me a few questions in Polish and as he did not receive any answer he left.

Soon he arrived back with W at his side and W started to question me, "Where have you been? How did you managed to get hold onto these potatoes?"

"I made it all the way to the kitchen and the Greeks have…" I started my reply … but I could not finish my sentence as W launched at me and started to beat me with his fist. Ábris watched his reaction with satisfaction. I lost consciousness for a short period of time. When I regained consciousness all I could hear was his voice, "Get up you grub, get up and get back into the tent!" he said. But I had no strength at all so, he picked up my light-as-a-flake body and threw me over his shoulder like a sack and carried me back inside the tent where he just threw me onto the ground. He continued my punishment but this time with his legs - kicking. I was crying loudly. Steinberger, another prisoner, who respected me, picked me up and placed me up onto my bed. This was the only reason why the kicking stopped. I could not stop crying. It came back every time I regained consciousness. I kept blacking out. I was hurt, again, but not just physically. It also hurt that the people who were hurting me had made the journey on the same designated train into the death camp for the same purpose. It hurt me too that my potatoes which I had been generously given by the Greeks had been taken away from me. At night, the delicious smell of my potatoes circled the tent. W was baking them on his hot plate, and when he bit inside them, he did not even look at me.

It was close to the end of April [115] when we first heard the American heavy artillery bombing. They were moving forward but not fast enough - not just fast enough for me, for all of us. I had 300 difficult days behind me, and I was weak. We had barely been given any food and I had parasites all over me. The sun's rays could give me enough food to make my skin brown, but that was not enough to make me stronger. My weakness had progressed so far that I could not leave my bed any longer. My only hope was the ever-increasing noise of the explosions of the bombing. We tried to guess the distance of the artillery, which we thought was about 50 to 60 kilometres.
Of course, we had secret hopes. We were waiting for the Air Force to drop the special forces with parachutes. We heard the noise of the reconnaissance aircrafts. We were naïvely hoping that they would push the warfront forward just to save our lives. We had to wait, but we still had to face a few problems. One, we knew the Germans would not spare our lives and they did not want to hand us over to the liberating army. Two, we were afraid we would starve to death. During these days we did not sleep at

---

[115] **Apr 3** 1945Nazis begin evacuation of camp Buchenwald concentration camp
Apr 4 Hungary liberated from Nazi occupation
Apr 11 Four soldiers in the Sixth Armored Division of the US Third Army liberate the Nazi concentration camp, Buchenwald,
Apr 14 World War II: US 7th Army & allies forces capture Nuremberg & Stuttgart in Germany
Apr 29 US Army liberates 31,601 in Nazi concentration camp in Dachau, Germany
Apr 30 Concentration camp Munchen-Allach freed
Apr 30 Soviet Army frees Ravensbruck concentration camp
Apr 30 **Adolf Hitler** commits suicide along with his new wife Eva Braun in the Fuhrerbunker in Berlin as the Red Army captures the city

all. We were just listening to the noises of the explosions. Suddenly the noises stopped. There was just silence, and the silence felt very strange. From then on everyone created their own hope and story until the morning sunrise, trying to guess why it was silent.

Next morning breakfast came unusually late. During the apportioning, the head of the kitchen arrived too. The Polish workers had big smiles on their faces when the coffee arrived. I could not believe what I saw in my mug. It was coffee with milk. Besides the coffee we received a larger the normal piece of bread. I squeezed the great smelling cup in my hand. The beautiful smell filled the whole tent. I could no longer smell the revolting odour of the place. All I could smell was the fresh coffee. Something had to have happened suddenly because we were being looked after. I tore off a small piece of bread and started to soak it in my fresh white coffee.
The extremely thirsty wanderer of the desert could not rejoice more when finding spring water, than I did when I ate the soft bread soaked in the coffee with great passion. I did not even look up. I did not think of anything else until I finished the last drop of my coffee and the last piece of the bread. All I could hear was the noise of the chewing and slurping of the others. I reached out with my mug for another portion and I was surprised to receive more coffee without any beating up.

The camp residents

Dead coloured skeleton, alive dragging himself,
Dull glossy eyes, looking down, little of flesh,
Yellow wrinkled skin, bent back, bony sunken chest,
Bold head, tapering skull, thin arms, feels like trash.

Scratched wounds, purulent, swollen ankles,
Frostbitten black skin, bluish nose in harsh cold,
Weightless body wrapped in rags with negligence,

Clumsy wooden shoes on wounded legs,
Such was the martyr Auschwitz residence.

This is how the skeleton-eyed man lived,
Chased to work on one leg marching slow,
The other leg on the doorstep of the gas chambers,
Whip-, tick-, fist-chasing, swinging, swaying shadow.

Wondering hungry, thirsty for water, hard bed
Full of greedy flees with great appetite,
Along with blood-sucking fat lice,
Lonely in the army of capos, hopeless every night.

He has no one anymore, the entire family
Gone up in a smoke, fighting with sleeplessness,
In a spacious mourning house, lying on his bed
Dreamless, he has no more weakness.

The beasts hiding in human skins,
The SS without judgement decease,
The inmates' last wish is to be there,
With the others in the eternal peace.

September 1966, Debrecen, Hungary

The free man[116]

After finishing the breakfast, some of the stronger men decided
to go to find out the reason behind this positive twist. Soon we
found out what had happened. Because of the heavy bombing
and the fast-forward movement of the Allied forces, some of
leaders of the Bayern state had started an independent
negotiation for a peace treaty. Favourable conditions were also

[116] Apr 29 1945, US Army liberates 31,601 in Nazi concentration camp in Dachau, Germany; Apr
30 1945, Concentration camp Munchen-Allach freed

helped during their negotiation by promising to treat the prisoners with humanity.

As soon we have heard this news the entire tent went into planning and dreaming about the future - what we would be doing next; how many family members we had to search for; to find our torturers and bring them to justice; what kind of food we would be eating as soon we arrived home; medical treatment, and so on - and so on. During the last months I had not seen any lager this happy. The hope of freedom and the start of a new life in my hometown shone before me. I had wished for this feeling for months, during the sleepless nights with a tormented heart. I was already close to realizing my dreams and it filled me with tremendous hope. It felt like I had received a big dose of vitamins.

During lunchtime, the large apportioning of the fulfilling meal continued. We received a thick stew with lunchmeat inside. In this stew we had already found some fat. The warm food felt great to our stomachs, and I already felt like I had been reborn. I began to find the miserable interior of the tent a bit more beautiful and to appreciate the forest with its bird voices, and everything which was around me in these late April days. Waiting for the dinner exuded a serene atmosphere during the afternoon sunset. The death statistics for that day dropped to zero. In the events of the last few hours there was much incentive and stimulating hope. Everybody wanted to stay alive. The sudden changes that took place resulted in a rapid turnaround in our bodies. The blood flowed faster, the blood vessels opened, the colour returned into the faces, the eyes were shining and even the bites of the lice did not bother us that much either. The night had fallen with us in these moods. The silhouette of the green pine forest did not infuse the atmosphere of seriousness. The German forest with the birdsongs had proclaimed a new spring. I watched longingly in the darkening silence. It would have been nice to put on some clothes and rush away quickly from imprisonment. I already felt the breeze of the freedom. I wished to step over the barbwire fences, out onto the grass field, and head East - to head home. Desires and thoughts flowed through my body. The quite spring night and the scent of the good-smelling earth rocked me into a deep sleep.

I woke up to the roar of cannons and the explosions of bombs. They were firing with more violence than before. Much happiness had been derived from the ceasefire. It was bitter knowledge that the gunfire had started again.

The news arrived later in the morning. The two sides could not agree, they continued the war, and this time they would not stop until the final fight, and it would be decided only by fighting. So, we would not be taken over by a liberating army so easily. We were in the middle of the battlefield. Our hopes had collapsed. The 52-person tarpaulin tent had become a mourning house again. We looked sadly forward to the future. Everything continued the same way as before, as if that one day had not even existed. The green grass soup had become our main food again, but this time even thinner than before. It was like they wanted to make up for the food they had lost on that one day. We did not receive any bread at all, so the future of our lives had become critical again.

We laid inside in silence, the happy planning had stopped. Our situation has become crucial.

In these conditions, two Hungarian doctors arrived. Without any introduction they advised the following, "The allied forces have been closing in towards the camp, and soon they will reach us. Therefore, the Germans have decided to evacuate the prisoners of this campsite and all patients should join in the march. You all will receive clothing. In their opinion it would be safer to leave the campsite than to stay here any longer."

Some of the patients were strong enough to stand up and walk away with the doctors. My bed companion got up with loud whimpering and said to me, "I am leaving too. I am more afraid to stay here than to go. I know these Nazis and they will execute everyone here in the hospital. I cannot give that a chance."

I did not have to think about this at all, to stay or to go - my body decided for me. I was too weak to get out of bed. I knew the dark future of the weak during a long march. I knew I could not walk even one kilometre let alone endure a march that would possibly be days long. If I must die, I chose the wooden bed instead of the side of the road.

We stayed in a reduced number in the tent. Soon my bed companion came back. He realized he did not have the strength for a long march. He cried aloud beside me from fatigue and fear. He, and all the rest of us, were afraid of the increasingly quiet forest. The pessimists whispered that after the camp was emptied, the life of the remaining few dozen patients would be ended.

After the liberation, I found out the horrific end for those leaving the camp. After a long walk they were all pushed inside many train wagons. These trains were hit by an air raid on the open track, and this caused severe damage. [117]

Picture: Dachau - May 3, 1945: Meméers of the 42nd Rainbow Division of the 7th Army uncover some of the horrors of the concentration camp at Dachau
Picture from: https://www.ibtimes.co.uk/ve-day-70th-anniversary-look-germanys-surrender-1945-end-ww2-graphic-images-1499979

---

[117] In April 1945, just prior to the liberation of Dachau by the Allied forces, the SS ordered approximately 7,000 prisoners to embark on a six-day-long death march to Tegernsee, located to the south. Those unable to maintain a steady marching pace were shot by SS guards. Other marchers died from starvation or physical exhaustion. - https://www.history.com/topics/world-war-ii/dachau

Picture from:
https://i.pinimg.com/736x/ff/01/c9/ff01c9f108b01d975ba3403013a30463--the-holocaust-concentration-camps.jpg - Dead bodies in the train wagon after the long trip

Picture from: https://collections.ushmm.org/iiif-b/assets/783273

May 1945: A pile of corpses found by troops of the US 7th Army at Dachau concentration camp in Germany. These prisoners had been gassed and their bodies were awaiting cremation

In these last few days we could rely only on our luck and good fortune. We could not do anything else.

The silence of the forest gave the SS-guards left behind every opportunity to get rid of the dying sick without witnesses.

The crucial night arrived. I got scared by every noise which came from outside the tent - branches moved by the wind, by birds, anything.

Next morning the camp prisoners came to our tents with some paint. They started to paint big red crosses on our tent. I had seen too many of these in the past almost 11 months. I had never found sincere intent behind any such action. I could not believe in anything the Nazis had done. There was always something terrible behind their actions. I took the painting of the tents as a tactical effort, yet it filled me with a bit of hope.

There were no walking patients in any of the tents so we did not know anything about what was really happening outside. Our commander W had disappeared somewhere. It was a good move by him to separate himself from us as many of us wanted to have a good chat with him for his way of treating us. He had inhumanely treated his fellow prisoners with religious fanaticism.

I did not take my eyes off the door. I was hoping someone would step through it and free my life - which had been almost ended a hundred times by now. I had waited for this never-to-be-forgotten moment for a long time.

The incoming light was overshadowed by a huge soldier at the door. His uniform was unknown to me, his helmet was covered with a green net, and across his chest hung a machine-gun. He stood there silently, and we looked back at him the same way. We did not recognise this man, and he could not say one word from the shock. He froze at the door. We could read the disbelief on his face.

He will remember for the rest of his life what he saw there and then. The light from the door that showed inside the tent allowed him to see the naked living skeletons, their big eyes staring at him, their swollen hands and feet from the infections, the pale skin colours, and all this mixed with the unbearable smell of rotting bodies and human faeces which had been kept inside in a pot in the middle of the tent.

The soldier took one step forward and he was right at beside my bed. Someone yelled out, "The Americans are here, we are free!" Hearing this, the entire tent became alive. Whoever had been lying still until now also started to move, started to yell with unrecognisable voices and sounds of happiness. They all started to crawl down off the beds and onto the floor towards him. None of us was strong enough to walk. He just stood there with wide-open eyes, witnessing what was happening in front of him. He could not believe what he saw. We must have looked like a bunch of zombies. When they reached him, those who had enough strength pulled himself up to hug him. Those who could reach only his hands kissed him there, and some who had no strength at all just kissed his shoes.

We all cried from happiness. Those who could not reach him cried and rolled over on their back on the ground. Everyone showed some sort of positive emotion. Amidst the variations of the reactions of unexpected joy, the eyes of the American soldier became teary, then ashamed, then he burst into loud sobs. The warrior soldier was deeply touched by the sight of so much human suffering and the outburst of gratitude towards the liberator. I could easily reach him and give him my gratitude. I did not even have to climb out of bed because he stood so close to me. I grabbed him from there. I leaned towards him and I kissed his back. He did not protest my thanking him. He looked at me, then he continued to cry. He was sorry for the many miserable people who had suffered so much.

On the 308th day, finally it had happened! What I had been thinking about and longing for every day, and made every effort with every part of my body to survive. This kind of momentous feeling does not happen often during one's life. My skinny body was almost unable to accommodate and process and the multitude of increasingly congested emotions. I felt I had to endure a straining, squeezing feeling, and overflowing joy. I wanted to run out into the forest, yell out that I had survived the 20th century's worst inhumanity to man. I wanted to breathe in some fresh air after the stinky air of the tent. I was on German soil, in a German forest, and my hangmen had gone into hiding from prosecution.

I dedicated this day to myself as the greatest of the great feasts. If I could play any kind of musical instrument, I would have played three anthems. First, the Soviet anthem for liberating Auschwitz, the most destructive camp in the world. Second, for the Americans for liberating Dachau and all the subcamps in the forest of Mühldorf. And third, I would play the anthem of my country, which would be for all decent Hungarians.

Along with the others I also sniffed sensitively and did not take my eyes off the American soldier.

He waved at us that he had to go but he would return soon. When he came back he had a small metal container in his hand and through a nozzle he started to pour some white powder with a strange odour on us from head to toe. We did not mind it as soon after, the itching and biting of the parasites eased. The yellow lice which had been sucking my blood with great persistence were fleeing, but in the end, their destiny was fulfilled - just as it was for our armed torturers. Getting rid of the bloodsuckers already made me feel relieved.

The American soldier took a sensitive farewell and went to join the fighting armies. He belonged to an armoured corps that chased after the remains of the retreating German army. Now we were left completely alone, hungry and naked. Some of our armed guards had fled, others had been captured by the Americans.

Some of the inmates who still had some physical strength took a trip to find some food. When they arrived in the kitchen they have found it completely empty and looted. In the corner of the storage area they found a few pieces of beans, potatoes and millet. They collected all of these and when they returned, they shared them around, leaving everyone to do whatever they wanted with them.

With help and a lot of effort I climbed down from the bed and took my place at the handmade brick cooktop of W's. I put my part of the fairly-distributed remnant in my little metal cup and sat down to cook it. Crouching down, I stirred the dusty mixture. No one was keeping order in the tent any longer. The beds had been taken apart and the wood used to make a fire. The pot in the middle of the room that had been used as a toilet, was knocked over and all its contents spilled onto the ground. The door was left open and I was afraid some of the hiding SS-guards would return and kill all of us unattended people. We had received a similar warning from the American soldier as well. Luckily, no one harmed us. I could cook my little meal without any disturbance. The ingredients were only water and the shared legumes. There was no need to do any testing to see if there was enough salt or whether other spices should be added. As the different legumes needed different length of time to cook, I could not wait long enough for them all to get soft enough. As soon as the water started to boil, I started to eat the nearly raw ingredients. I did not care if they were too hot and burnt my mouth, or were not ready to eat. The most important thing was to try to fulfill the screaming need of my empty stomach.

My fellow inmates acted the same way. We did not care too much about each other, we were only interested in looking after our own little bit of cooking. There were only Hungarians in the tent by that time. The good organization of the Poles ensured that, in the first hours of the liberation, the leaders of the Polish prisoners put their sick people in safety.

Their actions were driven by forethoughts. Many people died in the first few days following the liberation. On the second day we received a shipment from the close-by village. The pork meat dripped fat and that caused diarrhoea and painful stomach upset for many. We did not know who the sender was, but we guessed, because the next day the camp's SS doctor came by in civilian clothing to check on us.

The order had been to burn all the tents and the fugitives from the tents must be shot dead.
We later found out that the Jewish medical professionals had negotiated with the SS medical staff that if they would look after all the sick, and help with our survival and escape, they would be rewarded with good words to the American authorities for their freedom and mercy.
Therefore, to save his own life, the SS-doctor refused the order to execute us or transport all of us to Dachau. Instead of annihilation, the doctor painted the International Red Cross sign on the tents.

We stayed in the tents for another four days, until the 6th of May. We did not find any clothing, so those who could walk used their old rug to cover themselves as they moved around in the surrounding forest. On the Sunday morning, American medical vehicles arrived. I was very impressed by these signs of civilization. I was lifted onto a stretcher and placed inside the ambulance. I used all my strength to sit up so I could look back to see the place in which I had spent my previous two months. I did not feel sorry to leave this place, but I made sure I absorbed as much information and details as I could.
Lots of tears and blood soaked every square metre of the forest. Many last sighs were heard in the silence of the night. I farewelled so many of my friends and acquaintances. I also said good-bye to the tall green pine trees. The winter snow would cover this forest for many more years to come. Countless springs would provide space for the hatching bird chicks. Today's youth may never know the dreadful secret of the Mühldorf forest. If they could understand the rustling of the trees, they would hastily flee from them. No one would understand it if the pine trees were the only ones that lived, and were freed here, in the spring of 1945.
From the ambulance I said another farewell to the ones left behind - those with whom we dreamed of freedom, home and

family. They lay there in the soil of the forest and soon they would be placed in a proper grave, where no one would disturb their eternal peace anymore. I wished eternal peace over the bodies of my much-suffered companions. With this in mind, I said goodbye to all lost inmates, prisoners, and friends.

The ambulance soon rolled out onto the road. On both side of the road all I could see were big green meadows with lots of colourful flowers, as if nature was trying to make up for all the sufferings with this beautiful, heart-warming view.

Thousands of the liberated human groups flowed towards us dancing and singing. This brilliant picture of nature, which could not have been painted any more beautifully, was their backdrop. In the front there were Italians in shorts making music with a mouth organ and waving tricolour flags in their hands. Another group was waving the red flag of the Soviet Union and singing communist songs.

We just rolled slowly on amongst the celebrating crowd. The people sang into the ambulance through the open window, and even the American driver was amazed at seeing this endless happiness. They celebrated the peace and the liberating army of the Alliance.

The German citizens of the local village were hiding in their houses. They were afraid of the possible questioning of the liberated thousands. It is shame that these happy movements were not recorded and kept for the future generations. There can hardly be a better opportunity to capture such an international entanglement of faces radiating such joy.

When we cut through the crowd, I looked back again. I wanted to remember for this spectacle forever. I will never have another opportunity to see thousands of death-sentenced humans together. No one can celebrate the freedom with such huge joy as those who have been freed from their death sentence after surviving so many terrible tortures. The beautiful May spring and the defeated enemy on their home ground completed the picture.

I lay back on to the comfortable stretcher. My heart was full of joy. The Americans watched these events with interest but did not perceive this wonderful manifestation of the liberation with such a profound effect. They left me alone with my feelings. They did not disturb me. Only when we had left the joyful crowd well behind us did they offer me a cigarette. As I was a non-smoker, I thanked them for the gesture but refused to take one. Next moment, I was handed a bar of chocolate. Now that was my kind of treat, and I happily took it and munched on it.

The liberated patient

The ambulance transported me to the outskirts of Mühldorf into an old, shabby, monastery-like building with towers. I was allocated a room inside the building where there were nine similarly weak and physically run down patients. Our treatment was performed and we were looked after by the nuns who had been living there for a long time. They provided plenty of food as well as the medical treatment.

Before us, it was possibly used as a hospital for the wounded SS army. This was my conclusion because underneath my bed mattress I found a picture of an SS soldier, his handwritten mail, and a few small items. They must have been emptied out so quickly he did not even have time to gather his belongings. I think he would never have thought in his wildest dreams that he would need to make room for a fugitive death-sentenced Jew. Life does weird things, and maybe he was one of my torturers in one of the camps who gave me countless unpleasant moments.

The nuns performed their duties silently. They provided care, cleaning, cooking and serving the food. They became our full-time carers. I did not manage to find out from them whom they had served most faithfully. Their faces did not show any hatred nor any kindness towards us. They worked together diligently. As there was plenty of food, we were warned not to eat too much at once as that could cause complications. One man from Nagyvárad[118] did not listen and he ate so much he passed away by the next morning.

---

[118] Nagyvárad – in Romanian Oradea. The Romanian name Oradea originates from the city's Hungarian name. The city flourished both economically and culturally during the 13th century as part of the Kingdom of Hungary.

I became friendly with only one middle aged nun. She must have liked me as she always approached me with kindness. Before night time she always came and sought my assistance. Somehow she managed to get hold of a big can of fresh milk. We looked for the most disabled or sick patients and I carried the can after her from room to room. The seriously ill patients enjoyed a glass of refreshing milk.

On a funeral

A few weeks after our liberation I received information that some of my fellow inmates who had passed away, were to be relocated from a mass grave. The Americans ordered these corpses were to be dug up by the SS soldiers and buried in their final resting place, properly.

With some help from a walking stick, I managed to get myself to this ceremonial funeral organized the Americans. An announcement had urged all adult residents of the city to show up at the funeral. Soldiers made sure the instruction was followed. The male and female residents of Mühldorf city were all present, dressed in black, at the cemetery.

Lots and lots of graves had been dug. At each hole, a body was laid and next to them an SS soldiers stood stiffly with uncovered heads. They owed respect to their victims. There lay before them the silent, tortured, distorted, and blackened corpses. Many were already missing an ear, nose, or other limbs. These bodies accused their torturers in silence. They accused both their torturers and those who endured this as silent observers.

The Americans considered the residents of the city to be guilty also. They could only apologize for a small portion of their sins. The residents were ordered to walk up to the corpses and farewell the victims of the European countries respectfully. Many could not watch the open lips and accusing open-eyed looks of the dead. They turned their heads away, covered their eyes and some held handkerchiefs over of their nose to block the irritating smell. An American soldier of Polish descent stepped up in anger. He pushed and shoved the citizens and peeled the blocking hands from their eyes. "These are your sins!" he yelled angrily.

The ceremony was held by the army priest and when he said the words of the final farewell, deep silence descended over the entire cemetery.

After his final words, the SS soldiers placed the corpses into the graves. The new tombstones were embossed side by side and the entire city's residents stood beside them with their heads bowed. This new cemetery in the town of Mühldorf became the eternal resting place for many of my poor companions. I also said goodbye to the anonymous graves. When I looked back at the cemetery in the warm twilight of the early summer, a white cross had been lit by the setting sun on each grave.

The poster which was displayed after the liberation by the Allied forces on the wall in Mr. Schwarz's apartment.

Photo provided by the writer.

Wallposter on the wall in Mr Schwarcz's studio apartment from Mühldorf. When the Americans liberated the lager and all subcamps, they placed these posters all over the city and asking: "Whose fault?" Mr Schwarcz took one of these posters and kept it on his wall. Every morning before he went to work (especially when he was in the director position) he looked at this poster and reminded himself to be modest, humbled, to act with humanity and be optimistic.

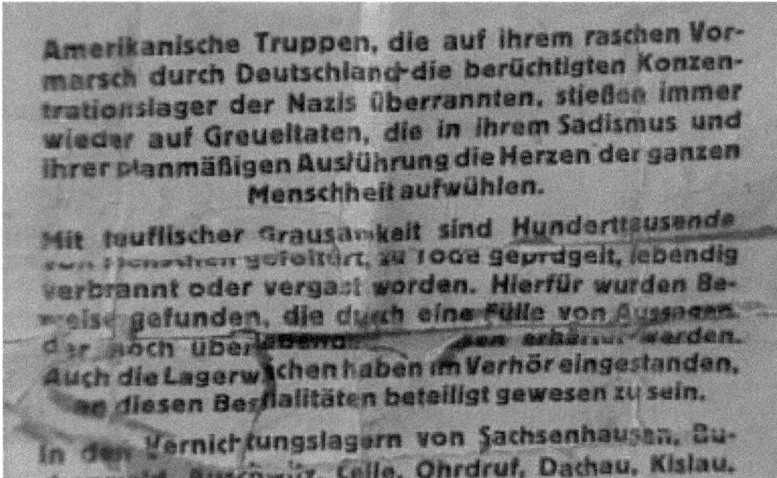

Amerikanische Truppen, die auf ihrem raschen Vor-
marsch durch Deutschland-die berüchtigten Konzen-
trationslager der Nazis überrannten, stießen immer
wieder auf Greueltaten, die in ihrem Sadismus und
ihrer planmäßigen Ausführung die Herzen der ganzen
Menschheit aufwühlen.

Mit teuflischer Grausamkeit sind Hunderttausende
von Menschen gefoltert, zu Tode geprügelt, lebendig
verbrannt oder vergast worden. Hierfür wurden Be-
weise gefunden, die durch eine Fülle von Aussagen,
der noch überlebenden ... werden.
Auch die Lagerwachen haben im Verhör eingestanden,
an diesen Bestialitäten beteiligt gewesen zu sein.
In den Vernichtungslagern von Sachsenhausen, Buchenwald, Celle, Ohrdruf, Dachau, Kislau.

Part of the poster

The mass graves

In a grave dug by themselves
They lie shot in the head,
Bone and soil all mixed together
They rest altogether in death's bed.
Many years later, green
Fertile bushes (growing) everywhere,
In the pine forest of Bavaria
And the wide Polish sunny bare.

The executioners marched contentedly
Returning home with bloodied hand,
They tell about their hero story
Fighting the unarmed, saving the homeland.

Awards given for machinegun killing
In glass cabinet shines the medal,
Grandchildren inherit the heroic deed
As they followed Hitler's devil credal

The ones who vanished

I received an invitation from a friendly nun who was living with her elderly mother on the side of the hill above the river Inn. She told me that the monastery had been used to treat SS soldiers before us. She also told me that before them, the monastery had been ordered by the Nazi party to look after mentally or physically disabled German citizens.

The monastery had a fruit and vegetable garden and a small farm as well. The disabled patients helped out under the supervision of the nuns.

Many secrets of fascist Germany have not yet been uncovered or recorded in historical chronicles. The majority of the Germans are silent, or rather, the tombs remain silent. Some are ashamed of the barbarism committed, but there are many who cover their sins by silencing themselves.

It took me a few weeks before I managed to uncover the secrets of the monastery. The nuns did not give me any information about the whereabouts of the disabled residents, despite the fact I was eager to find out.

I traced their whereabouts by accident. I managed to get so strong that I could go for some longer walks.

One warm afternoon, my walk stretched into the early night. On my way back to the monastery I came upon a park which was surrounded by a fence. The park stretched over a very big area and I looked for a gate in the fence. When finally I found one, a very strange scene inside the park welcomed me. In the middle of the park I could see trees, bushes, and flowerbeds. On the outskirt of the park I found some very strange little humps. Going a little closer I was surprised to see little crosses as well. The little humps that I could see from the distance were graves, and each little cross had a name on it. It was very odd to see graves inside this huge park. I walked all the way around the park and the graves continued all along the way. I was looking for someone, but the park was empty. I wanted to find out who was buried there.

It was becoming dark so I decided to hurry out of this strange and sad park. As I was walking towards the gate, an old man was walking inside the park with a bunch of flowers in his hands.

With my little German language knowledge, I greeted him, "Good evening, sir. May I ask you what these graves are?"

"These are the graves of the disabled German citizens who were gathered together earlier and were kept inside the monastery," he replied.

The "New Aryan ideology" of Hitler did not give mercy to these unfortunate people either.

For the sake of the clean German race, Hitler death-sentenced the Jews, the Gypsies, the gays, and the untreatably disabled, and he did not care if they were German citizens or not.

One day, German doctors appeared amongst the unfortunate people of the monastery. They came for the purpose of "examining, remedying, and healing". They brought many syringes with them. They injected a high concentration level of Benzonatate into the veins of the residents of the monastery, from which they "healed" so well that they all fell into a deep eternal sleep. The tombs of these residents were there in the park. I did not see anyone taking a walk there. The young and the old deliberately avoided this place. I do not know who decided to use this location and why these graves were dug there under the big trees.

Ábris

I was getting stronger and stronger from the food and the regular exercises. On one of these long walks my route led me towards the American kitchen. I was not hungry, it just happened by accident. Just then, good quality potatoes were being unloaded from the trucks. We had enough food, so I did not need more. Possibly, the one year of constant hunger made me lean forward and place some of the nicest pieces in my pockets. No one told me off, no one stopped me doing it. When I straightened up, the huge figure of Ábris' stood in front of me. He was alone, and he had just disembarked from a horse carriage which he had managed to get from somewhere. He recognized me as he questioningly narrowed his eyes. He found my action of getting potatoes in addition to the plenty of American food incomprehensible. We looked deeply into each other's eyes. I was not afraid of him anymore. I was putting on almost a half a kilogram each day. I was regaining my strength. I threatened him in Hungarian and called him many names - which he did not understand at all - but from the tone of my voice he realized the reason behind my outburst. I was strong now and I was ready to defend myself and my potatoes. He did not say one word. He pointed at his head, showing me that there was probably some problem with me there, then he boarded his carriage and drove away.

W.

There was another person who I needed to find - to get even with. It was our medical tent commander, the inhuman and evil W. I looked for him in many small surrounding villages and cities around Mühldorf. My tracing took me as far as a small house as Ampfing. I prepared myself for the meeting, which to me felt more like a personal battle. I did not forget all the hitting, beating, the suffering from the hysterical constant cries and inhumanity against those dying. I wanted to repay something. That was my intention and that is how I entered the front yard. An old woman was standing outside the house.
"I am looking for a man named Arthur Weberman," I stated.
"He is inside," she replied. "He is lying in bed. He has typhus," she added. "He does not have much time left, but you can go inside if you wish," she concluded.
"Oh, no, thank you. He has caused enough problems and pain for me. I do not need any more of his evilness," I replied and turned my back to the house. I was somewhat unsatisfied that I could not face him, but on the other hand I was happy that the suffering had finally caught up with him and I hoped he would receive his deserved ending.

He did end up healing and later returned to Hungary. He became part of the Hungarian Jewish church.

The choice

We were treated very well. The Americans organized clothing. Every family in Mühldorf had to supply two suits. We received a haircut and shave from the local barbers and the local dentists also had to come and treat us.

Every day we received a bar of chocolate and a box of cigarettes. As I was not a smoker, I was able to save some of the cigarettes. One day the American commander came to me and said:

"Hungary has been bombed very heavily so we would like to offer you the opportunity to settle in another country - Sweden, Switzerland, America or any other place. You name it and we will make it happen."

"Thank you for the generous offer, but I born in Hungary and I would like to return to my hometown Debrecen," I replied.

"That is good, but we cannot help you with your safe return." he said.

One man from Debrecen also said: "Come with us to Paris".

Of course, I did not take my place on the beautiful bus which came to pick them up.

Our Hungarian government had proven itself again. They did not care about us. They had not provided any help for us during the war, and we did not receive any help after the war was over. There was no bus or train which I could take to return home. I had to find my own way.

On the 1st of July 1945 I ended up joining the Czechs. I did not say one word of course - as I did not trust anyone. When we arrived at Pilsen, I took my place with them in a hotel. One Hungarian staff member, a young boy, was made to work extra hard in the hotel and I did not like the way he was being treated. One day when he was cleaning the floor under my bed in our room, I gave him a box of American cigarette. The Czechs did not like me for this gesture, so I felt the need to continue with my journey to get home.

I embarked on a train which took me to Brno[119]; then I continued my trip to Pozsony[120]. From there I arrived at Budapest and registered myself at the Bethlen Square Synagogue[121]. Here I could take a shower and I received food, fresh clothes and shelter.

---

[119] Brno; German: Brünn, is a city in the South Moravian Region of the Czech Republic and the second-largest city after the capital, Prague.

[120] Pozsony, county was an administrative county (comitatus) of the Kingdom of Hungary. Its territory is now mostly part of Slovakia (Bratislava), while a small area belongs to Hungary.

[121] The neo-Renaissance building was built in 1876 for the National Institute of Israelite Deaf Mute, and in 1931 the prayer room was expanded into a synagogue by Leopold Baumhorn.

Picture from:

I continued my trip home the next day and in the early morning of the 15th July 1945, after two weeks of travel, I arrived in heavily bombed Debrecen.

I took the road towards our house at Hatvan street. I felt free and I knew I could live there now as a free man and no one could call me a Jew in a disparaging way anymore. Someone walked close behind me, but I did not look back, I was not scared of anything or anyone anymore. I was happy to see our family home and I was hoping to meet some of my relatives.

When I have entered through the gate and made my way through the internal front court, an old lady said to me, "Who are you, and where are you heading?"

"This is our home and I have just returned from the war," I replied.

"There is no longer anyone here from the original Jewish families. There are only new owners living here," she said. So, I had to turn my back on my family home once again, which was deeply upsetting.

I did not know what to do or where to go, so I just started to walk the streets in the American army jacket which I had worn since leaving Mühldorf.

Someone recognized me: "Sandor!" he said. "Have not seen you for long time. Where have you been?" he asked.

"I have just returned from the Nazi concentration camps," I replied. "I went to look for my family home and my relatives, but someone else has the ownership of our old family home. Besides, I do not even know if I have any relatives left as all of us were deported."

"As far as I know, your parents arrived back home a long time ago," he said.

"My parents? But they were old and ill," I argued.

"I am pretty sure they came back long time ago," he continued.

"Would you know where I can find them?" I asked.

"No, sorry," he replied. We wished each other a good day and I continued my lingering on the street but this time, with my heart full of joy. I did not know where to start my search for my parents. As I walked on the streets, another friend spotted me, "Sandor, is that really you? How are you? Where have you been?" he bombarded me with his line of questions, being excited to see me returning.

"I am well, thank you. I have just returned from Hell, from the Nazi concentration camps," I said. "I just heard that my parents may be alive. Do you know anything of their whereabouts?" I asked in hope.

"Yes, they have returned, and so has your sister."

"Do you know where I can find them?" I asked him impatiently.

"Yes. They live on the Csokonai Street, I think number 24," he said.

"I cannot believe it. Thank you. I must go now to find them!" I said back over my shoulder, as I could not wait to see my parents and my sister after such a long time, and after so much suffering. On the way there I could not stop thinking about the incredible luck of their survival as well. I saw everything in the camps, and I knew they would not be selected for life by Mengele. They were on a train before me which had also been sent to Birkenau, and by the time I got there I was sure they already had been sent to the gas chambers.

When I arrived at the door my heart was racing and wanted to jump out of my chest. I knocked on the door. My old and skinny mother opened the door. She could not believe what she saw. She reached out to place my head into her hands so she could believe her eyes. "Sandor," she said, and she fainted. I grabbed her and picked her up, walked inside the house and placed her on a couch. My father was lying on the floor as he was very ill and weak, just like many strong men I had seen before.

"I have prayed for you and my prayers have been listened to by God whose name must be praised," my mum said when she had won her strength back.

I had a few energy snacks in my pocket, and I started to strengthen my father up from that point.

"We heard you had a stomach bleed and that you have passed away from it," my mum said.

My parents did not go to ask for any help or any reimbursement from the city for their loss. This house was an old place with damp walls, but we were free citizens.

My father suggested a walk down to the church to say a thank-you prayer for my and everyone's return.

The deporting train which had taken my parents away had been sent to Austria by a human mistake. This was the only reason they managed to survive.

Next day I had to walk to the birth and death office to register myself. In 1944 I had been deleted from the list of living citizens.

A few years later my sister got married to a very great man, Sándor Garai and moved to Békéscsaba[122]. I agreed to take care

of our old parents. My father had an asthmatic problem which did not get better in this damp house, and my mother had epilepsy.
There were many nights when I had to get the ambulance and take my father to hospital to get him a bit better.
I patiently looked after my mum as well.

My older brother, Jozsef, who had been taken for forced labour work to the Soviet front, returned home about three years later. My other brother Zoltán also returned as he had been deported to Austria too, but he had been placed in a different camp than our parents and our sister.

Mr Schwarz on 20 July 1945 – after his return – Picture from personal collection

Back to work

---

[122] Békéscsaba is a city in Southeast Hungary, the capital of the county Békés

A few day after my return, I went back to the textile factory where I used to work before the war and presented myself for work. It all went well and I received my job back.

I had hidden 39 files. These files belonged to the 39 Jewish workers the German factory owner employed as essential workers during the war until the final evacuation.
After the war when I returned home, the factory owner's wife came to see me and asked for my help as the new communist government had put him into jail. I went to see the Committee Secretary of the Communist Party, Elemér Balogh, and I explained to him what happened before the war. I suggested that the communist government needed to weigh the situation as Selényi had saved the lives of 39 people before the war and put his own life on the line by doing that, as many who helped the Jews could, and did, face the death penalty during the war. Mr Balogh and the Communist party did not like my interference but I said, "Here are the files of these Jews Mr Selényi employed and perhaps saved their lives. He was there for us when we needed him. Please have a look at these papers and make a balanced judgement about him. He is a good man."
Mr Selényi was released a few days later and a grand piano was also returned into their possession. I was not sure of the reason behind confiscating the piano.

So, in other words, Mr Selényi had been questioned by the local Ispán at the peak of the war for employing 39 intellectuals who could not fulfill their position any longer as doctors, lawyers, etc., by law. Now, after the war, he had been questioned again because he was a German.

In 1948, two representatives of the Communist Party asked for a meeting with me and they said: "We would like you to become the director of this textile factory, but we have two conditions. One, you will help to rebuild this factory from its ruins (it was heavily bombed). Two, you have to change your name into something more Hungarian."
"Well," I said, "I can fulfill your first request, but I will not change my name. This is who I am," I said to them.

Somehow this conversation made it to the Central Communist Commission in Budapest. The two representatives were fired for their odd request and later I found out they were also Jews. I did not understand their conditions at all.

So, I did what I always do, I worked hard. I carried the bricks for the bricklayers, I assisted with the water and sewage systems. I did not act like a fancy director and I definitely did not walk around in expensive suits amongst the workers. My belief was, I am not more important than a cleaning lady, I am also a worker. I just have more responsibility.

One of these personal documents which has been hide by Mr Schwarcz. – Picture from personal collection

I continued to look after my ill parents until they passed away and, in the meantime, I fulfilled my position as a director.

We built up the factory and our company was first in line (of which I was very proud) during the 1st of March Labour Day parade in 1949. This was a personal and a collective great achievement.

For the next two years I did not take one day off, and I worked hard to rebuild the textile factory from its rubble. I paid a big prize for this. The gastric bleeding virus I had managed to catch in Mühldorf, recurred and I ended up in hospital. It turned into bowel cancer and two-thirds of my bowel had to be surgically removed. After the surgery the doctors ordered me to stay in bed and not to move. So, for the following two weeks, I did not move an inch.

The nurses and the patients kept poking their heads through the door to see if I was still there - if I was still alive. Many could not understand the will power I had to follow the onerous instructions of the surgeon. Even other specialists came to see me. I became the role model for the surgeons as many patients who were supposed to stay in bed could not follow this simple instruction, and thereby slowed down their own recovery process.

One of the doctors who was looking after me was particularly interested in me. One night after he finished his work he came to my bed and sat down. "Sandor, could you please tell me about how you can be so still? What makes you so strong-willed?" he asked.

It was very hard for me to talk, but telling my story took my mind off the pain. I told him my story in a nutshell, but I placed more emphasis on the days when I was hiding under the bed in building 4 in Auschwitz.

When I was discharged I had to make the decision to give up my position as company director in 1951. I stayed there as a group leader in one of the factory's sections and continued to live with this motto: "The best investment is care (towards my staff)".

Mr Schwarcz, the director of the Centrum shopping complex - Picture from personal collection.

The Communist Party

In 1945 after my return to home, I joined the Communist Party. I strongly believed this would be the party which would lead the

re-building of the country. However, I have never understood and agreed with the ideology of the Party.
Here are some memories why:

I was appointed to be an adjudicator along with a high-level judge. My decisions on the outcome of the verdicts were not the same as those of a highly educated lawyer.
There was a case against an 85-year-old man who had no money to pay his taxes. When we listened to the case, the judge and myself went inside a room to make our decision. My verdict was that we should not put this old man in jail just because he was poor. The Judge was not very happy to hear my verdict. The next day I gave my authority back to the Party. I did not want to undertake this kind of work for the Communist Party any longer.

I was also appointed to be the 'number 1' adjudicator for the Hungarian football federation. It was my decision to determine the punishment/s for football players who received a red card during a game or committed some kind of irregularity on or off the field. A case that appeared before me was that a player had received a red card. I got a phone call from above, "What will be your verdict?" the communist party representatives asked.
I said, "This is my decision; I will make my own judgement."
"Stop talking so much. Your decision will be so and so," they said and outlined their verdict.
The next day I walked into the headquarters and handed back my authority, along with the privilege of having free entry to any football game in the country.

I had been asked on multiple occasions to be a speaker at Communist Party events. I was never keen to do this - to speak for a long time in front of an audience, and to be in the spotlight. So, when I had no choice anymore my speech would be as follows: "There have been a few long speeches before me and I am very tired, so I would like to close my remarks, and go home." I was never asked to speak on any Communist Party event again.

I never used the opportunity to take free holidays like many others in management or political positions, but I received a free weekend away as a reward for my work. I had only one suit, one set of pyjamas, one set of clean underwear, and one clean shirt. I packed these into a small package and travelled like this - light. When I arrived, the receptionist could not believe I had no suitcase. There were about 200 people at the dinner party from various factories around the country. The Master of Ceremonies decided to appoint only two people to tell their story. He appointed one lady and for some reason he chose me as the male speaker. Once the lady had finished her speech it was my turn. I talked about the ghettos and the concentration camp life. When I had finished, the Master of Ceremonies proposed a toast: "And now let's lift our glasses and drink!" Suddenly, everyone wanted to be my friend and drink with me. I did become a bit tipsy that night.

Next morning we had been organized to take a walking tour in the mountain area. Many people were around me and all wanted to know more about me and my story. I wanted to rest. That was the reason for me taking this trip. So I cut the hiking short, walked back into the hotel, packed up my few belongings and left to get back home. This was my only trip - which became shorter than planned, and the one and only day off in the two years of everyday work.

I did not follow the orders from the Communist Party.

On another occasion the Communist Party called me in for a meeting.
They asked me, "Are you part of the Zionism?[123] Are you a Zionist?".
"When the American army freed me from the concentration camp in the forest of Mühldorf, they looked after me and fed me.

---

[123] **Zionism**, Jewish nationalist movement that has had as its goal the creation and support of a Jewish national state in Palestine, the ancient homeland of the Jews (Hebrew: Eretz Yisra'el, "the Land of Israel"). Though Zionism originated in eastern and central Europe in the latter part of the 19th century, it is in many ways a continuation of the ancient attachment of the Jews and of the Jewish religion to the historical region of Palestine, where one of the hills of ancient Jerusalem was called Zion. - https://www.britannica.com/topic/Zionism

They wanted to look after me further. They offered to move me to Switzerland, Sweden or America, but I decided to come home to my hometown and to my motherland Hungary. Your accusation that I am a Zionist is highly offensive and has no evidence. Therefore, please accept my resignation. from the Communist Party. Here is my membership handbook," I said and slid my Party booklet across the table. I was a bit nervous for a few days that I would be taken away for questioning, as many I know had been, just for quitting their membership. After two weeks I had to believe they had accepted my resignation without any consequences.

After all of this, I became the newly appointed director of the marketplace in the heart of Debrecen.
In 1951 the previous director had been caught on fraud charges. It was nearly a year since I had retired from the director position at the textile factory and had enough time to recover.

Living inside the mouldy walls in our house I managed to catch bronchitis twice. On the second time the doctor said to me, "The third one will take you to your grave if you don't change your house!"
As I did not use my power as a Director of a government company, I decided to find somewhere dry to stay until I recovered. I walked down to the train station and asked the porter to let me sleep in the waiting room. I paid him with some beer for his kindness. In the morning I walked home, had a shower, shaved, changed my clothes and went to work, and sat in my director's chair to fulfill my duty. I stayed at the train station until I had recovered fully.

One of my staff members, István Kovács, and his wife, came to me and they said, "We heard that you will soon receive a flat as part of a bonus as the director position. We would like you to help us by giving the flat to us."
"Why would I do that?" I asked.
"Because we are living in a shed with our three children," the wife replied.
"And? I live in a house with my parents surrounded by mouldy walls and the doctor has ordered me to move out. If I do not

move out, I will catch bronchitis again and this time it could be deadly for me," I said.

"Yes, but at least you have a roof over your head which keeps you dry. Our place does not have walls and the roof is leaking too," she continued.

"Well, then I will give you my flat," I agreed.

"Would you be able to write that down and sign it?" she asked. I did as she asked.

Of course, the Communist Party was very upset with me and said, "You cannot just give away an entire flat to someone!

"But these people need a flat more than I do," I replied.

"But we cannot give you a flat every time you gift it away," they advised.

The Kovács family still lives at 9 Ispotály street.

Due to the political pressure from some communist party members I decided to give up my director position. There were some people that I had difficulty tolerating, particularly one woman that I did not like. I could not, and did not, want to deal with that communist woman any longer. She was treating everyone, and acting, disgustingly.

My next job was outside of the city in Téglás[124] and I was helping to teach young farmers. I had to get up at 4 am and did not return home until 10pm. My mum got up early with me and heated the water on the stove for me to wash myself. The wages were half the amount I had been receiving as director, but at least I did not have to deal with that unpleasant communist women. Then came The Uprise of 1956 against the Soviet Union. It was sparked by the university students and many young residents. They knocked down all the "Red Stars" and anything which was a symbol of the Communist regime. I did not believe this was a clean reform because the anti-Semitism had also returned. There were anti-Jewish slogans painted all over the walls.

Three of the Communist Party members came to see me in our home.

"Schwarcz comrade, we would like you to come back and be the director of the Market House once again," they said.

---

[124] **Téglás** is a town in Hajdú-Bihar county, in the Northern Great Plain region of eastern Hungary.

"Is that so? I can just come back and be the director again, just like that?" I asked. "I tell you what, you organize a secret ballot and if the majority of the workers would like me to come back and once more fulfill the director's position, I will do so."

A few days later they came back and delivered the result. The majority of the workers elected me as the managing director.

I returned to this position in 1956. The old marketplace was starting to become too small and the Party decided we would be building a new shopping complex which would be the first and the most modern shopping building in Hungary.

In May 1959, in the presence of a newspaper journalist and photographer, I laid the foundation stone of the new building. The irony behind this was very interesting. On 3rd of June, 1944, police officers wearing a Yellow Star had escorted me and a few more Jews from the ghettos, to remove the rubble after the first air raid on the city. I had been working there as an outlaw. Now, a few years' later, I was appointed as the director of this newly-built Centrum shopping complex.

I could not have been happier that this had happened.

The construction went on for three years, and on the 16th of August 1962 I was there at the official opening with some very high-ranking politicians. I continued to be the managing director until my retirement in 1970. We named the building as the Hajdúsági Áruház (later it was called Centrum shopping complex). [125]

One Christmas I decided to erect a huge Christmas tree. It was six metres tall, and it was the first Christmas tree ever erected during the holiday season for the public, publicly. When it was done and as I was standing next to it, all I could think of was the Christmas tree in Auschwitz in 1944. I would never have thought I would ever be a free man again or that I would celebrate Christmas in my own hometown ever again. This time we did not have execution by hanging. This time we enjoyed this holiday season the way it supposed to be - in peace, with love, and with friendship.

---

[125] **Centrum Stores** was one of the largest supermarket chains in Hungary, next to The Scale. For decades, the supermarket chain sold its products in major cities in Hungary. The department stores were nationalized in 1948, after which they operated in different forms.

I continued to live between the mouldy walls until I turned 56 years old, in 1967. In April 1976, I took up residence in my new studio apartment at 4 Hollo Street, Debrecen.

In a speech in front of about 1,500 people where everyone from the trading organizations was present, the Minister of Commerce, János Tóth, said, "There is one director amongst us, his name is Sándor Schwarzc from Debrecen, who has managed to synchronize humanity and efficiency." I stood up so everyone could see the person he mentioned.
A few years later our shopping complex became the best performing in the commerce sector of the entire country. János Tóth came to Debrecen in person to deliver the award medal to me in front of thousands of people in local indoor stadium. It was a very proud moment for the entire Centrum's board and staff members.

The new Centrum shopping complex. Only the ground and the first floor were used as a shopping area. The 6-level building's top 4 levels have been hosting privately owned flats. Picture from:
https://egykor.hu/images/2010/preview/debrecen-hajdusagi-aruhaz.jpg

Picture from personal collection – Mr Schwarcz's unit marked on the photo

One Saturday in 1970, with a typewriter and a dictaphone in my hands, I left the building and said to the people I saw "I wish everyone a great future. I will not be coming in to work from Monday."

I did have some bitterness in me, and for 17 years I did not even walk on that side of the street if I had to go in that direction. I had no car so most of my transport was walking or public transport. Then, 17 years later, I was invited for a dinner party where I forgave everyone for everything and accepted their apologies.

The next Monday after my retirement I asked myself, "What will you do with your free time now?" I decided to learn how to operate the typewriter and write down all of what had happened to me, starting from the forced labour work until our liberation. I had a few copies of these books and many journalists and many writers approached me. They wanted to receive a copy of this book and they promised me it would be published. None of them got as far as publishing. However, one part of my story from this book did make it as far as being published by Gabor L. Kelemen, who was the director of the Magyar Hírlap, a

Hungarian newspaper. However, it was without acknowledging me as a writer and without thanking me for it. I received no financial benefit from it, nor have I received one free copy. I had to purchase my own published book with my own money. Of course, as I had many friends, who exerted some pressure, this was corrected for the second edition and my name is also on the cover. For this reason, I have forgiven him for his mistake. All 8,000 copies of this re-printed edition have been sold. The title of this book is: Gól a halál kapujában (Goal in the gate of death). These kinds of disappointments have happened to me time after time, but as I said earlier "the best investment is kindness" and it has returned 80 per cent of the happiness and kindness to me. As in any case of investment, I had to deal with an about 20 per cent loss.

This is one of the reasons I decided to publish my own book with my own life story, titled as, A Halál Árnyékának Völgyében (In the Valley of the Shadow of Death).

Other activities were used to educate the new generation about the history of World War II, and the Holocaust.
I have visited 118 primary schools, high schools, vocational schools, universities and jailhouses. I also gave interviews on radio stations and TV stations as well, and have published numerous articles in the newspapers and have won some writers' prizes with some of them. I have made thousands of photocopies of my writings and paid for them from my own pension. I have either handed them out or mailed them to my friends. I did all this purely for educational reasons.
One particular presentation was at a monastery. Of course, I have talked about my days after our liberation and the times I have spent at the monastery in Mühldorf.

When my presentation was over, we all stood up and the head nun asked everyone to say a prayer to all who were lost in the war and to pray to God for my miraculous homecoming. I had two young students by my side holding my hands. When we reached the prayer, which said "…just as we forgive those who sin against us" I spoke out loudly. At the end of the prayer, the students asked me why I had done that? I told them. "When I was on my death bed in Mühldorf, I promised that if I ever got out of there alive, I would live the rest of my life without hatred. If I see a teardrop, I will wipe it off."

Since then, if I have seen hatred anywhere, I have tried to stop it. I tried to comment on it in the newspapers through my writings, or I have switched off the television. For the same reason, I have not watched any of the parliamentary coverage either, as all I could feel and see was hatred.

Translation of published articles and other memoirs:

Reuniting with my mother

I have returned from hundred deaths. I knocked on our door on a warm dawn in July. My mother opened the door. After a few silent seconds I was reaching for my head-scarfed mother's arms. I managed to catch her before she hit the ground because I came unexpectedly.

I arrived home from Birkenau, Auschwitz, Gross-Rosen, Dachau, Mühldorf. I arrived from a very long journey. I managed to avoid the gas-chambers, crematoriums, and mass graves.

It was easy to hold my mother's fragile and light body. The early morning washing, poverty problems, the depravation of the lager near Vienna had already worn out my fragile mother's body. The boy, who was considered lost, was found. I had returned. I did not give up easily to the executioners who reached for me thousands of times. I was cruelly vulnerable to the fascist executioners every minute of the month. I avoided the tentacles of death lurking from a hundred directions. I had to stay alive because I felt in the human smelling smoke of the camps that I was being missed; and they were missing me very much back home. This determination was missing from many of my fellow inmates who were destroyed; they surrendered themselves more easily to the hangman. In me there lived a high degree of the will to live. I trampled the snowy roads in the harsh cold between the rows of SS-guards. Hunger, thirst and the constant beating had worn me out thoroughly, but I did get up again and again and I did not let myself be trampled down. I am sure others were longingly awaited by their mothers, but only a few could return from the world of the crematoriums into the hugging arms of their mothers. The first victims of the gas-chambers were also the mothers. They held and squeezed the hands of their children. For these mothers, children become their deadly end, because for many mothers their children were the passport into the gas-chambers. They were destroyed by the cyan gas hugging and embracing each other.

Mothers rarely returned to their homeland. They could not meet their daughters and sons.

We were lucky that met each other again – myself and my mother.

All of us were destined for destruction. For this purpose, they erected death factories. We were scattered, knowing nothing about each other, into the concentration camps which were built in many places. All we knew was that we had been sentenced to death. At the time of the separation, we were aware that there would be no reunion. In spite of this, I did reunite with my mother on one July morning in 1945.

During the months of torment, my mother and I were miles apart, but only physically. In thought we were in constant contact with each other. We overcome the distance. Not even the electric fences could stand in the way of this. The mysterious telepathy with which no SS-soldier could interfere nor intervene with, had worked. From the distance we encouraged each other to hold on. We did not see each other but our relationship had maintained our connection despite hundreds of kilometres. My mother wanted me to persevere against all the atrocities of the executioners. The wave of my mother's strong desire always circulated around me. She took care and looked over me, helping me through the hours of my hardest sufferings.

I managed to stay alive, I returned home, I came back. We both survived among the inhuman evils of fascism, which few could only succeed, which was like a special miracle.

First letter to my mother, Mária Risányi (8 February 1985)

Mr Schwarz and my mother Mária Risányi were in contact by letter after we moved from Debrecen to Veszprém. Here are some of the letters (The writer).

Dear Mária,

I have received your short-worded postcard.
I will reply longer.
You asked me what I am doing?
I lay down, reading, warming up and I visit some of my good friends. I am avoiding the bad and the inhuman people, of which there are plenty nowadays. However, I do not complain about my relationships as "I am a lucky man" with great genes, and besides the top hundred, many other people are looking for my friendship. I am alone, I live by myself and still never bored, I fulfill my days well.
Before I wrote this letter, two chief medical doctors came to me for a "chat". With them was a female doctor who would like to look after me.
A couple days ago a few young workers visited me and asked me to give an experience talk in their factory. We had a few conversations. They said they would like to listen to me all day, but in spite of everything, there are limits and I am not full of myself, as you know me! I will never forget where I came from – I have become someone out of poverty.
My home is a studio apartment; it has central heating, it has hot and cold water and from the miserable place on Csokonai street and escaping from the Hell of Auschwitz, for me this is very satisfying.
So, I lay, I read, I keep myself warm, I visit my friends for a cup of coffee, and between I clean, and I cook potato and rice in water and besides that, sausage and debreciener[126]. This is my daily menu. I am pleased with this narrow menu. By the way,

---

[126] A debrecener (Hungarian: debreceni kolbász, German: Debre(c)ziner, Italian: Salsiccia di Debrecen) is a pork sausage of uniform fine texture and reddish-orange colour, named after the Hungarian city of Debrecen.

rice is everyday food for the Chinese and if it is an excellent food for them then I do not have to resent it either.

In the days, my friend Imre Précz visits me. He noted the 1985-year calendar in front of me. He found out from me that you have left town and moved to Veszprém[127]. I believe you will get used to the city and I am sure the people are kinder than here. I think of you and your sons often. We did not have a very big friendship between us, but however, I did enjoy talking to you all; and now you have moved very far away.

I believe I wrote these lines much more abundantly so I cannot get blamed for short response.

I am wishing you very good health and good luck with real sincerity and love for your new home.

Sincerely: Sándor S.

From Balmazújváros[128] to the Inter[129] - Football manager in Auschwitz

Article from the Hungarian Newspaper's Sport section (Sport Revue 21st August 1991)

Dezső (Solti) Steinberger's name has been intertwined with football. He started from Balmazújváros and he reached the high command of the World known Internazionale. Meanwhile, the manager also served on the Nazi-organized football team at the Birkenau death subcamps of Auschwitz. Gábor L. Kelemen has written extensively about Dezső (Solti) Steinberger in his "Goal at the gate of death" book which was released a few years ago and published by "Sportpropaganda" company. Sándor

---

[127] Veszprém is one of the oldest urban areas in Hungary, and a city with county rights. It lies approximately 15 km north of the Lake Balaton and approximately 110 km west from Budapest. It is the administrative center of the county of the same name.

[128] Balmazújváros, is a town in Hajdú-Bihar county, in the Northern Great Plain region of eastern Hungary.

[129] Football Club Internazionale Milano, commonly referred to as Internazionale or simply Inter, and known as Inter Milan outside Italy, is an Italian professional football club based in Milan, Lombardy.

Schwarcz who was deported from Debrecen, and was the protagonist of the book, remembers him and recalls the dialogues with him. It was unknown what fate became of Mr. Steinberger. Recently, however, he appeared in Hungary and our reporter met him in Siófok[130]. In the interview on the 8-9th pages he extends the chapter from the "Goal at the gate of death" book which remembers Dezső (Solti) Steinberger, and illustrates what role he played in the death camp.

Dezső (Solti) Steinberger visited Debrecen which I did not know about; but he knew I lived here. He did not make the effort to look for me and to come and see me although he knew I was alive. He has invited many people from Debrecen to his house in Italy; he has talked about how wealthy man he has become and how great a "hotshot" he is.
This was another disappointment in my life.

---

[130] Siófok is a town in Somogy County, Hungary on the southern bank of Lake Balaton.

Auschwitzi futballmenedzser

BALMAZÚJVÁROSBÓL AZ INTERBE

Exkluzív

Steinberger (Solti) Dezső neve összeforrt a labdarúgással. Balmazújvárosról indult el, s a világhíres Internazionale vezérkarába jutott. A menedzser időközben az auschwitzi és birkenaui haláltáborban a nácik által szervezett futballcsapatnál is szolgált.

L. Kelemen Gábor Gól a halál kapujában című könyvében, amely évekkel ezelőtt jelent meg a Sportpropaganda Vállalat gondozásában, hosszan írt Steinberger (Solti) Dezsőről. Schwarz Sándor debrecenei deportált, a könyv főhőse emlékezett rá, visszaidézte a vele folytatott párbeszédeket. Azt nem lehetett pontosan tudni, hogy mi lett a sorsa Steinberger úrnak. A közelmúltban azonban feltűnt Magyarországon, s riporterünk találkozott vele Siófokon. A 7. oldalon levő interjúnkat a 8-9. oldalon kiegészíti a Gól a halál kapujában című könyvből idézett Steinberger (Solti) Dezsővel foglalkozó fejezet, amely érzékelteti, hogy milyen szerepe volt a haláltáborban.

Dezső (Solti) Steinberger (on the left) in the Newspaper article with Ferenc Puskás[131] (On the right) - Original copy of the writer

I belong with the small people

---

[131] **Ferenc Puskás** (1 April 1927– 17 November 2006) was a Hungarian footballer and manager, widely regarded as one of the greatest players of all time and the sport's first international superstar. A prolific forward, he scored 84 goals in 85 international matches for Hungary, played 4 international matches for Spain and scored 514 goals in 529 matches in the Hungarian and Spanish leagues. He became an Olympic champion in 1952 and led his nation to the final of the 1954 World Cup where he was named the tournament's best player. He won three European Cups (1959, 1960, 1966), 10 national championships (5 Hungarian and 5 Spanish Primera División) and 8 top individual scoring honours. In 1995, he was recognized as the top scorer of the 20th century by the IFFHS (**International Federation of Football History & Statistics**).

Part of an article from the Hungarian Newspaper (Magyar Hírlap- January 15, 1992)

...I have been invited and presented my life experience in over one hundred schools. I have never included politics into my story telling. After my presentations I have always given the opportunity for the students to ask questions. After one of my presentations, I was asked a very interesting question:
"How much hate do you have towards the Germans, who caused all those sufferings to you in the lagers?"
I was quite surprised about this question so I took my time to give the right answer: "A people or a nation cannot and must not be hated globally. A German who is today 40-45 years old, was not even born in those times; furthermore, why should I hate someone who did not hurt me? ..."

Letter to my mother – 1st October 1992

Dear Mária Risányi,

Thank you for thinking of me during your trip in Spain. You must have had many beautiful experiences.
I never longed to travel, to see the World. When I was working as a director, I probably would have had the opportunity, however, I am feeling fine at home in my solitude. Really, I am not at all in solitude, as I lately enjoy great popularity, which means that I hardly even have time to peel these few pieces of potatoes because of the many invitations and visitors.
Furthermore, I do my own housework alone because I do not want to use others, of course not financially. I am an obsessed bachelor who cannot leave his usual habits behind.
On the 6th of September the Debrecen radio gave a fifty minutes broadcast about some of the events of my life. The reporter of the city radio visited me unexpectedly and made the recording - after which I received a lot of great comments.

A few days ago, I have received a postcard from Imre Précz, and he would like to correspond more frequently with me from Israel, where he and his wife settled down with their children. I have no desire to inform him more frequently about the events that are happening here; he should come home and see for himself if he is so interested about Debrecen! I will stay because this is my hometown and I could have had the opportunity to live easier somewhere else, but many of my nostalgic memories bind me here.

It is nice for you that you wish to sell your car to be able to travel to Israel. I am very sorry that I cannot be your travel companion as I have written above, I do not want to go much further from this little one room.

The radio reporter who came to me also remarked on how modest my home was - which we discussed further in the recording.

I was very happy when your two sons came to visit me a few weeks ago because attention is good, and I think it helps to slow down my aging and will lead to less wrinkles on my face.

I have a typewriter. When I retired from the Centrum shopping complex and left without receiving not even one piece of a flower, I purchased the typewriter and a cassette radio, and that is how I left and walked home on that Saturday afternoon from my workplace. But because of this I did not become a depressed man. This much about myself. Greeting you and your two sons.
Sándor Schwarcz

On the food market:

One day I was walking in the food market shopping for myself, when from behind one of the stands a young salesman called after me, "I remember you Mr Schwarz. Years ago, you came to the school which I was attending at that time and I clearly remember one sentence from your presentation," he said.
"And what was that?" I asked him with much interest.
"You said, "I can be happy for every little thing!" he replied.

"And so, I am happy for you to recognise me and to remember a little about my presentation. You have made my day. Have a great one for you too!" I said with a smile on my face.

Without name again

One day, someone scratched my nametag of my unit entrance door. I lost my name once when I arrived at Auschwitz, so I have written my other name on the door A- 17854, and next to it "My name was scraped off!" Someone in the unit block must have seen this and with kindness, they have replaced my nametag. As I did not know who it was, I have written a "Thank You" beside it. It is still on the door which is never locked. I am not afraid of anyone and anything anymore. Anyone can enter here anytime. If I hear a knock on the door, all I have to say: "Come in please, it is open".

Picture of the unit door. Picture from own collection

Schindler's list – (1993)

In 1993 the movie Schindler's list was released. I was asked to speak before the premiere of this movie at the Kossuth University[132], and give my personal opinion of the movie afterwards, in front of hundreds of students and viewers.

(Tuesday, 17 March, 1998)

Picture of the University's main building. Picture from:
https://i.ytimg.com/vi/EOjyh-Z8pls/maxresdefault.jpg

Two half-times in Hell (1961 – Drama/Sport movie)

My story as a football player in Auschwitz has spiked some interest from many angles. I have provided my story for a movie called "Two half-times in Hell" (Két félidő a Pokolban). When

---

[132] The **University of Debrecen** (Hungarian: *Debreceni Egyetem*) is a university located in Debrecen, Hungary. It is the oldest continuously operating institution of higher education in Hungary (since 1538). The university has a well-established programme in the English language for international students, particularly in the Medical field, which first established education in English in 1986.

the movie was finished, I did not receive an invitation to the premiere. I called the writer and director, Zoltán Fábri, and expressed my deepest disappointment at not being invited, and the response was as follows: "We have re-written your memory in a degree that it is no longer matches what was made in the movie. Therefore, we did not feel the need for inviting you."

The graves are defaced

In the middle of 1999, some of the graves in Szombathely were defaced. Some tombs were broken into and above all, the Swastika[133] was painted on them. The local radio has asked me to give them a report about my life. On the 10th July 1999 I was able to speak about my experiences during the Second World War. This was one way the radio tried to educate the grave-insulting perpetrators what the Nazism really was, and what it stands for.

The change of regime (1989)

As I have mentioned earlier, I never mixed politics into my presentations. Unfortunately, the 3 political parties which have been elected after the fall of the Berlin Wall and the evacuation of the Soviet Army from Hungary, were unable to tackle the problem of anti-Semitic laws. This has caused great pain to a man who had lived through the Hell of five concentration camps.

---

[133] In Nazi Germany the swastika (German: *Hakenkreuz*), with its oblique arms turned clockwise, became the national symbol. In 1910 a poet and nationalist ideologist Guido von List had suggested the swastika as a symbol for all anti-Semitic organizations; and when the National Socialist Party was formed in 1919–20, it adopted it. On September 15, 1935, the black swastika on a white circle with a red background became the national flag of Germany. This use of the swastika ended in World War II with the German surrender in May 1945, though the swastika is still favoured by neo-Nazi groups. - https://www.britannica.com/topic/swastika

It should just stay as János Holló [134] street –

Article from the Hajdú-Bihar Napló[135] (7th April 1990)

In the Saturday edition I read an article entitled as a proposal for the "Review of the street names in Debrecen", written by a University Student.

I born in Debrecen, but still I had to leave my hometown in an animal wagon during the WW2 to the concentration camps of Birkenau, Auschwitz, Gross-Rosen, Dachau and at the end in the Bavarian Mühldorf.

I was found by the American liberating army, with my body weighing about thirty something kilograms.

Thanks to the fascist Hungarian government I was tormented by inhuman suffering.

For a short period of time, István Bethlen [136] and Kuno Klebelsberg ,[137] along with other names suggested by the University student as a new street names, were members of the fascist Horthy-government. I live in the János Holló street. I was a prisoner in Dachau in February 1945 when János Holló was executed by the German fascists. Does the young university student know the history of that inhuman cruel era, because there were also other martyrs of that area, whose names should not be erased? My presence has been requested at many institutions and schools to give an eyewitness history of that

---

[134] He was part of the communist party before the WW2 and has been deported as the enemy of the Horthy-regime

[135] Independent newspaper of the Hajdú-Bihar county

[136] István Bethlen statesman and Hungarian prime minister from 1921 to 1931, who maintained the old order in Hungary after World War I.

[137] Count Kuno von Klebelsberg de Thumburg was a Hungarian politician, who served as Minister of the Interior and Minister of Culture of the Kingdom of Hungary between the two world wars.

inhuman period by speaking to many young pupils in their
history classes.
I have many friends in the János Holló Street, and nobody there
would like to have it renamed.

Due to this letter and some other interested comments, the street
has not been renamed.

(The 1989 change in politics caused the renaming of many
streets). Writer's note.

Letter to my mother – 10 March 1993

Dear Maria,

I thank you very much for your letter and the Name-day [138]
wishes. These kinds of remembrances are helping my survival
and lengthening my life, as I am very well into old age. I am
reading with happiness your letter that you are thinking of me. I
am very happy for you that soon your long-awaited dream will
come true and you will be able to get to know the land of Israel
in person. I am sure you will return with many great memories,
and I am also happy for your sympathy for the Jews and
friendship with the Jewish people, and that you do not forget
about me either. I wish you a lot of good and beautiful
experiences along your entire trip.
Imre Précz lives in Be'Er Sheva in Israel. He sends me his letters
from there and he would like to receive my replies more
frequently. I do reply to his letters every time, because I receive
so many letters daily that I have to respond to at least one every
day. I have become especially popular since the Kossuth Radio
broadcasted some of my life's experiences on the 11th and the 18th
of October in their morning Sunday program. Furthermore, the

---

[138] A name day is a tradition in some countries in Europe, Latin America, and Roman Catholic
and Eastern Orthodox countries in general. It consists of celebrating a day of the year that is
associated with one's given name.

Debrecen Radio has also broadcasted some of my memories in a 50-minute-long broadcast on the 6th of September.

A few weeks ago, I received an invitation from the nuns from the Svetist Catholic High School (Debrecen) to give their students a short presentation of my struggling past.

I am never bored - on the contrary. I think I have never been as busy with people as I have been lately. It seems that in this hateful world, people are still searching for humanity. They say that I project serenity and calmness which is a great feeling. I was a resident in five concentration camps and around me tens, hundreds, and millions have died - and I am still alright. I do not own a fortune and I do not own valuables. I was a director for 25 years, but I do not own land, garden, car, or phone and I did not even take advantage of the free holidays.

I told on the radio that "I can be happy for every little thing". I am alone. I do not have a wife - a spouse, therefore I do my house duties by myself. I do not visit restaurants and beside the potatoes I cannot cook anything. I have canned food and conserved fruits. I eat lots of vitamins and I do not crave fancy dishes, but this is not because of frugality. I cannot and I do not like to cook, but you do not have to feel sorry for me.

Unfortunately, my old cartilage detachment, which is already incurable, is becoming calcified and because of it I suffer a lot. Several doctors care for me without being financially compensated - just out of love. Firstly, Rácz, chief medical officer- from friendship, Dr Piroska Vincze internal medicine, and many more - even that they are all are Christians.

Maybe with these few lines I have just typed on this paper will provide some information about how I live my everyday life.

Again, thank you for thinking of me and it makes me very happy because I feel your respect towards me from your lines.

I am greeting you with warm heart and I also greet your boys with love.

Sándor Schwarcz

Letter to my mother – 3rd June 1993

I have received your postcard, and soon after, your letter with the photographs. Probably you have a great camera, as the pictures are very clear. I also thank you specially that during your travel and visiting so many places, you did not forget about me either. You must have had a great experience in what you saw there - and from the interaction with people from other cultures. I am a pretty damned person because I never wanted to see the world and I even though have had the opportunity to do it. Despite my Jewish religion, I still did not want to visit Israel. A lot of people have already asked me if I have ever been to Israel, and then they are surprised when I tell them I have never been there and do not even intend to travel.

I just mailed my reply letter to my friend Imre after two months. Imre wishes to receive my letters more frequently because he wishes to know more about the life in Debrecen. I would like to write to him to say that if he is so interested about this city, then why did he leave it? I think this, but in my letters, I do not write it down. I also mailed another letter to Israel this week, to someone who is also interested. It is good that I am not such a curious person. This is my birth town and I do feel good here, and my life did become colourful. I have many friends now and I have so many invitations. This afternoon I received an invitation to a family as one of their relatives is visiting from Brazil and he wanted to meet and to know me. I had to stop writing this letter too, as Dr Rácz has arrived for a friendly chat. Besides them I also had two more visitors today.

Even when I walk about on the street doing my own thing, so many persons want to chat with me about how I live, what I cook and things like that. Sometimes I am so annoyed that I just want to get home and I sometimes think I should have a mask on so I can just walk home in great comfort.

People say that calmness and serenity flow from me and in this troubled world this is greatly appreciated.

I know that life has become difficult and it looks like it will continue to become more difficult, and the people are full of problems, they are nervous, and they are in bad moods. Many had an established standard of living that they could no longer sustain. From these people I differ in that I live and I have always lived very modestly compared to the average person. I continue to cook my four or five potatoes in a beef stock water. I do this not for reason of frugality, but because I have no need for more or for different.

Yesterday I ran into someone from your old workplace who took over the position after Imre. He wishes all the best for you.

The typewriter ink decided to give up. I thank you one more time for your attention and I am thinking of you and the boys too.

(Tomorrow, I have to buy a new ink ribbon for the typewriter) – *"written by hand"*.

Letter to my mother – 31 March 1994

Dear Mária,

Thank you very much that you have thought of me on my name day and you have wished me well.

I am still well, even though I have received too many chances from life. As you well know how especially hard it was for me to survive from thousands and thousands of deaths. A few weeks ago, I received an invitation from the Vénkerti primary school to talk about my memories. Soon after I received another invitation, but this time, they video recorded my presentation. The school's leadership know that the human life is not endless, and they have wished to capture my tragic life. This way the school can show my story - our story - for years to come.

You know that I am not full of myself. However, not many people can tell their life story with as much passion about the humiliation of the forced labour work; the inhumanity of living with the yellow star; the life in the ghetto; the evacuation into the brick factory; and the embarkation into the animal train wagons towards Auschwitz: my meeting with Dr Mengele and my life in five concentration lagers.

This is what they are asking about, and I can tell them. I have done so in hundreds of primary schools and different level of educational institutions. It is not easy to do this over and over, but I am doing this as a crown witness. I therefore have no recognition before the various Jewish organizations, but I do not care. I am not a church attendant and I am not a religious person, but I feel like I am a chosen person so that I could survive amongst the hundreds and hundreds of thousands.

In the lager of Mühldorf living with lice, with purulent wounds, with abdominal bleeding, people dying around me daily - and surviving all this - I believe that God wants me to stay alive. I was brave enough to say this during the Communist era too. Otherwise, I am very busy. So many people need respect and love that I have hardly any time to do my house duties. I have to do most of it myself. Luckily, I do not have much problem with cooking as I do not have too many needs either. A few potatoes with a cube of soup stock with butter or margarine, and some orange soft drink fulfils my needs. I do all this, not for reasons of frugality, but because I do not have need for more.

Every day I accept one invitation for a coffee, but I cannot accept every invitation. In this hateful anti-semitism world, I do not feel I should accept more. If I can, I avoid the wickedness and for my peace of mind I have not listened to the radio for years. For months I have not switched on the television to watch the news or the political programs, because I do not want to disturb my night sleep with these incitements.

This is how I live in Debrecen. I respond to Imre's letters only after a long wait. I think he wants to hear news from here more often, where our life started to become tragic. I met your colleague, Péter on the street and he briefed me about the life of all from the property and planning department and about himself as well. He was very happy to see me. It is very difficult for me to get to home from the market as I get stopped every five or six metres by my interested chatting partners.

I think of you and the boys often. I wish you a lot of strength and health to carry out your work of.

Sincerely Sándor Schwarcz

Letter to my mother – 28 March 1995

Dear Mária,

Thank you very much for your great wishes. This kind of wish I can respect even when it comes late. I read the news about your son Farkas' great opportunity in Graz with interest. I also read it with great interest that you all think of me often, which means I got close to your hearts.

I can write to tell you that I have fast recovered from my accident. I go personally to buy my groceries without any supportive equipment. That very old football player cartilage detachment in my knee is in a very calcified stage and it bothers me - however I live with it in peace. My chief physician friend Dr Rácz told me three years ago after an X-ray, that many people would not be able to walk on it. However, I am different. Someone who managed to put up with five concentration camps must be able to put up with much more than an ordinary human. A few months ago, this great friend of mine, Dr Rácz passed away suddenly.

Otherwise, I am fulfilling my bachelor duties the same way as I have done it in the past. I am being treated as a 'miracle' in the hospital as well.

I had to be in the hospital for two months. During this time, I did not take any painkillers and after the fifth day I was able to visit the toilet by myself. Lots of people have visited me in the hospital. However, no one from my religion has come to see me. There is a newspaper called EREC, which is getting delivered to my address even though I have never ordered it. This is a Zionist-ideology newspaper. Even though I have never been a Zionist and I am not one today either, I found in it a communication about me. I have submitted my writing, from which I am sending you a photocopy.

When I was in the hospital in October, there was a program on the TV in which I said a few sentences. This program got aired in Israel where one woman recognised me, and she said we worked together in the Union ammunition factory. This kind of Union-group has their own community - however they just found out about me. They have asked me to send over a few of my writings because they have found my historical memories very interesting. One woman in San-Francisco is translating this Union-group's memory into English. They found my story so interesting they have asked my permission to include it in the book. I should have raised myself to their attention a long time ago, but I did not know how to do it, and also, I am a humble man.

I believe I have gone through so much difficulty in my life that I have to be thankful for every new day. I have received so many second chances and put up with many tortures, and survived. I live with this kind of attitude. I receive so many letters from every corner of the country and I try to respond to many. Two reply letters have been scheduled for each day, but I do not type every letter with as much love as the letter to your family.

I am wishing you a great resting time and peace for the upcoming Easter holidays.

Sincerely Sándor Schwarcz

Letter to my mother – 8 July 1995

Dear Mária,

Thank you very much that you have thought of me in Greece (sent a post card), and furthermore, that you are thinking of me. Me too.

I am sending you a copy of sequels of my story, which has been published in the local newspaper for retirees. I do not know how my life story ended up in the newspaper, because I did not give it to them for publishing. I did not know about this newspaper in the past. However, one of my friends brought it to my attention that I am featured in this paper.

I purchased this paper on my own money, because they have forgotten to send me an honorary copy.

In April Julia Széll from the Kossuth radio visited me and recorded approximately two hours of interview - however nothing has happened with it since.

I have such encouragements and similar disappointments that they do not bother me. I know this is the kind of world we live in now. However, I have some great friends as well, so the attentiveness balances out the inattention in my life.

Fifty-one years ago, I was suffering in the Auschwitz subcamp of Birkenau, when in the great heat I would have given a few years of my life for a glass of clean water. Now there is a glass of cold clean water sitting front of me.

My thirst due to water shortage started from the 1st of July 1944. Symbolically during this month, I have a glass of water on my desk, and during July, I only drink water and I avoid any soft drink. I assure you I have not gone insane, and I do not have any brain problem.

Sorry, I got a bit side-tracked.

Thank you that you do think of me, I am surrounded with love.

Sándor Schwarcz

Ps.: Tomorrow, Sunday the 9th, there will be a commemorative martyr ceremony in the city's Jewish cemetery. I do not have a great relationship with the local Israelite community, I will not attend on the ceremony.

Article from the Kurir[139] (24th September 1996)

I was very hurt when I read in the Monday's National Sport (newspaper) that during the MTK[140] – DVSC[141] match on Sunday

---

[139] The oldest Catholic news agency in Central Europe, which was founded 95 years ago, provides news and information about the life of the universal and the Hungarian Church. Their foreign sources are websites of Catholic news agencies and newspapers in Italian, English and German languages. They publish the news of the Hungarian Church based firstly on the information received from the Press Office of the Hungarian Catholic Bishops' Conference and from the diocesan press referents, secondly on the coverage of their colleagues. – www.wideweb.hu

[140] A multi-sport club founded in Budapest 1888.

[141] DVCS – (Debreceni Vasutas Sport Club) Railway Sport Club of Debrecen - were formed on 12 March 1902.

some called the players gypsies, and sometimes anti-Semitic shouts were heard. On the 29th of June 1944 I was transported in an animal wagon from the brick factory of Debrecen to Auschwitz-Birkenau. After our arrival, an SS-guard was looking for good football players. I applied and after a technical test the SS-officer considered me to be good enough to be part of the team.

Returning to my hometown, Debrecen, having been through five concentration camps, I hoped that never ever would I witness someone display anti-Semitism either in public life or on the football pitches.

Letter to my mother – 3 August 1999

Dear Mária,

Thank you for your question. However, I have two painful knees, which are very disturbing to my movement and almost ties me to my flat. In the meantime, many invitations are waiting, and new friendships are forming. On the other hand, my life is not boring. Even in this enraged world, my interaction with other people who are looking for a friendship with me, feels good. To write about this in a letter would be challenging, because it would be difficult to explain.

On the 10th of July I talked about the events of my life on the Kossuth radio, and after it I received a lot of phone calls - as now I own a phone, although I also made the number a secret. American movie director Spielberg is organizing contact with holocaust survivors. On the 19th of July some video technicians visited me. From 8 in the morning till 9 of the night the recording about the events of my life went on without stop. They recorded eighteen 30-minute tapes. I was talking for almost nine hours without a break about my life. A few days later they have asked me to do some more recording at some locations where some of my events happened. At the end, twenty half-hour recordings had been made after ten hours of conversation - which may be a record length. The recordings have been sent to America. Based on their information they will send a copy as a gift in about six months' time.

In my calendar I can find the Mária name-day on a few different dates. I will use one of them to greet you and to wish you good health and happiness in everyday of your life first, and please do not forget about me in your thoughts, just because the distance between us is huge.

I have mentioned before that the pain in my knees has restricted me more. I am not writing so many letters at present. However, this time I made an exception, as I find you are still interested in the fate of my life. It is very difficult to express my thoughts in a letter, so I will not go into that in more detail.

Luckily, my head and brain are still quite active which is also a disadvantage. Otherwise, I know I would need more exercise, but I am disabled in some degree due to my knees.

I hope your two sons are in a great position in life, and they continue to keep me in great respect.

I hope you are satisfied with this full page of my letter. I will say goodbye. I am still grateful for our friendship.

Bye for now.
Sándor Schwarcz

Article from the Népszabadság[142]

(National newspaper) – 13th February 2001
The soap from Auschwitz

I arrived at Auschwitz amongst about three thousands-five hundred death sentenced people, where Dr Mengele, with a wave of his hand, sent me to the right. I later learned that this

---

[142] Népszabadság was founded on 2 November 1956 during the Hungarian Revolution as successor of Szabad Nép (meaning Free People in English) which was established in 1942 as the central organ of the dissolved Hungarian Working People's Party. Népszabadság was also the organ of the party.

hand gesture meant staying alive for a while. Whoever he sent to the left, found their death in the gas chambers.

Our briefing took place in the barrack number 9 in Birkenau and one of the SS-officers was looking for professional football players. Along with nine gypsy males and a Hungarian man from Pest called Wagner, I became the eleventh player.

From foreign radio broadcasts, we had previously learned that there were gas chambers and crematoriums in Poland where executions were taking place, but I had not known what was behind the football.

I was a football player for four weeks in the Birkenau camp. The camp's gypsy prisoners were executed - not even my football teammates being spared.

The football field was separated only by a few meters from the gas chambers and from the crematoriums. Right at that time, the tens of thousands of Jews from the Eastern side of Hungary had been delivered for execution. I saw them marching into the gas-chamber, and later saw their thick smoke elevated towards the sky through the crematorium's chimney.

As a football player during these four weeks, I was "privileged". For cleaning ourselves, we even received soap. I was washing myself with this little, angular, greenish-gray, odourless soap. One of the capo informed me that the soap was made out of human fat which dripped from the fat of the dead burning bodies in the fire of the crematoriums using the technology of German chemists. In this evil place the genocide took place in three work-shifts. The soap made from human fat was another "addition" to the horrors of Auschwitz. Millions of children and adults were destroyed on the conveyor belt into dark ashes in a matter of hours.

I suffered in five concentration camps: Birkenau, Auschwitz, Gross-Rosen, Dachau, Mühldorf.

Trusting in some miracle I looked after these tragical "medallions". I had a small cotton bag hanging in my neck. Here I have guarded four little greenish-gray soap, the diced remains of my fellow human beings, which I managed to hide and bring home. We buried it in the Jewish cemetery in Debrecen and a tombstone is erected above it.

Now when I can choose between branded soaps, I never forget the little soap of Birkenau-Auschwitz, which was small and angular like a toy brick.

Soap: Its colour is greenish-gray;

Odourless: Made out of human fat;

R.J.F.: Reinnes Juden Fett: (Clear Jewish Fat) from human fat, which dripped down from the fire of the crematoriums, with the technology of German chemists.

Product of Auschwitz: for the use of the prisoners, for washing; Made for the son from the fat of his own mother, cooked for the daughter from the flesh of her own father.

Parents pressed into small cubes, moulded for cleaning.

Sándor Schwarcz - Debrecen

Theatre Premier

The Attila József Theatre in Budapest had booked my survival story for the 2002/2003 season. But despite the fact that it has been advertised, the theatre Director used his right to change the program for the season. The new performance was Fateless, by the Nobel Prize winner Imre Kertész [143] who was also a Holocaust survival. The director of the theatre, Péter Léner, did not even bother to call me and apologize for the change. So, to express my disappointment I have written the following letter to one of the Hungarian newspapers called Népszabadság.

Dear Editorial, Budapest
My friends from Budapest notified me a few month ago, that the wall posters of the Attila József Theatre have been advertising for their 2002-2003 season a "Premier with Sándors Schwarcz, the A-17854 numbered survival".

---

[143] **Imre Kertész**, (born November 9, 1929, Budapest, Hungary—died March 31, 2016, Budapest), Hungarian author best known for his semiautobiographical accounts of the Holocaust. In 2002 he received the Nobel Prize for Literature. - https://www.britannica.com/biography/Imre-Kertesz

The director, Péter Léner, assured me over the phone, and the Secretery General of the theatre personally visited me and assured me that my life story would be performed in a monodrama during the new season. The director asked for photocopies of my additional stories and a copy of my collected life story which was typed and bonded on 240 pages. This collection then ended up in the possession of Péter Léner and the director of the Csokonai theatre[144].

I have received the yearly program plan of the theatre on a small copy of the advertising wallpaper, on which my name appears the same way as on the real size poster. Here is a comment on the bottom of the poster: "The theatre reserves the right to change the program". This change can be used by Péter Léner, the director.

The Nobel-prize winner Imre Kertész is more known around the World then Sándors Schwarcz from Debrecen, therefore I have to accept the "branded name".

I know the Auschwitz survival story of Imre Kertész, and where he lived his tortured life for a while.

My destiny turned out to be suffering through Auschwitz until the evacuation day and I continued to suffer through five concentration camps. I am still a living survivor with the A-17854 tattoo on my arm.

I have told my survival story and the experience of watching the death of thousands of people closely in hundreds of primary, secondary, high schools and universities, in front of thousands of children and adults.

I must acknowledge the cancellation of my performance. Along with careless inhumanity, plenty of failures have touched me in the last few decades. Nevertheless, I have armoured myself with the strength of living through Auschwitz.

I want to know if Imre Kertész has any knowledge of the role change which he may not find as a fair procedure. He may also object that the director Péter Léner of The Attila József Theatre did not even respect me enough to give me a plausible

---

[144] The **Csokonai Theatre** is the oldest and largest theatre in Debrecen, Hungary. It was named after one of the first Hungarian Modern Age playwrights, Mihály Csokonai, who lived and created many of his works in Debrecen.

explanation. Perhaps, he did not think of this. This 91-year-old lonely man with two femoral neck fractures can live without needing any explanation.

Maybe I will meet of someone who could tell Imre Kertész and István Darvas[145] (who has performed the reading) that I was appointed for the performance in 2002-2003 in the Attila József Theatre.

Perhaps, the presence of the Nobel-prized Imre Kertész was more attractive for the theatre's cashbox.

I also attached a letter to this article which was addressed to Imre Kertész, in which I have congratulated him for his workmanship as a Hungarian writer and for his Nobel Prize win, in these times when anti-Semitism is still well alive.

None of the leading political parties after the revolution have managed to step up strongly enough against the anti-Semitism in Hungary.

Message for the New Generation

Every young person should start some kind of sport early in life. You need to be in a good health, be strong and in a good optimistic spirit to face any difficulty that life may throw at you from time to time. Do not smoke! Do not take drugs! Do not drink too much alcohol or become an alcoholic! Show love and respect to everyone at all times. This will be your best investment in life.

Life without hate and inhumanity.

Other memories after my return:

---

[145] Hungarian born actor.

Mr. Veres - As now a free man, I have decided to look up Veres to thank him for his human treatment during the war and my forced labour work in Szolnok at the wagon factory and the railway. He was very happy to see me and he was honoured that I have taken my time to visit him. I have written about this important moment and visit in the newspaper of Szolnok city. I also have sent this story to the Budapest newspaper too, which had a writer competition. With this article I won the first prize which was a tape recorder.

Mr. Fritzi - One day I received a visitor. It was Rudolf Fritzi. He was one of the army guards when we were in forced labour work. He was treating us Jews with as much humanity as it was possible. Nowadays he lives in Switzerland with his family. He has returned home because his son was very sick and was looking for some speciality treatment. He asked for my help to talk to Juhász professor[146]. So, I did, and said, "Rudolf was treating the Jews well during the war, and he asked my help to talk to you to please look after his son." The professor did. Rudolf said to me, "I have to return to Switzerland. Please look after my son while l I am away. When I return, I will bring you a big piece of original Swiss cheese."
So, I visited his son every day for few hours in the hospital for about 2 weeks. One day I was again in the hospital to perform my daily visit when there was an empty bed. I asked the nurses where the boy was. "He has recovered and has been discharged this morning," they said. "His father came this morning and picked him up," they continued.
I was a bit bitter that there was no thank you - nor cheese. I have never heard from them again.
I was not disappointed - as bigger disappointments happened to me in my life.

---

[146] Associate Professor Surgical Institute, **DUHSC-Debrecen University Medical and Health Science Center**, Debrecen/Hungary/Europe, Ferenc Juhász, M.D., Ph.D., Associate Professor, Head of Division of Endocrine Surgery and Breast Center Institute of Surgery, Medical and Health Science Center University of Debrecen

Dr Kallos - One day walking on the street I ran into Dr Kallos and I have thanked him for behaving so humanely with the Jews. He recognized me, and he was happy to receive my gratitude.

My old friend Sándor Friedman,

Last time I saw him it was on the other side of the barbed wired electric fence along our football filed in Birkenau. He was selected to be part of the sonder commando working in the crematoriums. He asked me, if I ever made it out alive, to tell the World about this terrible place. I never saw him again.

After my arrival back to our hometown I went to find his parents. I did not tell them about the terrible place where he had to work. I lied about him and I said he was working as a builder and lived in another country.

I have never had the strength to tell the parents the truth.

After they passed away, they left behind a daughter who had disability. I have supported her mentally and financially as much as I could.

Mr Pál - After the war I have visited Mr Pál who was the army major of my younger brother Béla in the village of Biharnagybajom and personally thanked him for the great humane behaviour with which he treated my brother before the war.

The twins of Auschwitz,

It was about 50 years later after our liberation when there was a knock on my door. When I flung the door open there was a middle-aged man at the door. I did not recognize him, but I invited him inside like I always do with everyone.

He said: "I am here in Debrecen for a short trip and I have heard about a man who once played as a football in Auschwitz. You may not recognize me, but once I gave you a piece of cooked potato through the fence in Auschwitz. You were training as a football player," he said. "I was one of the twin boys in the Mengele medical testing centre," he continued. "I live in Switzerland and my twin brother in America."

I was very happy for his visit and we talked for a few hours.

March 1981, Mr Schwarcz visiting the Textile factory – Picture from personal collection

Wednesday, 7 March 2007, Hajdú – Bihari Napló – Debrecen

In Memorium

Valley of the Shadow of the Death
Debrecen – The Auschwitz man is gone. Sándor Schwarcz survived the last century. As a forced labour worker, in the ghetto, then he went through the death camp, where he had to face the gas chambers seven times and left it seven times. On the

2nd of March the recognized, respected and former director of the Centrum shopping complex passed away.

His death and the way of his life were brought to the Naplo's attention by his friend Károly Balló. Sándor Schwarcz was a public figure: he wrote and published several articles in various journals, and two years ago his book with the title "Valley of the Shadow of the Death" was published. Sándor Schwarcz, who called himself the "The Man of Auschwitz" died at the age of 96.

Sándor Schwarcz, the A-17854 prisoner –
Picture from personal collection

Auschwitz message

Swirling ashes, grey ripples,
Bursting towards the clear skies,
Spread by wind to five continents

As whispering wind of Fascist sin, it flies.
From the chimney mother's cry shatters the ears,
The outcry of fathers hissing grimly,
And amongst them children screaming,
All embodied as millions dead in the smoke slimly.

Mother, father, child disembodied and
Hugging each other under the sky,
Four million are accusing, searching
And looking for the evil, bad guy.
It doesn't grey the night sky
Red like lava and glows far by.
Takes signs into the dark night,
Course fall on the executioners without cry.
The Martyr's army warns with history,
Waiting for the judgement by the Heavenly.

Anger and revenge are covered in ashes,
Its humus fertilizes, ripens grape bunches
Tasty fruit grows on barky trees,
Multicolour flowers blooming on the branches.
The fertilized land, the sea, the river
And the salty taste of their tears
Blended into the flesh of the cow and fish,
And the invisible still helps to benefit for years.

The four million is sending in their will
Without the stamp from the court of justice,
To destroy the chimneys of the crematoriums
From the red bricks houses to be constructed.
The entire world should gather against
Those who want to feed this fire,
From mass graves we cry out loud,
Neo Nazi! Stop, and do not Inspire!
We protect the world with our army,
Armoured with our ashes,
Surrounding by our patronage
Every newborn, races and fleshes.

The poems of Sándor Shwarcz translated by Farkas and Eszter Pungur

TIMELINE RELEVANT TO EUROPE'S JEWISH COMMUNITY
https://www.onthisday.com

1942

Jan 20 Nazi officials hold notorious Wannsee conference in Berlin to organise the "final solution", the extermination of Europe's Jews

Feb 27 1st transport of French Jews to nazi-Germany

Mar 11 1st deportation train leaves Paris for Auschwitz Concentration Camp

Mar 17 Bełżec Concentration Camp opens with the transport of 30,000 Lublin Polish Jews

Mar 23 2,500 Jews of Lublin massacred or deported

Mar 25 1st 700 Jews from Polish Lvov district reach the Bełżec Concentration camp

Mar 26 First "Eichmann transport" to Auschwitz & Birkenau concentration camps

Mar 30 1st RSHA-transport from France arrives in camp Birkenau

Mar 30 SS murders 200 inmates of Trawniki concentration camp

Apr 27 Belgian Jews are forced to wear stars

Apr 29 Jews forced to wear a Jewish Star in Netherlands & Vichy-France

May 3 Nazis require Dutch Jews to wear a Jewish star

May 4 German occupiers imprison 450 prominent Dutch as hostages

May 7 Nazi decree orders all Jewish pregnant women of Kovno Ghetto executed

May 12 1,500 Jews gassed in Auschwitz

May 15 Nazi occupiers in Netherlands arrest 2,000 Dutch officers

May 17 Dutch SS vows loyalty to **Hitler**

May 27 Nazi leader **Reinhard Heydrich** is shot and mortally wounded by Czech rebels in Prague during Operation Anthropoid

May 27 Hitler orders 10,000 Czechs murdered

May 28 1,800 Czechs murdered by Nazis during attack on Heydrich

May 30 Reichsfuehrer Herman **Himmler** arrives in Prague

Jun 5 USA declares war on Bulgaria, Hungary & Romania

Jun 9 Nazis kill all inhabitants of Lidice, which had been implicated in the assassination of Reinhard Heydrich, Nazi controller of Bohemia and Moravia, to "teach the Czechs a final lesson of subservience and humility"

Jun 9 German-Neth press reports, 3 million Dutch sent to East-Europe

Jun 12 Hitler orders enslavement of Slavic peoples

Jun 20 **Adolf Eichmann** proclaims deportation of Dutch Jews

Jul 10 Himmler orders sterilization of all Jewish woman in Ravensbruck Camp

Jul 13 5,000 Jews of Rovno Polish Ukraine, executed by nazis

Jul 13 SS shoots 1,500 Jews in Josefov Poland

Jul 14 Riots against Jews in Amsterdam

Jul 14 1st transport of Amsterdam Jews to Westerbork **Jul 15** 1st deportation camp at Westerbork, Jews sent to Auschwitz

Jul 15 Dutch Jews invoked for "Labor camps"

Jul 16 French police arrest 13,152 Jews in Paris

Jul 16 Jews transported from Holland to extermination camp

Jul 17 Transport #6 departs with French Jews to nazi-Germany

Jul 22 Warsaw Ghetto Jews (300,000) are sent to Treblinka Extermination Camp

Jul 28 Nazis liquidate 10,000 Jews in Minsk Belorussia Ghetto

Jul 30 German SS kills 25,000 Jews in Minsk, Belorussia

Jul 30 German occupiers set night curfew on Jews in Netherlands

Jul 31 German SS gases 1,000 Jews in Minsk, Belorussia

Aug 4 1st train with Jews departs Mechelen Belgium to Auschwitz

Aug 7 Transport 16 departs with French Jews to nazi-Germany

Aug 10 200 Jews escape Mir Ghetto in Poland

Aug 11 - Sept 30] SS begins exterminating 3,500 Jews in Zelov Lodz Poland

Aug 11 999 Jews are taken from Mechelen transit camp in Belgium

Aug 17 Transport #20 departs with French Jews to nazi-Germany

Aug 21 Transport #22 departs with French Jews to nazi-Germany

Aug 24 Transport #23 departs with French Jews to nazi-Germany

Aug 25 SS begins transporting Jews of Maastricht

Aug 26 7,000 Jews are rounded up in Vichy-France

Aug 26 Transport #24 departs with French Jews to nazi-Germany

Aug 28 Transport #25 departs with French Jews to nazi-Germany

Sep 4 Transport #28 departs with French Jews to nazi-Germany

Sep 7 Transport #29 departs with French Jews to nazi-Germany

Sep 11 Transport #31 departs with French Jews to nazi-Germany

Sep 21 Transport #35 departs with French Jews to nazi-Germany

Sep 23 Transport #36 departs with French Jews to nazi-Germany

Sep 29 French Government in exile of De Gaulle cancels agreement of Munich

Sep 30 SS exterminates 3,500 Jews in Zelov Lodz Poland in 6 week period

Oct 5 5,000 Jews of Dubno, Russia massacred

Oct 5 Budy Massacre at Auschwitz sub-camp, 90 French-Jewish women beaten to death by prison guards

Oct 10 1,300 Austrian Jews transported to Theresienstadt concentration camp

Oct 18 Hitler orders captured allied commandos to be killed

Oct 29 Nazis murder 16,000 Jews in Pinsk, Soviet Union

Nov 5 Nazi raid on Greek Jews in Paris

Nov 6 Nazis kill 12,000 Jews in the Minsk ghetto

Nov 9 Transport number 44 departs with French Jews to nazi-Germany

Nov 11 745 French Jews deported to Auschwitz

Nov 11 Transport #45 departs with French Jews to Nazi-Germany

Dec 4 Holocaust: In Warsaw, Zofia Kossak-Szczucka and Wanda Filipowicz set up the Żegota organization

1943

Jan 10 Soviet offensive against German 6th and 4th Armies near Stalingrad

Jan 13 Hitler declares "Total War"

Jan 13 Soviet offensive at Don under general Golikov

Jan 15 1st transport of Jews from Amsterdam to concentration camp Vught

Jan 15 World War II: The Soviets begin a counter-offensive at Voronezh

Jan 18 Soviets announce they have broken the long siege of Leningrad by Nazi Germany by opening a narrow land corridor, though the siege would not be fully lifted until a year later

Jan 19 1st Warsaw Ghetto Uprising begins

Jan 20 Operation Weiss: German, Italian, Bulgarian & Croatian troops attempt to retake land liberated by Tito's partisans

Jan 24 Adolf Hitler orders German troops at Stalingrad to fight to the death

Jan 24 Jewish patients, nurses and doctors incinerated at Auschwitz-Birkenau

Jan 31 Field Marshal Friedrich Paulus surrenders to Soviet troops at Stalingrad

Feb 2 German 6th Army surrenders after Battle of Stalingrad in a major turning point in Europe during World War II

Feb 14 The Soviet Union recaptures the city of Rostov-on-Don, liberating Russia from the German 17th Army during WWII

Feb 16 World War II: The USSR reconquers Kharkov.

Feb 17 Adolf Hitler visits field marshal Erich von Manstein's headquarters in Zaporozje, Ukraine and stays until the 19th

Mar 1 Jewish old age home for disabled in Amsterdam raided

Mar 2 1st transport from Westerbork Netherlands to Sobibor concentration camp

Mar 9 Greek Jews of Salonika are transported to Nazi extermination camps

Mar 13 Failed assassin attempt on Adolf Hitler during Smolensk-Rastenburg flight

Mar 14 World War II: Kraków Ghetto is "liquidated"

Mar 21 Assassination attempt on Adolf Hitler fails

Apr 19 Jews refuse to surrender the Warsaw Ghetto to SS officer Jürgen Stroop, who then orders its destruction, beginning the Warsaw Ghetto Uprising

May 16 SS General Jürgen Stroop orders the burning of the Warsaw Ghetto, ending a month of Jewish resistance. 13,000 Jews have died, about half burnt alive or suffocated, German casualties less than 300

May 19 Berlin is declared "Judenrien" (free of Jews)

Jun 10 Heinrich Himmler ordered the final liquidation of Lodz ghetto in occupied Poland

Jun 20 German round up Jews in Amsterdam

Jun 25 Crematorium 3 at Birkenau is finished

Jul 12 World War II: Battle of Prokhorovka - Russians defeat German forces in one of the largest ever tank battles

Jul 13 Greatest tank battle in history ends with Russia's defeat of Germany at Kursk, almost 6,000 tanks take part, 2,900 lost by Germany

Jul 28 Italian Fascist dictator Benito Mussolini resigns

Jul 28 Operation Gomorrah: RAF bombing over Hamburg causes a firestorm that kills 42,600 German civilians

Jul 31 Transport #58 departs with French Jews to Nazi Germany

Aug 2 Uprising at Treblinka Concentration Camp (crematorium destroyed)

Aug 18 Final convoy of Jews from Salonika, Greece, arrives at Auschwitz

Sep 7 987 Dutch Jewish transported to Auschwitz Concentration Camp

Sep 11 Jewish ghettos of Minsk & Lida Belorussia liquidated

Sep 15 Concentration Camp Vaivara in Estonia opens

Sep 15 Concentration Camp Kauwen in Lithuania opens

Sep 18 Adolf Hitler orders deportation of Danish Jews (unsuccessful)

Oct 6 Himmler wants acceleration of "Final Solution"

Oct 14 600 Jews escape during an uprising at the Nazi concentration camp in Sobibor, Poland

Oct 23 First Jewish transport out of Rome reaches camp Birkenau

Nov 2 Jewish ghetto of Riga Latvia is destroyed

Nov 6 Stalin says: "The issue of German fascism is lost"

Dec 2 First RSHA (Reichssicherheitshauptamt -Nazi Reich Security Head Office) transport out of Vienna reaches Birkenau camp

Dec 17 Transport 63 departs with French Jews to nazi-Germany

Dec 26 Earl Claus von Stauffenberg vain with bomb to Hitlers headquarter

1944

Jan 11 Crakow-Plaszow Concentration Camp established

Jan 27 Siege of Leningrad lifted by the Soviets after 880 days and more than 2 million Russians killed

Mar 18 Nazi Germany occupies Hungary

Mar 31 Hungary orders all Jews to wear yellow stars

May 15 14,000 Jews of Munkacs, Hungary, deported to Auschwitz

May 16 1st of 180,000+ Hungarian Jews reach Auschwitz

May 19 240 gypsies transported to Auschwitz from Westerbork, Netherlands

Jun 20 Nazis begin mass extermination of Jews at Auschwitz

June 29 US 7th army corps conquers Cherbourg - German counter attack at Caen - Nazi Paul Touvier shoots 7 Jews dead - Rommel & von Rundstedt travel to Berchtesgaden - Soviet Armies join in Bobroesjk

Jul 12 Theresienstadt Family camp disbands, with 4,000 people gased

Jul 17 Soviet troops cross Bug River and march into Poland

Jul 19 1,200+ 8th US Air Force bombers bomb targets in SW Germany

Jul 20 Death March of 1,200 Jews from Lipcani Moldavia begins

Jul 20 Flying Fortresses of US 8th Air Force attack Leipzig/Dessau

Jul 20 **Adolf Hitler** survives an assassination attempt led by German army officer Claus Von Stauffenberg

Jul 23 Soviet Army marches into Lublin, Poland

Jul 24 Soviet forces liberate concentration camp Majdanek

Jul 26 Soviet troops arrive in Weichsel

Jul 27 Soviet Army frees Majdanek concentration camp

Aug 2 Jewish survivors of Kovono Ghetto emerge from their bunker

Aug 3 Auschwitz-Birkenau concentration camp gases 4,000 gypsies

Aug 5 German forces begin the mass killing of between 40,000 and 50,000 Polish civilians in the Wola district of Warsaw during the uprising

Aug 6 All 1,200 Jewish death marchers from Lipcani Moldavia have died

Aug 6 Deportation of 70,000 Jews from Lodz Poland to Auschwitz begins

Aug 14 Soviet offensive at Weichsel

Aug 17 Soviet troops arrive at Austria-Prussia border

Aug 17 US 320th regiment infantry occupies Châteaudun

Aug 22 Last transport of French Jews to nazi-Germany

Aug 23 US 20th Army corp enter Fontainebleau/Melun de Seine

Aug 25 US Army XII Corps reaches Troyes, France

Sep 3 68th & last transport of Dutch Jews (including <u>Anne Frank</u>) from Westerbork leaves for Auschwitz concentration camp

Sep 3 Tank division of British Guards free Brussels

Sep 4 2,087 Jews transported for Westerbork to KZ-Lower Theresienstadt

Sep 4 British 11th Armoured Division frees Antwerp

Sep 4 US 1st Army frees Namen (Namur)

Sep 11 A reconnaissance squadron of the US 5th Armored Division "Victory Division" is 1st allied force to enter Nazi-Germany

Sep 28 Nazi forces begin killing civilians in the Italian village of Marzabotto

Oct 6 Soviets march into Hungary & Czechoslovakia

Oct 7 Uprising at Auschwitz-Birkenau concentration camp, Jews burn down crematoriums

Oct 13 US 1st army begins battle of Aachen, first German city captured during WWII

Oct 15 The Arrow Cross Party (very similar to Hitler's NSDAP (Nazi party)) takes over the power in Hungary.

Oct 16 Hungary: Horthy government falls/nazi count Szalasi becomes premier

Oct 18 Soviet troops invade Czechoslovakia during WW II

Oct 20 US 1st army wins battle of Aachen

Oct 21 World War II: US troops capture Aachen, 1st large German city to fall

Oct 23 Soviet army invades Hungary

Oct 30 Last transport for Auschwitz arrives in Birkenau

Nov 2 Auschwitz begins gassing inmates

Nov 8 25,000 Hungarian Jews are loaned to Nazis for forced labor

Nov 23 US 7th army under General Patch conquers Strasburg (close to Muldorf, Germany)

Nov 26 Himmler orders destruction of Auschwitz & Birkenau crematoria (Leading Nazi and Reichsführer of the SS **Heinrich Himmler**)

Dec 3 Hungarian death march of Jews ends

Dec 3 US 5th Armoured division occupies Brandenburg Hurtgenwald

Dec 23 Beginning of harsh winter

Dec 26 Budapest surrounded by Soviet army

Dec 29 Belgian Nazi Leon Degrelle sentenced to death

Dec 31 World War II: Hungary declares war on Germany.

1945

Jan 2 Allied air raid on Nuremberg

Jan 4 Germans execute resistance fighters in Amsterdam

Jan 12 German forces in Belgium retreat in Battle of Bulge

Jan 12 The Soviets begin a large offensive against the Nazis in Eastern Europe

Jan 16 Adolf Hitler moves into the Fuhrerbunker, his underground bunker in Berlin

Jan 15 Red Army frees Crakow-Plaszow concentration camp

Jan 17 Auschwitz concentration camp begins evacuation (after Christmas story of Sandor)

Jan 17 Soviet army enters the devastated city of Warsaw and clears German resistance

Jan 17 Swedish diplomat Raoul Wallenberg, credited with saving tens of thousands of Jews from the Nazis, arrested by Soviet secret police in Hungary

Jan 18 Soviet Armed Forces enter Krakow, Poland and push Germans out, only to eventually occupy entire country

Jan 20 The Hungarian Provisional Government concludes an armistice with the USSR, US, and Britain, agree to pay reparations and to join the war against Germany

Jan 26 Soviet forces reach Auschwitz concentration camp

Jan 27 Soviet troops liberate Auschwitz and Birkenau Concentration Camps in Poland

Jan 31 US 4th Infantry division occupies Elcherrath

Jan 31 Soviet troops reach the Oder River, less that 50 miles from Berlin

Feb 1 US Army arrives at Siegfried line

Feb 2 Escape attempt at Mauthausen concentration camp (Mauthausen-Gusen concentration camp complex)

Feb 4 Roosevelt, Churchill & **Stalin** meet at Yalta in the Crimea to discuss the final phase of the war

Feb 6 US 8th Air Force bombs Magdeburg/Chemnitz

Feb 6 Russian Red Army crosses the river Oder

Feb 11 Yalta agreement signed by FDRoosevelt, Churchill & **Stalin**

Feb 13 USSR captures Budapest, after a 49-day battle with Germany; 159,000 die

Feb 21 US 10th Armour division overthrows Orscholz line

Feb 23 Operation Grenade: US Lieutenant General Simpson's 9th Army crosses Ruhr

Mar 1 US infantry regiment captures Mönchengladbach

Mar 5 World War II: The Battle of the Ruhr begins

Mar 6 Erich Honnecker & Erich Hanke flee nazis

Mar 10 Fieldmarshal **Albert Kesselring** succeeds **Gerd von Rundstedt** as commander of German Army Command in the West

Mar 12 30 Amsterdammers executed by nazi occupiers during WWW2 many executions have been taken places in the Dutch

Mar 19 **Adolf Hitler** issues "Nero Decree" to destroy all German factories

Mar 21 During WW II Allied bombers begin 4-day raid over Germany

Mar 24 Operation Varsity: In the largest one-day airborne operation of all time, British, US & Canadian paratroopers land east of the Rhine in Northern Germany

Mar 24 Operation Varsity: In the largest one-day airborne operation of all time, British, US & Canadian paratroopers land east of the Rhine in Northern Germany

Mar 25 US 4th Armored div arrives at Hanau & Aschaffenburg

Mar 30 USSR invades Austria

Apr 3 Nazis begin evacuation of camp Buchenwald concentration camp

Apr 4 Hungary liberated from Nazi occupation (National Day)

Apr 4 US forces liberated the Nazi death camp Ohrdruf in Germany

Apr 4 US tanks and infantry conquer Bielefeld

Apr 11 SS burns & shoots 1,100 at Gardelegen (slave laborers)

Apr 11 Four soldiers in the Sixth Armored Division of the US Third Army liberate the Nazi concentration camp, Buchenwald

Apr 11 US troops conquers Mulheim, Oberhausen, Bochum, Unna, Essen

Apr 12 Canadian troops liberate Nazi concentration camp Westerbork, Netherlands

Apr 13 Red Army occupies Vienna

Apr 14 World War II: US 7th Army & allies forces capture Nuremberg & Stuttgart in Germany

Apr 15 British Army liberates Nazi concentration camp Bergen-Belsen

Apr 15 US troops occupy concentration camp Colditz

Apr 16 Colditz Castle, the high-security prisoner of war camp in Germany, is liberated by American troops

Apr 20 US 7th army captured German city of Nuremberg

Apr 22 Concentration Camp at Sachsenhausen liberated (later has become a Soviet camp!!! – 43,000 did not survive during the Cold War from here)

Apr 23 Concentration camp Flossenburg liberated

Apr 25 "Elbe Day" - US and Soviet forces meet at Torgau, Germany on the Elbe River during the invasion of Germany in WWII

Apr 29 US Army liberates 31,601 in Nazi concentration camp in Dachau, Germany

Apr 30 Concentration camp Munchen-Allach freed

Apr 30 Soviet Army frees Ravensbruck concentration camp

Apr 30 **Adolf Hitler** commits suicide along with his new wife Eva Braun in the Fuhrerbunker in Berlin as the Red Army captures the city

May 1 Radio Budapest, Hungary re-enters shortwave broadcasting after WW II

May 2 More than 1,000,000 German soldiers officially surrender to the Western Allies in Italy and Austria

May 5 Mauthausen Concentration camp in Austria liberated by US forces from 41st Reconnaissance Squadron

May 7 World War II: Unconditional German surrender to the Allies signed by General **Alfred Jodl** at Rheims

May 8 German General **Wilhelm Keitel** formally surrenders to the Allies represented by the United States, the UK, France and the Soviet Union in Berlin - V-E Day: WWII ends in Europe after Germany signs an unconditional surrender

May 9 Czechoslovakia liberated from Nazi occupation (National Day)

May 9 Nazi propagandist Max Blokzijl arrested

May 9 World War II: **Hermann Goering** is captured by the United States Army

May 9 World War II: The Soviet Union marks Victory Day

May 15 World War II: The final skirmish in Europe is fought near Prevalje, Slovenia

May 21 Nazi SS-Reichsfuehrer **Heinrich Himmler** captured

May 23 The Allies arrest the members of the Nazi Flensburg government, including Admiral Karl Donitz, formally dissolving Nazi Germany

References:

Book by Sándor Schwarcz: A Halál árnyékának völgyében – Oliver Games International 2005

Relevant information and further research can be found on the links below:
Video library link of Mr Schwarcz:
http://vhaonline.usc.edu/viewingPage?testimonyID=53084&returnIndex=0
https://www.britannica.com/place/Galilee-region-Israel
https://www.jewishvirtuallibrary.org/berettyjfalu
https://docplayer.hu/1994119-Egyesuletek-debrecenben-a-harmincas-evekben.html
http://www.blackseagr.org/learn_hungary.html
https://www.history.com/topics/world-war-ii/world-war-ii-history
https://encyclopedia.ushmm.org/content/en/article/sonderkommandos
https://www.thoughtco.com/kapos-prisoner-supervisors-1779685

Further research:

http://www.deathcamps.org/gas_chambers/gas_chambers_rav ensbrueck.html

http://www.holocaustresearchproject.org/othercamps/chainofc ommand.html

http://auschwitz.org/en/history/the-ss-garrison/trials-of-ss-men-from-the-auschwitz-concentration-camp-garrison

Gipsy lagers: http://en.auschwitz.org/lekcja/1/

Human experiments: http://en.auschwitz.org/lekcja/1/

Extermination of the Hungarian Jews:

http://en.auschwitz.org/lekcja/1/#

Final days in camp Buchenwald-

https://metro.co.uk/2016/01/27/holocaust-memorial-day-2016-the-horrors-of-the-holocaust-in-pictures-5647192/ - A freed Hungarian Jew, dying from starvation, is examined by Czech doctors at the liberated Buchenwald concentration camp, while other sick prisoners look on in Buchenwald, Germany on April 13, 1945

http://www.holocaustresearchproject.org/survivor/shlomo.ht ml

Relevant movies:

Escape to victory -

https://cinema.tesionline.it/img/news/cinema/escape81.jpg

Death Match – Russian movie from 9 Aug, 1942

 https://www.dailymail.co.uk/news/article-2127854/The-banning-Death-Match-Ukrainian-authorities-halt-showings-film-notorious-1942-Nazi-killings-Kiev-footballers-fearing-spark-trouble-Euro-2012.html

Jewish football story WWII -

https://www.haaretz.com/opinion/.premium-how-the-nazis-destroyed-a-golden-age-for-jewish-soccer-1.5978782

The twins – timeline - https://www.timetoast.com/timelines/a-day-in-the-life-of-a-twin-in-a-concentration-camp

www.ingramcontent.com/pod-product-compliance
Lightning Source LLC
Chambersburg PA
CBHW080509090426
42734CB00015B/3009